GOD *and* CHARLES DICKENS

GOD *and* CHARLES DICKENS

RECOVERING THE CHRISTIAN VOICE OF A CLASSIC AUTHOR

GARY L. COLLEDGE

BrazosPress

a division of Baker Publishing Group
Grand Rapids, Michigan

© 2012 by Gary L. Colledge

Published by Brazos Press
a division of Baker Publishing Group
P.O. Box 6287, Grand Rapids, MI 49516-6287
www.brazospress.com

Printed in the United States of America

Library of Congress Cataloging-in-Publication Data

Colledge, Gary.
    God and Charles Dickens : recovering the Christian voice of a classic author / Gary L. Colledge.
       p.   cm.
    Includes bibliographical references (p.   ) and indexes.
    ISBN 978-1-58743-320-7 (pbk.)
    1. Dickens, Charles, 1812–1870—Criticism and interpretation. 2. Christianity and literature. 3. God in literature. I. Title.
PR4592.G6C65 2012
823'.8—dc23
                                    ·   2011050111

12   13   14   15   16   17   18   7   6   5   4   3   2   1

For Aurora, Collin, William, David, and Ethan

"I love these little people; and it is not a slight thing when they, who are so fresh from God, love us."

—Charles Dickens, *The Old Curiosity Shop*, chapter 1

May you each find joy, as did Dickens, in our Savior

Contents

Acknowledgments

I would certainly be remiss if I failed to express my deepest appreciation and sincere thanks to the handful of family and friends who contributed to the writing of this book in ways that most of them are probably unaware.

Let me begin by thanking everyone at Brazos for their warm reception of the manuscript, their interest in the project, and their careful work on it at every stage of the process. It has been my privilege and a joy to work with such capable and friendly folks.

I would also like to express my gratitude to Dr. Bruce Longenecker (Baylor University), who was instrumental in providing opportunity for the work and research that would eventually produce this book. From the inception of the original project to its publication here, Bruce's unobtrusive support and sincere interest has helped give it shape. Thanks, too, to my friend Craig Clapper, pastor of Trinity Evangelical Free Church (South Bend, Indiana), who queried with his characteristic frankness, "What does Dickens have to say to the church?" and who then invited me to share my answer with his congregation. The conversations I enjoyed with Craig on Dickens and the church provided the impetus for the rough outline of this work.

Don Alexander, my good friend and mentor, read and discussed chapters five and six with me and provided a careful critique in a very short time. Over the years, Don and I have had countless discussions concerning the church and I have benefitted greatly from his wisdom and insight. I thank him for his contribution to this volume.

My work colleagues and friends at Summa Western Reserve Hospital (Cuyahoga Falls, Ohio) have consistently expressed a genuine excitement for the project and regularly offered generous words of encouragement, for which I am grateful. I extend special thanks to Joe Spiros, my supervisor at work, for his accommodation of my writing schedule and his enthusiastic support for the project.

I could never have completed this project without the unwavering support of my family. While that may seem a tired and clichéd expression to some, anyone who has ever undertaken the sort of solitary and time-intensive project writing sometimes can be knows how true such an expression is. My children—and my best friends—Emily, Kristen, Jonathan, and Rachel, always exhibited an extraordinary excitement for anything and everything related to the writing process—whether that was the turning of a phrase, the working out of an argument, the completion of a chapter, the finishing of the manuscript, or the final submission to the publisher. And they always made me feel like this would be the most important book the world would ever see. Saying a simple thank you to them seems quite inadequate.

My deepest gratitude goes to Marla, my wife. She endured endless conversations (and even more ramblings) about Dickens, about religion, about Dickens and religion, about all things Dickensian, and even about the writing process. She read, she thought, she formulated, she outlined with me. And she did it all with patience, grace, interest, and selfless love. Her influence is inscribed on every page of this book. A mere thank you is surely not enough. Nevertheless, I express that thanks, and while doing so I am reminded of how Dickens brings his *David Copperfield* to a close. As David reflects on the many "faces" in his memory, he is soon brought to reflect on the face of his wife, Agnes. "But one face," David writes, "shining on me like a Heavenly light by which I see all other objects, is above them and beyond them all. And that remains. I turn my head, and see it, in its beautiful serenity, beside me. My lamp burns low, and I have written far into the night; but the dear presence, without which I were nothing, bears me company." I know exactly what David is talking about.

Introduction

This is a book not so much *about* Charles Dickens as it is a book *of* him. At least it tries to be. By that I mean, I have attempted in these pages to let Dickens speak—through his fiction, through his letters, through his journalism, through his speeches—with as little interference as possible but also without letting the book become simply a compendium of quotations. Specifically, I have attempted to let him speak so that we might hear Dickens the Christian. That voice, the Christian voice of Charles Dickens, for whatever reasons, is not often heard. Yet, Dickens's Christian voice is conspicuous and pervasive in his work, even though that fact is not always recognized or acknowledged.

Michael Slater, in his definitive biography, *Charles Dickens* (2009), makes some significant gestures toward Dickens's faith. First, in the several instances where Slater mentions the faith of Dickens, it seems clear that Dickens's faith was no small matter in his life. Dickens's faith, Slater implies, is part and parcel of who he was and is evident throughout his life. Second, Dickens's faith, says Slater, finds expression in his work, whether in the deliberately spiritual *The Life of Our Lord*, his social journalism, or his fiction. Third, and not unexpectedly, Dickens's faith sustained him in difficulty and tragedy, particularly as he grappled with the deaths of various friends and family members. Of course, Slater says little, if anything, substantial about the nature or the substance of Dickens's faith. Given the intent and design of *Charles Dickens*, it would be a bit misinformed, not to mention unfair, to expect Slater to speak extensively to Dickens's faith or to suppose that he should. That is the subject and the purpose of another book, a different book. The book you are reading is an attempt to be that other book.

As such, then, this book purposes to speak to the Christian faith of which Slater writes. It is a book that will attempt to lead you into Dickens's Christian thought but to guide you only sparingly. Once you are acquainted with Dickens and introduced to his understanding of the life of faith, my hope is that you will examine him on your own and test my observations against yours. Certainly, I have made every effort to be honest and accurate in what is written here, and to the best of my knowledge, it is honest and accurate. Furthermore, I am hopeful that my treatment of Dickens will be adjudged to be reasoned and fair. And, of course, any errors in content or judgment are certainly my own and for which I accept full responsibility.

My study of Dickens has convinced me that he was a Christian and that he wrote unapologetically as a Christian. So, I write here not simply to prove that Dickens was a Christian but in order that the Christian voice of one of the great literary geniuses of all time might be heard; the voice of one who was neither theologian nor biblical scholar nor churchman but a layperson, one who thought seriously and deeply about the life of faith, following Jesus, and just what that should look like.

As Dickens was not a theologian, a biblical scholar, or a churchman, we should not expect to find anything approximating a systematic theology or even theological speculation. Even so, in his *The Life of Our Lord*, Dickens does come near to an explicit and deliberate expression of his faith—and I would argue that *The Life of Our Lord* is, in fact, an explicit and deliberate expression of his faith, substantive and definitive. But Dickens's Christian faith and his Christian worldview undergirded all that he wrote. As such, *The Life of Our Lord* is not an anomaly in the Dickens corpus. It is an inevitable and integral volume in it. In chapter 2, I will deal more extensively with *The Life of Our Lord,* and we will see how it becomes, in some instances, a valuable guide to help us navigate the Christian landscape of the Dickens corpus. In any case, *The Life of Our Lord* is a central and definitive source for our understanding of Dickens's Christian thought.

Reading This Book

As a stage for Dickens's Christian voice, I hope these pages serve at the same time as an introduction to this important aspect of Dickens's writing, especially for those who are not familiar with his work or who are not familiar with the Christian aspect of his work. I have quoted extensively from Dickens himself, from his fiction and his correspondence, and to a lesser degree, his journalism and his speeches. I have done this deliberately so that the reader can hear Dickens's voice. I have also included, again quite deliberately, a number of extended quotations to reveal the fuller context, thereby offering a better understanding of what Dickens intended to say. When it seems appropriate for the sake of clarity or to provide some context, I add some words of explanation; however, this book is not a formal commentary on Dickens's work. On occasion, and especially in the last chapter, I will engage in some limited and nonacademic interpretation. Notwithstanding, interpretation is not a primary purpose or goal of the book.

I am well aware of the danger of identifying the voice of a novel's narrator and characters with the novelist himself. Accordingly, I have attempted to associate material in such a way that the quotes I have cited from novels represent concepts and ideas also found expressly in his letters and his journalism—a sort of multiple attestation, if you will. I have also tried to show, perhaps less conspicuously, that Dickens's worldview is multiply attested. There are times when it is reasonably clear that the characters and the narrator have stepped out of the way—or perhaps Dickens shoves them out of the way—and Dickens the author speaks. In any case, then, I have taken deliberate care that what we are considering at a given point in a given chapter is indeed the Christian voice of Charles Dickens.

The latter portion of each chapter (except chapter 1 and chapter 7) has been given over to what I informally refer to as, "what Dickens has to say to the church." In these sections, I have tried to draw out the implications of Dickens's observations, comments, criticisms, and declarations for the church today. The church to which Dickens spoke was a church in transition, not unlike the church today. As such, Dickens's words may resonate for us in particular ways that remind us of what the church should be and how the church might become what it should be in the days ahead.

In view of this, then, it is important to bear in mind that Dickens writes to those who claim to be Christians—he writes to the church. He does not write to try to make people Christians. He writes to try to make Christians attentive and active. He writes to rouse Christians from a comfortable lethargy of affluence and self-preoccupation to their moral responsibility to the needs around them. And Dickens would think first of the needs of those in his immediate circle of influence—the culture and community around him. The inward and ingrown focus of the church, both individually and institutionally, was unacceptable to Dickens and was the central point of his criticism of the church. In this regard, Dickens anticipated in some respects the missional notion so popular in today's ecclesial setting. If we read Dickens otherwise, ignoring this basic orientation, we will certainly misread him and misconstrue much of what he has to say that is of value for us today.

Toward a Greater Understanding of Dickens

I have provided a selected bibliography for those interested in some further reading on Dickens's Christianity and Christian thought. Of course, the best way to get to know Dickens and his thought is to read his novels. Dickens himself said as much in his will.[1] Most authors, of course, will make a similar claim. Still, there are some excellent secondary sources that are informative, engaging, and worthwhile.

A handful of volumes have been written on Dickens and religion, each employing their own method and, as I see it, complementing each other. Dennis Walder's *Dickens and Religion* (George Allen & Unwin, 1981) is the seminal work. Walder traces the religious themes in selected Dickens novels and provides an excellent introduction to the subject of Dickens and religion and how Dickens employed his faith in shaping his art. *Charles Dickens, Resurrectionist* (1982) by Andrew Sanders discusses Dickens's thematic and artistic use of death and resurrection in his work and does so in a Christian context. As such, Sanders's work also serves as a valuable commentary on Dickens and Christianity.

The more recent *Literature and Religion in Mid-Victorian England: From Dickens to Eliot* (2003) by Carolyn W. de la L. Oulton is an excellent volume that situates Dickens and his work in the context of his peers and of nineteenth-century religion. Her portraits of the mid-Victorian religious landscape seem to me to be the strength of her work—compelling and second to none. My *Dickens, Christianity and "The Life of Our Lord": Humble Veneration, Profound Conviction* (2009) is a study of *The Life of Our Lord*, the harmony of the Gospels that Dickens wrote for his children. My viewpoint is that *The Life of Our Lord* is the definitive work in the Dickens corpus, bringing clarity and greater precision to our understanding of his Christian thought.

I should add that the books I have listed tend to be more academic than popular in their approach. I include them here not for that reason but because (1) they are four among only a few more volumes that variously include a full and knowledgeable treatment of Dickens and Christianity, and (2) they are extremely readable. Only rarely do they resort to jargon and academic-speak.

Those with an interest in biography have any number of Dickens biographies from which to choose, but I have found three in particular that are especially noteworthy. Dickens's most recent biographer, Michael Slater, has written and published what is being hailed as the definitive Dickens biography. Slater's *Charles Dickens* (2009) is the product of a lifetime of the study of Dickens by a scholar who knows Dickens and his work probably better than anyone living. Slater works through Dickens's life novel by novel, placing each one quite meticulously in the context of Dickens's everyday life and work. It is a large volume (nearly seven hundred pages), but it is highly readable and will reward those who will invest in reading it. John Forster, Dickens's original biographer, was a contemporary and a close friend of Dickens and his family. Forster wrote *The Life of Charles Dickens* between the years 1872 and 1874. The Forster biography is often criticized today because it is alleged to intentionally paint a very flattering portrait of Dickens despite what Forster knew of his shortcomings and failings. Whatever its faults may be, it is still an important biography for Dickens studies and is an essential read for Dickens enthusiasts. Edgar Johnson's *Charles Dickens: His Tragedy and Triumph* (1952) is said to have corrected much of Forster's one-sided account. But it is possible that Johnson has erred in the other direction. In any event, Johnson's is an informative and capable account of Dickens's life and work.[2]

Two other works deserve attention here. George Orwell's essay "Charles Dickens," in *Critical Essays* (1960), is as good a piece as has been published on Dickens and should be read by those with any interest at all in Dickens. Obviously, it is not a biography, but it serves as an excellent introduction to Dickens. Also, *The Dickens Christian Reader* (2000), edited by Robert Hanna, is an excellent little volume—if you can get your hands on one. In just over one hundred twenty pages, Hanna has compiled a selection of passages from Dickens's writing that give voice to his Christian thought and ideas.

An Invitation to Dickens

When Joseph Gold described Dickens as a radical moralist he meant that Dickens was both moralist and reformer at the same time. Developing this idea further and with greater clarity, Gold summarized: "The moralist as artist is someone who believes in and reveals to us our own possibilities for living more meaningfully. The reformer is someone who wants to see a different society appear by some means or other. . . . Dickens is not concerned with the philosophical question of whether such a world is possible. He makes it happen in his art."[3] For Dickens, this all emerges from his decidedly Christian worldview. To live more meaningfully for Dickens is to live according to God's design and order within a world created by God and in which God is active. And doing that means nothing more, and nothing less, than committing to follow the example and teaching of Jesus; to imitate Jesus as we give our lives in service to others; to be forgiving, generous, and compassionate. Dickens was convinced that it was in just this way that society would be transformed. And he truly believed that.

As we hear Dickens, however, we are listening to more than just a mere moralist. Dickens was a Christian with his moral sensibilities attuned to the world around him. And he was anxious that the church begin to embrace its moral responsibilities in tangible and concrete ways. For Dickens, doing so was not difficult. In fact, he understood the task as simply imitating Jesus. And so, he would write in his *The Life of Our Lord*:

Remember!—It is Christianity TO DO GOOD, always—even to those who do evil to us. It is Christianity to love our neighbours as ourself, and to do to all men as we would have them do to us. It is Christianity to be gentle, merciful, and forgiving, and to keep those qualities quiet in our own heart, and never make a boast of them, or of our prayers or of our love of God, but always to show that we love Him by humbly trying to do right in everything. If we do this, and remember the life and lessons of Our Lord Jesus Christ, and try to act up to them, we may confidently hope that God will forgive us our sins and mistakes and enable us to live and die in peace.[4]

George Orwell said of Dickens: "He is always preaching a sermon, and that is the final secret of his inventiveness. For you can only create if you can *care*."[5] Orwell was right.

Notes and Abbreviations

All references to Dickens's novels are to The Oxford Illustrated Dickens, Oxford University Press, unless otherwise indicated. For *The Life of Our Lord*, I have used Simon & Schuster's 1999 edition and have used the abbreviation, *TLOL*.

To make the citations from Dickens's letters more accessible, I have endeavored to provide precise dates from the Pilgrim Edition of his letters, which I have used throughout.

I have used the Everyman's Edition of John Forster's biography.

When discussing Bible references that pertain to Dickens and the nineteenth century, I refer to the King James Version. In all other instances, I quote from the New American Standard Bible unless otherwise indicated.

In referring to Dickens's novels, particularly in the notes, I have used the following standard abbreviations:

AN	American Notes and Pictures from Italy	MC	Martin Chuzzlewit
		CHE	Master Humphrey's Clock and
BR	Barnaby Rudge		A Child's History of England
BH	Bleak House	ED	The Mystery of Edwin Drood
CB	Christmas Books	NN	Nicholas Nickleby
DC	David Copperfield	OCS	The Old Curiosity Shop
D & S	Dombey and Son	OT	Oliver Twist
GE	Great Expectations	OMF	Our Mutual Friend
HT	Hard Times	PP	The Pickwick Papers
LD	Little Dorrit	TTC	A Tale of Two Cities

1

Charles Dickens

THAT GREAT CHRISTIAN WRITER

In his introduction for the Everyman's Edition of *Reprinted Pieces*, G. K. Chesterton remarked,

> If ever there was a message full of what modern people call true Christianity, the direct appeal to the common heart, a faith that was simple, a hope that was infinite, and a charity that was omnivorous, if ever there came among men what they call the Christianity of Christ, it was in the message of Dickens.[1]

Even in light of the fact that more recent Dickens scholarship has given some critical attention to Dickens's religious beliefs and concerns[2] and that this aspect of Dickens's work is becoming gradually more familiar to readers, such a statement as Chesterton's remains provocative and, for many, surprising and perhaps even astonishing. To suggest that Dickens's work is implicitly Christian may seem quite bold and unexpected. Yet, it seems apparent Dickens thought of himself unequivocally as a Christian, and he was confident that his work was deeply rooted in the New Testament and that his characters exhibited the teachings of Jesus and were expressly disciples of Jesus.

In his *The English Novel: Questions in Literature* (1976), editor C. T. Watts offers a collection of dialogues in the form of essays on the English novel and particularly on English novelists. In the third chapter, A. E. Dyson and Angus Wilson discuss Charles Dickens. What is especially intriguing—and noteworthy—about this dialogue between Dyson and Wilson is that they begin their discussion speaking of Dickens's religion, or more properly, of his Christianity. Wilson observes from the outset that Dickens "thought of himself as centrally a Christian" and that the Christian aspect of his work is "an absolutely essential part of his development as a novelist." He goes on to remind us that both Tolstoy and Dostoevsky refer to Dickens as "that great Christian writer."[3]

Why, then, do statements such as those from Chesterton, Dyson, and Wilson elicit such surprising and strong reaction? Such reaction may likely be attributed to earlier Dickens scholars and critics who played down the role of religion in the work and life of Dickens and were quite skeptical of any significant Christian conviction on Dickens's part. For instance, in the early 1940s the eminent Dickens scholar Humphry House observed of Dickens, "His practical humanist kind of Christianity hardly touched the fringes of what is called religious experience, and his work shows no indication of any powerful feeling connected with a genuinely religious subject."[4] Earlier, Sir Arthur Quiller-Couch, in coming to terms with the "atmosphere" of Dickens's world, offered, "To begin with, we must jettison religion; or at any rate all religion that gets near to definition by words in a Credo."[5] As far as Quiller-Couch was concerned, Dickens had "simply disregarded" religion and the religious issues that "were agitating men's thoughts" in Dickens's day. Philip Collins was bold to remark in his *Dickens and Education* (1964) that if Dickens had any deep religious convictions "his novels would have contained more explicit and insistent references to Christian worship and belief,"[6] while Robert Newsom, in his *Charles Dickens Revisited* (2000), described Dickens's religious views as so inconsistent that they are scarcely intelligible as religious at all.[7]

Certainly, not all Dickens scholars are as dismissive or indifferent as those just cited, and as was pointed out above, more recent scholarship is at least recognizing—even if a bit superficially and inconsistently—the presence of the religious aspect of Dickens's work. Still, there can be little doubt that such assessments as those cited above have been influential in shaping the thought of many readers and students concerning Dickens's religious ideas. A further muddying of the waters occurs through the negative interpretation by some scholars of Dickens's religious parodies and caricatures—interpretation that maintains Dickens must have been nonreligious or even antireligious. It is not difficult to see, then, why any suggestion of Dickens holding Christian convictions and to a Christian worldview is met with a certain amount of surprise, if not mild incredulity.

Nevertheless, as I will try to demonstrate, such negative assessments seem quite unfounded and even misinformed. Dickens's fiction, letters, and essays are charged throughout with humble veneration for our Lord, passionate Christian conviction, and a thoroughgoing Christian worldview. More importantly, the Christian nature of his work is straightforward and conspicuous. And it is no wonder, because Dickens was deliberate and intentional in expressing his Christian convictions in his work.

Dickens and His Faith

That the Christian aspect of Dickens's work was deliberate and intentional becomes more apparent when we hear Dickens himself on the matter. In 1861, Dickens wrote to the Reverend David Macrae in response to Macrae's criticism that Dickens lacked a positive portrayal of strong Christian characters, what Macrae called "specimens of earnest Christianity."[8] Dickens replied:

> With a deep sense of my great responsibility always upon me when I exercise my art, one of my most constant and most earnest endeavours has been to exhibit in all my good people some faint reflections of the teachings of our great Master, and unostentatiously to lead the reader up to those teachings as the great source of all moral goodness. All my strongest illustrations are derived from the New Testament; all my social abuses are shown as departures from its spirit; all my good people are humble, charitable, faithful, and forgiving. Over and over again, I claim them in express words as disciples of the Founder

of our religion; but I must admit that to a man (or woman) they all arise and wash their faces, and do not appear unto men to fast.[9]

In Dickens's mind, his work was fundamentally Christian in orientation—and was so deliberately. His narrative world emerged from his own uncompromising Christian worldview, and his characters were measured against the teaching and example of Jesus. As a result, Dickens wrote with a characteristic sense of Christian commitment and moral obligation that was firmly rooted in the Scriptures, particularly the New Testament, and with what Andrew Sanders so brilliantly refers to as the desire for a "continued awakening of the Christian conscience."[10] When we read Dickens we hear a decidedly Christian voice, one that qualifies him as "that great Christian writer."

This is a book, then, about Dickens's Christianity and his Christian worldview. It is intended to focus attention on the Christian aspect of Dickens's work and how he thought about the life of faith. My interest in these pages is not simply to acknowledge the presence of Christianity and Christian themes in Dickens's work but, more significantly, to consider the nature and expression of the Christianity and the Christian worldview that informed and shaped Dickens's work. Most importantly, I hope to give the Christian voice of Charles Dickens a hearing.

In doing so, it will become apparent, if we are listening carefully, that Dickens's words resonate in and for the church. Consequently, this book is also about what Dickens can teach the church today. Dickens could be scathing in his criticism of the church of his day and of Christians, but his always seemed to be the voice of the reformer from within rather than the detractor from without, urging the church toward its true calling and Christians toward genuine discipleship—what Dickens would call "real Christianity."[11] He had become especially exasperated with an ingrown institution that had become preoccupied with its own ecclesial polity and theological minutiae at the expense of the many pressing social needs around it. Dickens wanted more from the church—he expected more from the church. He even wrote a short piece in which he offered some pertinent advice to pastors about preaching.[12] Dickens's Christian voice was sometimes subversive, often prophetic, and always passionate.

And he can remind us in humorous, profound, simple, or uncomfortable ways what our faith should look like. It would probably be wise for us to listen.

Arthur Clennam's Four Sundays[13]

Sometimes Dickens's Christian voice was direct and personal. By that, I am referring to those instances when Dickens spoke directly to religious issues in a personal way, as he did in his correspondence and, to a lesser degree, in his speeches and journalism. There are other times when Dickens was just as personal, perhaps, but addressed religious issues in the course of a narrative, in a character's reflections, or in the portrayal and descriptions of his characters. One such instance of this latter method occurs early in *Little Dorrit*, when Arthur Clennam, having been abroad, returns to London on a Sunday evening to the "maddening church bells of all degrees of dissonance, sharp and flat, cracked and clear, fast and slow . . . urging the populace in a voluble manner to Come to church, Come to church, Come to church!" Arthur, relieved by the eventual ceasing of the pealing of the bells, can only respond, "Heaven forgive me and those who trained me. How I have hated this day."[14]

For Arthur, Sundays represent "a long train of miserable Sundays" in his life, a "procession [that] would not stop with the bell[s] but continued to march on." Dickens goes on to outline Arthur Clennam's four Sundays, representative of his upbringing and his training in Christianity. In this way, Dickens introduces an important theme of the novel as well as a significant line of thought in his larger body of work and in his own life. It is quite likely, of course, that this speaks as much to Dickens's thought and experience, certainly his perceptions, as it does to Arthur Clennam's.

Arthur's first Sunday is the Dreary Sunday of childhood. Arthur remembers being "scared out his senses by a horrible tract which commenced business with the poor child by asking him in its title why he was going to Perdition." Dickens refers to this tract as "a piece of curiosity that he really in a frock and drawers was not in a condition to satisfy." Clearly, Dickens is targeting the ploy here that was so common in the Christianity of Dissenters and Nonconformists—that of using Christian teaching to frighten children into desired religious and moral behaviors. Further, there is a veiled gesture toward what Dickens saw as the mistaken and dangerous representation of God as Lawgiver and Judge over and against the representation of God as Father. This kind of approach, particularly with children, always raised Dickens's ire considerably, and he was always ready to speak to the issue in the strongest language.

The Sleepy Sunday of Arthur's boyhood is remembered as one on which "like a military deserter he was marched to chapel . . . three times a day, morally handcuffed to another boy." The language that Dickens employs in the larger description of the Sleepy Sunday, as well as his use of the word "chapel," may suggest a combination of his own experience at William Giles's School and his perception of the habits of Dissenters and Nonconformists. Whatever the case, as a reflection of Arthur's experience, he would just as soon have traded "two meals of indigestible sermon for another ounce or two of inferior mutton" for dinner. The "indigestible sermon" seems to be a reference to Dickens's exasperation with those preachers and teachers who remained forever insensitive to their audiences and employed theological jargon that was rarely understood by educated adults, let alone young children. And Dickens had little patience with those who preached or taught about "religious mysteries that young people with the best advantages can but imperfectly understand."[15]

Of course, there is the Interminable Sunday of Arthur's middle years. Here, by way of Arthur's memory, we have our first intimations of Mrs. Clennam, Arthur's mother. Especially revealing is Dickens's designation of this Sunday as an interminable one, for indeed this Sunday extends to the end of the novel in the heart and demeanor of Mrs. Clennam, providing Dickens with the thematic antithesis to his heroine, Amy Dorrit. And Dickens uses the opportunity of an Interminable Sunday to offer an indirect description of the embodiment of the distorted Calvinism that he understood as the Christianity of most Dissenters and Nonconformists. For this Sunday, Arthur remembers his mother sitting behind her Bible all day, a Bible "bound, like her own construction of it, in the hardest, barest, and straitest boards, with one dinted ornament on the cover like the drag of a chain, and a wrathful sprinkling of red upon the edges of the leaves—as if it, of all books! were a fortification against sweetness of temper, natural affection, and gentle intercourse."[16]

Dickens was surely no enemy of the Bible. In fact, just the opposite is true. He insisted in a farewell letter to his son Edward that the New Testament "is the best book that ever was, or will be, known in the world; and because it teaches you the best lessons by which any human creature, who tries to be truthful and faithful to duty, can possibly be guided."[17] And this, as we will see, will be a constant theme of Dickens's life and writing. His point here in the context of *Little Dorrit*, however, seems to be that, in the hands of Mrs. Clennam, and those like her, the Bible itself has been turned into a weapon of sorts to be wielded against those who were not given to a like understanding of the Christian life. The Bible has become lifeless, stilted, and deadly. And even its pages, with their "wrathful sprinkling of red upon the edges," serve as a reminder of God's demand for a sacrifice to appease His wrath.[18]

Furthermore, for Mrs. Clennam and others of her religious persuasion, the Bible had become "a fortification against sweetness of temper, natural affection, and gentle intercourse." For whatever reasons, Dickens often portrayed the Dissenters and Nonconformists who embraced Calvinism as sullen and bad-tempered, and he attributed this to their misunderstanding of and an ungodly reversal in their religion. In *David Copperfield*, for instance, Mr. Murdstone and his sister are characterized by a religion which "is a vent for their bad humours and arrogance." Even more telling was that Murdstone "gloomily profess[es]" his Christianity as he "sets up an image of himself, and calls it the Divine Nature." And when Murdstone preaches, it is observed, "that the dark tyrant he has lately been, the more ferocious is his doctrine."[19] Dickens revealed the fullness of his sentiments in this regard in *Barnaby Rudge*: "Ye men of gloom and austerity, who paint the face of Infinite Benevolence with an eternal frown; read in the Everlasting Book, wide open in your view, the lesson it would teach. Its pictures are not in black and sombre hues, but bright and glowing tints; its music—save when ye drown it—is not in sighs and groans, but songs and cheerful sounds. Listen to the million voices in the summer air, and find one dismal as your own."[20] Mrs. Clennam was a part of this fellowship that "gloomily profess" Christianity and "who paint the face of Infinite Benevolence with an eternal frown," and that created for Arthur an Interminable Sunday.

Finally, there is the Resentful Sunday of his later years, which seems to extend to his present. The Resentful Sunday is aptly named in that Arthur passes this prolonged, slow-moving Sunday in sullenness, umbrage, and bitterness. There comes along with this Sunday "a sullen sense of personal injury in his heart," which explains why Arthur introduces his four Sundays with the prayer, "Heaven forgive me and those who trained me. How I have hated this day." As Dickens develops this passage, we get the sense that Arthur is not sure what is the root cause of his loathing Sundays, but he certainly connects his feelings with those who trained him. But Dickens subtly interrupts the narrative; as he sees it, the root cause is that Arthur has "no more real knowledge of the beneficent history of the New Testament, than if he had been bred among idolaters." Arthur has been cheated out of a vibrant, life-giving Christianity and knowledge of the Saviour. And because of that, he has passed "a legion of Sundays, . . . [in] unserviceable bitterness and mortification." For Arthur, his Sundays have been useless, meaningless exercises in superstitious religiosity and forced self-abasement.

Dickens, of course, was using this masterful description of Arthur's four Sundays not only to characterize Arthur's upbringing but also to provide a foreshadowing of the religion of Mrs. Clennam, which is held in contrast to Amy Dorrit's expression of Christianity as a follower of Jesus throughout the entirety of the novel. And in describing Arthur's experience of Christianity and his Christian upbringing, Dickens was drawing attention to all that he saw as counterfeit, superficial, and deadening in Christian religion.

Clearly, then, Dickens made extraordinary use of Arthur Clennam's four Sundays in order to speak to those religious issues that stirred his passion and aroused his Christian voice. And for Dickens, these were words to the church, reminders or alerts intended to speak to the church for its good and for its advancement.

Esther Summerson as Disciple

If Arthur Clennam's four Sundays come to us from the negative side, demonstrating what Christianity and the life of faith is *not*, Dickens presents from the positive side Esther Summerson, the heroine of *Bleak House*. Esther represents what Dickens refers to in his letter to David Macrae (see above) as one of his "good people," all exhibiting "some faint reflections of the teachings of our great Master" and all "humble, charitable, faithful, and forgiving." Clearly, Esther was intended by Dickens as a "[disciple] of the Founder of our religion"; but she arose and washed her face and did not "appear unto men to fast." She is, in fact, a disciple of Jesus in the precise way that Dickens understood the idea of discipleship—the imitation of Jesus.[21]

In at least three instances in the course of the narrative of *Bleak House*, Esther either prays or remembers her prayer "to be industrious, contented and kind-hearted and to do some good to some one."[22] This is noteworthy, especially from Dickens's pen, because it is similar in nature to the prayer that Jesus prays in the wilderness before he embarks on his public ministry in Dickens's *The Life of Our Lord*. Jesus prays, "that he might be of use to men and women."[23] In fact, Dickens implies that this represents Jesus's prayer for the entirety of his sojourn in the wilderness. Significantly, what both prayers emphasize is a primary concern to serve others. In Dickens's mind, it is precisely such servanthood that characterized Jesus. Just so, it is Esther's aspiration to follow her Master in the same manner of service.

To have an even clearer understanding of Esther as disciple, it is important to be familiar with Dickens's caricatures in *Bleak House*—Mrs. Pardiggle, Mrs. Jellyby, and the Reverend Chadband. Each one of these characters represents a slightly different Christian perspective of the nineteenth century. Mrs. Pardiggle appears to have some connection to High Church Anglicanism, Mrs. Jellyby is perhaps an Anglican Evangelical, and Chadband likely a Dissenter or Nonconformist. Whatever the case, Esther is seen in contrast to each one, and in this way, Dickens shows the difference between "religion and the cant of religion, piety and the pretence of piety, a humble reverence for the great truths of Scripture and an audacious and offensive obtrusion of its letter and not its spirit."[24]

In Matthew 23, Jesus speaks to the crowds and to his disciples concerning the religious leaders of his day. Jesus tells those listening "but do not ye after their [the scribes and Pharisees] works; for they say, and do not" (Matt. 23:3). Jesus then goes on to specify particular instances of things the religious leaders say but do not do. Further,

Jesus declares, "But all their works they do for to be seen of men" (Matt. 23:5). Then, Jesus teaches the crowds and the disciples, "But he that is greatest among you shall be your servant" (Matt. 23:11). Whether or not Dickens had this particular passage in mind as he developed the contrast between his caricatures and Esther is not known. But he certainly had a similar passage in mind, if not this one.

For Dickens, Pardiggle, Jellyby, and Chadband are the religious leaders of the day; they are the scribes and Pharisees, so to speak. They are the ones who should be doing something in service to humankind, looking out for the welfare of others and taking care of the needy. But they are not. Rather, they are involved in their own self-absorbed projects and self-serving religiosity from which they see very little of the real needs about them, even in their own families. And in each case Esther stands in the gap narratively to be the example of Jesus in their places.

Early in the story, Mrs. Pardiggle visits Bleak House in an effort to solicit funds for her charitable projects from the generous and kindhearted John Jarndyce, Esther's (and Ada's) guardian. On this occasion, Mr. Jarndyce is not at home, and so, as she is on a mission of visitation, Mrs. Pardiggle apprehends Esther and Ada, taking them along with her (and her five sons—"ferocious with discontent") to the camp of the poor and destitute brickmakers and into the hovel of a particular family that she has been visiting regularly. Dickens takes this opportunity, then, to create a distinct and conspicuous contrast between Esther (and, in this case, Ada) and Mrs. Pardiggle.

Mrs. Pardiggle, upon entering the home uninvited, exhibits only a feigned friendliness and even less sensitivity to the needs of the people she is visiting. And as Mrs. Pardiggle continues through the motions of her religious project, Esther observes that, in her demeanor, tone of voice, and sermonizing, she takes the whole family "into religious custody . . . as if she were an inexorable moral Policeman carrying them all off to the station-house."[25]

Prior to setting off on this goodwill visit back at Bleak House, Esther had attempted to excuse herself from this round of visitation. In Esther's excuse, Dickens anticipates Mrs. Pardiggle's manner and conduct, setting up the thematic contrast between the two. Esther questions her own qualifications for such a service. She explains that she "was inexperienced in the art of adapting [her] mind to minds very differently situated, and addressing them from suitable points of view," and that she "had not the delicate knowledge of the heart which must be essential to such work." Further, she insists that she "had much to learn . . . before [she] could teach others, and that [she] could not confide in [her] good intentions alone."[26] Esther finally observes, "For these reasons, I thought it best to be as useful as I could, and to render what kind services I could, to those immediately about me; and to try to let that circle of duty gradually and naturally expand itself."[27]

Dickens does two things here. First, he articulates what he believes to be wrong with this sort of philanthropy. Second, he shows in Esther's sensitivity to the needs of the specific situation that she is more qualified to meet those needs than Mrs. Pardiggle. Indeed, once Mrs. Pardiggle has finished her moral assault on the family and is satisfied that she has fulfilled her own agenda, she leaves, "expressing her hope that the brickmaker and all his house would be improved when she saw them next." Clearly, Dickens speaks through Esther again as she remarks, "I hope it is not unkind in me to say that she certainly did make, in this, as in everything else, a show that was not conciliatory, of doing charity by wholesale, and of dealing in it to a large extent."[28]

Moreover, upon Mrs. Pardiggle's departure, Esther and Ada immediately and naturally attempt to attend to the needs they see in the home. Obvious to both Esther and Ada is the need of the brickmaker's wife, who had been intensely caring for and caressing an obviously ill infant during the entire Pardiggle visit. Esther and Ada approach the mother and child to help and as they do so the child dies. Esther and Ada again immediately attend to both the physical and emotional needs of the mother by taking the child from the mother and doing what they can "to make the baby's rest prettier and gentler." Then, as Esther recalls, they tried "to comfort the mother, and . . . whispered to her what Our Saviour said of children."[29] Dickens shaped the entire narrative to show the contrast between Mrs. Pardiggle and Esther, between true service and the pretense of service, between the religionist and the disciple.

Mrs. Jellyby is another character in *Bleak House* whom Dickens uses to contrast the earnest and genuine Christianity of Esther with a superficial and misdirected religiosity. On Esther's initial trip to Bleak House, Mr. Jarndyce arranges for her to stay an evening with the Jellybys. Mrs. Jellyby is a prolific letter writer soliciting funds for what she calls the Africa project. She was hopeful, "by this time next year to have from a hundred and fifty to two hundred healthy families cultivating coffee and educating the natives of Borrioboola-Gha, on the left bank of the Niger."[30] Actually, Mrs. Jellyby's daughter Caddy, her amanuensis, does the letter writing, but does so with great disdain for both the Africa project and her mother. This is because, as Esther observes, although Mrs. Jellyby has "handsome eyes . . . they had a curious habit of seeming to look a long way off. As if . . . they could see nothing nearer than Africa."[31]

Indeed, Mrs. Jellyby sees little else. Her home is in extraordinary disarray and she, for all intents and purposes, ignores her family, including Caddy, an unnumbered brood of younger children, and her husband. Although Dickens develops this narrative with a lighter, more comic tone than the Pardiggle narrative, his point is similar. It is Esther who comes into the Jellyby home and begins to do quite naturally what Dickens would have expected Mrs. Jellyby to do. Esther attends to, nurses, and reads to the children at bedtime, "until Mrs. Jellyby accidentally remembering them, sent them to bed."[32] Esther is also surrogate mother to Caddy through the remainder of the novel, helping her through young adulthood and into marriage. Again, it is Dickens's point to question the passion of such mission-minded Victorians when they had hoards of homeless, marginalized, needy people on their own streets—men, women and children—all of whom were just as sacred as the natives of Borrioboola-Gha. Osbert Sitwell has commented on what he refers to as the "Mote-Beam School of Philanthropy," in which Mrs. Jellyby participates: "[They] rescue, clothe, and feed [natives] in islands lost among the Antipodes, but allow their own children to grow up totally neglected and those of their neighbors to die of starvation."[33] Again, it is Esther who sees that perhaps the most generous and most Christian thing to do would be "to render what kind services I could, to those immediately about me; and to try to let that circle of duty gradually and naturally expand itself." In a word, this would probably be Dickens's philosophy of mission in a nutshell.

Dickens drew one more contrast to Esther in *Bleak House* in the character of the Dissenting or Nonconformist Reverend Chadband. While Chadband is not as directly connected to Esther by way of narrative device as Mrs. Pardiggle and Mrs. Jellyby, he is no less a foil. Chadband is a pompous, rambling, self-appointed preacher who talks overly much but says substantially nothing. And for that very reason, Chadband seems harmless. But Dickens sees such preachers as dangerous, for in their self-absorbed, empty preaching they obscure the message of the gospel.

In one important scene in which Chadband had been preaching at Jo, the street sweeper, Dickens interrupts in an editorial aside to let Jo know of a book, "a history so interesting and affecting . . . it might hold thee awake, and thou might learn from it yet."[34] But, the narrative continues, "Jo never heard of any such book. Its compilers, and the Reverend Chadband, are all one to him—except he knows the Reverend Chadband, and would rather run away from him for an hour than hear him talk for five minutes."[35]

Esther, of course, is just the opposite. Esther talks little, but does much. She simply wants to live up to her prayer, to be of help to someone and to serve others in that place in which God had placed her. These are not idle words for Esther. She does just that. And for Dickens, that is the difference between superficial piety and true Christianity. While Pardiggle, Jellyby, and Chadband go about their religious activities, Esther serves those about her in concrete and tangible ways. In this way, Dickens claims her "in express words as [a disciple] of the Founder of our religion."[36]

The themes and the characters we have considered here are representative of Dickens's writing. They are neither curiosities nor exceptions. His stories and his people consistently emerged from and were shaped by his Christian worldview. Just as he insists in his letter to Macrae, his good people, his strong characters are disciples of Jesus. And for Dickens, that discipleship was demonstrated in practical ways in service and care for others. Just so, he wanted to demonstrate what Christianity and a life of faith looked like lived out. And those times when Dickens showed what Christianity is *not* speak as loudly and are just as instructive in reminding us of what Christianity is intended to be.

A Clarifying Perspective

In light of all that has just been said, one would be justified in wondering if I am attempting to make Dickens out as Christian novelist, churchman, or theologian . . . or all three. Let me say from the outset that he was neither theologian, churchman, nor Christian novelist—at least in the way those ascriptions are normally used. While I will say more about this concern in later chapters, it should be established here that I do not believe Dickens was a theologian either by aptitude or interest, and I do not wish to make him one. Nor was he a churchman. I do believe, however, that Dickens was a serious Christian layperson, one who took his beliefs seriously and one who was at least aware of and, to some degree, informed about some of the theological ideas that were provoking discussion in his day.

As a serious layperson, Dickens did invest time thinking carefully about his faith and, as we will see, had clear and certain notions about Christianity and the life of faith. Moreover, like most laypeople in his day, Dickens probably would have subscribed to a simple set of core beliefs characteristic of a popular lay Anglicanism.[37] In her *The Nineteenth-Century Church and English Society*, Frances Knight outlines these core beliefs: (1) the efficacy of prayer, (2) belief in the reality of heaven and hell, and (3) a composite but undefined view of salvation by works and by faith. Knight suggests further that those who embraced this popular lay Anglicanism (4) would have felt no particular allegiance to the parish church and (5) that the Bible and the Book of Common Prayer would have played an important role in (6) an Anglican piety that had its source largely in the home rather than the church.[38] As will become evident as we consider his Christian views and practices, Dickens's Christianity resembles the popular lay Anglicanism that Knight describes.

Dickens, then, is neither churchman nor theologian. Neither would I try to shove him into that class of Christian writer who writes overtly Christian novels for a popular audience, particularly as we understand those today or even as they were understood in the nineteenth century. Accordingly, Dickens could not be considered a Christian novelist by any means. Dickens was, however, a novelist who possessed deep and passionate Christian beliefs and who wrote from a thoroughgoing Christian worldview. As such, Dickens's Christian thought was simply part of the whole fabric of his work. It is precisely in this sense that Tolstoy and Dostoevsky refer to Dickens as "that great Christian writer."

A conspicuous Christian thread runs through almost all of Dickens's novels and books. And in cases where we find such a thread, it provides a formative element in the theme and plot of the work. More importantly, Dickens made expressly clear that his heroes and heroines were intentionally created as those who aspired to the teaching and imitation of Jesus. It makes sense, then, that Angus Wilson would comment, "In profound ways the Christian religion makes sense of his work."[39]

Still, with all that has been written about Dickens over the years—from his marriage to his social involvement; from his parenting to his acting—rarely have his religious beliefs and Christian convictions been brought into popular discourse in any substantial way.[40] So often, when Dickens's life is discussed, his Christian convictions are virtually ignored. But unless we account for Dickens's committed Christian worldview, we may very well miss much of what regularly helped to shape his ideas and his meaning. Without question, our understanding of Dickens will be substantially altered, becoming more nuanced and complex, when his Christian worldview is brought to bear on his life and work. For this reason, his profound sense of an authentic and practical Christianity cannot be ignored if we hope to understand him correctly and if we hope to read him in all his richness and breadth. For good or bad, then, this Christian orientation must inform and contribute to our understanding of Dickens's life and work.

A recent BBC production of Dickens's *Little Dorrit* may serve as a case in point. This production seemed almost perfectly crafted—except, of course, for the absence of the strong Christian themes that run throughout the novel.[41] They were, for all intents and purposes, omitted from the production. In Dickens's mind, Amy Dorrit significantly represents a humble Christ-like Christian faith lived out. She represents a New Testament ethic and a disciple of Jesus, while Mrs. Clennam represents, with the same significance, a heartless religiosity and an Old Testament ethic—in the form of a distorted Calvinism—based on a God who was exclusively Judge at the expense of being Father. Some might argue that the production was quite well done and was none the worse for the editing out of the Christian material. They might insist that the basic storyline remained intact. In some respects, that may be true. The fact remains, however, that Dickens as creator of the story and the characters deliberately and purposefully developed this line of Christian thought in order to shape the story and give it the thematic emphasis he wanted. And he placed significant and conspicuous emphasis on this line of Christian thought. The sustained and passionate development of the contrast between Amy and Mrs. Clennam is as much a part of the story for Dickens as is "Do Not Forget" or the symbol of the prison. To ignore the development and presence of this line of thought, then, is to do an injustice to Dickens and to his intent as author.

The same might be said about the 2008 BBC production of *Bleak House* or Roman Polanski's 2005 movie adaption of *Oliver Twist*. While both, like *Little Dorrit*, are excellent productions and fine interpretations of Dickens, they misrepresent Dickens, at least to some degree, by leaving out what for him were central elements of theme and character development. It is understandable that time constraints in most Dickens productions demand that material be omitted—novels of nearly one thousand pages are not always adaptable even to six-or eight-hour productions. But the Christian themes and worldview in Dickens are aspects that do not require much on-screen time; they are part of the fabric of the narrative and of the lives of the characters. A proper gesture in this direction would be faithful to the spirit of Dickens's art and a more accurate depiction of his characters and narrative world.

My point here is not to dismiss these productions offhandedly. Rather, it is to point out with some sense of clarity that both popular culture and the literary world seem to ignore this important aspect of Dickens's life and work. Were it because Dickens used cryptic, obscure, enigmatic references to religion, such negligence could perhaps be overlooked. But Dickens is clear and straightforward in his Christian themes and characters, and intentionally so. As such, it is incumbent upon us as responsible readers not only to acknowledge the presence of his Christian worldview but also to let it inform and shape our understanding of Dickens's work and message.

Meeting Dickens

Dickens's faith was a simple one—he was not much interested in theology and was certainly not given to theological speculation—but he thought seriously and perceptively about Christianity and the life of faith, and he wrote passionately from his convictions. His was a thoroughgoing Christian worldview in which Jesus occupied the center. In fact, Jesus was, for Dickens, essentially the heart and whole of Christianity. That is, for Dickens, taking the teaching of Jesus seriously and embracing an authentic commitment to imitate his example was the mark of the true Christian.

In Dickens's mind, Christianity was not, as it never had been and never should be, about guarding a system of doctrine, advancing the programs of the church, or giving intellectual assent to a given data set. Christianity was about imitating Jesus in the concrete realities of everyday life. That may seem naïve to some; it may seem simplistic; it may seem short-sighted; or it may seem overly reductionist. Certainly, Dickens's Christianity has been alleged to be one of the four at one time or another. But there is nothing simplistic or naïve about a faith that seeks to imitate Jesus, for the imitation of Jesus means a life given away in service to others. It requires a selfless humility, an unwavering confidence in God's faithfulness, an abandonment of self-centered preoccupations, and an untiring love. Like all the rest of us, Dickens fell short of his ideal, but he was wise enough to know what he should aspire to be. In any case, his sense of the life of faith was penetrating and his concept of Christian discipleship provocative.

The Inimitable Boz

But then, Dickens was an interesting and provocative fellow. There is little question about his genius. He was a great crafter and teller of stories; his descriptions are some of the most affecting in literature; his characters, unforgettable; his ability to turn a phrase, unmatched. He was a great observer of things and people; and he knew people, understood the human condition, and had an uncanny sense of human nature. His oldest child Charley would recall his father's ability to read the character of his school friends when they came to the Dickens home to visit. Charley remembered how his father seemed to know exactly what to say to them and how to say it.[42]

As a novelist and writer, Dickens was a humorist. Had he lived today, he likely would have fallen somewhere in the line of our popular comic satirists, our great stand-up comedians, our finest comic actors, and our most accomplished comedy writers. He brought so many skills and talents to his craft, but his humor, with an incisive wit and cleverness, and his penetrating ability to assess the social and human condition comprised a talent that surely was a major strength in an individual that possessed so many. It is not uncommon to laugh out loud when reading Dickens (neither is it uncommon to weep).

And not everyone knows that during his career as a writer, Dickens was an amateur actor—a rather talented one—involved in any number of stage productions with both friends and family. In fact, had it not been for a serious cold he developed that caused him to miss a theatrical audition early in his life, the world may never have met Charles Dickens the author.

As to his personal habits, Dickens was all about order, propriety, and hard work. An article in the *Dickensian* in May of 1967 chronicles the informal interview the Rev. Dr. G. D. Carrow had with Dickens that took place 8 August 1867. Carrow questioned Dickens about his work habits, and Dickens replied with a basic outline of his daily schedule:

> I rise at seven; at eight I breakfast; until ten I walk or ride and read the morning papers; at ten precisely I go to my desk and stay there till two, and if particularly in the vein keep at it until four. Then I take the open air for exercise, usually walking. At six I sit down to dinner and remain at table until ten, during which time I discuss domestic matters with my family or entertain such friends as may honor me with their visits. This, the great occasion of the day, over, I retire to my study, amuse myself a little with the flute, read up the reviews, or examine such original publications as may have been sent to my table; and exactly at twelve I extinguish my lights and jump into bed. So rigid is my conformity to this method of work that my family say I am a monomaniac on the subject of method.[43]

This brief overview suggests at least two things. First, it speaks to Dickens's rigid schedule and his almost unhealthy preoccupation with order, routine, and punctuality. And while it reflects Dickens's schedule as he was managing it in 1867, just three years before his death, it is indicative of the basic schedule Dickens maintained throughout his adult life and career. Second, filling in the gaps that he provides here with what is known further of his life reveals a full and demanding day. Again, it must be born in mind that this was his schedule in 1867, when his pace of work and responsibility had slowed considerably—at least compared to his earlier life. Notwithstanding, the gaps seem easy to fill.

The writing that Dickens would take on in a portion of his day at any point in his life was enough to provide an entire day's work for any other person. He was a prolific letter writer, and his correspondence itself seems almost overwhelming at times. His surviving letters fill twelve very hefty volumes. Still, it was quite normal for Dickens to be working at a novel (or two), writing an article for a paper here or a journal there, and managing the enormous amount of correspondence that came across his desk. Moreover, his charitable work and involvement in itself could have been a fulltime job. Whether he was working, writing, and speaking on behalf of the Ragged Schools, managing and supervising his and Angela Burdett-Coutts's Urania Cottage, working tirelessly to help the various needy individuals whose predicaments were brought to his attention, or participating on a board, committee, or commission, Dickens was always ready to offer assistance and to be involved.

As a journalist, Dickens was a social journalist. When he wrote, he was not simply writing opinion pieces or entertainment. Often he was asked to contribute an article to a newspaper or a journal that would speak knowledgeably and persuasively to any one of a variety of social issues. Likewise, Dickens was in demand as a speaker to lend his voice and his influence to causes, from sanitary conditions to education, and from the housing conditions of the poor to the needs and development of hospitals. Dickens was more than willing to oblige all of these requests. When the entertaining that he and his wife, Catherine, did in their home is reckoned into the equation, it is easy to see that he managed a rather full schedule, and it makes sense that his family saw him as "a monomaniac" with regard to order, routine, and punctuality.

Dickens as Father

In all of this, Dickens found time—somehow—to be involved with his family. He loved his children and he involved himself in their lives. Dickens had a reputation among his friends and family as one who especially enjoyed the company of his children and was more than willing to help create and join with them in their fun. In her article, "Dickens's Philosophy of Fathering," Natalie McKnight speaks to Dickens's "playfulness" with his children.[44] She refers to instances cited in the biographies of Dickens by John Forster, Edgar Johnson, and Peter Ackroyd that all highlight Dickens's spirit of fun. As Forster relates a specific instance, one that Dickens asked expressly that he remember and write in his biography, "Little Mary [Dickens] and her sister Kate had taken much pains to teach their father the polka, that he might dance it with them at their brother's birthday festivity . . . ; and in the middle of the previous night as he lay in bed, the fear had fallen on him suddenly that the step was forgotten, and then and there, in that wintry dark cold night, he got out of bed to practise it."[45] Forster remarks in this context, "besides the dinners, the musical enjoyments and dancings, *as his children became able to take part in them,* [my italics] were incessant."[46] Michael Slater adds his own observations of what must have been one of Dickens's first children's parties in which Dickens himself entertained as a magician, complete with magic lantern and dressed in full magician's regalia. Slater quotes the daughter of William Makepeace Thackeray as she remembered such parties: "There were other parties, and they were very nice, but nothing compared to these: not nearly so light, not nearly so shining, not nearly so going round and round." Slater notes that she saw the Dickens parties as "shining facts in our early London days."[47]

His oldest son, Charley, remembered his father sitting in his "American rocking-chair" in the evening "singing comic songs to a wondering and delighted audience consisting of myself and my two sisters." For Charley, "the impression of the singer, as he sat in that rocking-chair with us three children about or on his knees" left an indelible mark on his memory. Similarly, Charley recalled the child-like fascination that Dickens exhibited with a sizeable toy theatre belonging to Charley. He remembered his father immersing himself so entirely in the toy that he recruited his good friend Clarkson Stanfield to stage a production called *Elephant of Siam*, for which they designed and painted several new backdrops. And Charley remembers most vividly the energy and enthusiasm that Dickens brought to all of this. "Whatever he did he put his whole heart into and did as well as ever he could," Charley recalled. "Whether it was for work or for play, he was always in earnest. Painting the scenes for a toy theatre, dancing Sir Roger de Coverley at a children's party, gravely learning the polka from his little daughters for a similar entertainment . . . it was all one to him."[48]

Beyond the merriment and play, Dickens involved himself in the lives of his children in more serious, but no less significant ways as well. For one, he composed *A Child's History of England* expressly for his first child, Charley, to provide him with a proper understanding of English history in order that he might not, in later life, develop wrong notions of his country and his culture. Dickens wrote to his friend Douglas Jerrold, 3 May 1843, about *A Child's History of England* and its purpose:

> I am writing a little history of England for my boy, which I will send you when it is printed for him, though your boys are too old to profit by it. It is curious that I have tried to impress upon him (writing, I dare say, at the same moment with you) the exact spirit of your paper. For I don't know what I should do, if he were to get hold of any conservative or High Church notions; and the best way of guarding against any such horrible result, is, I take it, to wring the parrots' necks in his very cradle.[49]

Certainly, *A Child's History of England* is revisionist and marginally propagandistic, but that's precisely the point. As a father, Dickens was anxious that his children develop the values and attitudes that he thought were right and proper and that he wished to instill in them. I do not mean to suggest at all that Dickens was distorting, recasting, or rewriting history to bring them in line with his beliefs. Rather, he was interpreting history and commenting on it from the standpoint of his worldview, his values, and those he wished to impart to his children.

Dickens's composition of what we know today as *The Life of Our Lord* follows along similar lines. He wrote *The Life of Our Lord* in order that his children might know Jesus, "who He was and what He did."[50] But quite unlike *A Child's History of England*, *The Life of Our Lord* was never intended to be published, for Dickens saw it as a private and intimate gift from a father to his children.[51] It was for the family alone. Indeed, it was written exclusively for his children and for their instruction. Perhaps one of the least understood facts about *The Life of Our Lord* is that Dickens wrote it to be *read* to his children, not for them to read. And it is almost certain that sometime during the Christmas holiday, Dickens would perform a dramatic reading of *The Life of Our Lord* for his ever-growing family and probably did so annually for a number of years.[52] Dickens wrote to David Macrae in 1861 concerning *The Life of Our Lord*: "All of them [Dickens's children], from the first to the last, have had a little version of the New Testament that I wrote for them, read to them long before they could read, and no young people can have had an earlier knowledge of, or interest in, that book. It is an inseparable part of their earliest remembrances."[53]

Dickens and the Life of Faith

Dickens reiterated time and again to his children the beauty of Christianity as it comes to us in the New Testament and urged them to follow the teaching and the example of Jesus as the one true expression of genuine Christianity. But he hoped they would see Jesus on Jesus's own terms, apart from "the vain constructions and inventions of men,"[54] and the New Testament on its own terms, apart from any person's "narrow construction of its letter here or there."[55] To this end, Dickens wrote *The Life of Our Lord*.[56] The qualifications that Dickens offers here, of course, are pregnant with his hesitations and misgivings about the state of Christianity in the nineteenth century as it was mediated not only by the established church and its churchmen, but also by the Dissenters and Nonconformists. And so, while in Dickens's mind there were plenty of vain and narrow constructions and human inventions relative to Jesus and the New Testament to go around, he was confident that *The Life of Our Lord* provided an unadulterated, nonsectarian presentation from which he was so anxious for his children to learn.

It is this centrality of Jesus as he emerges unaltered from the New Testament—at least in Dickens's mind—that defines Dickens's faith and makes the reading and study of Dickens so fascinating. Søren Kierkegaard said that a Christian's life should be marked by what must be "an effort in the direction of what the New Testament calls Christianity."[57] Kierkegaard couched this, of course, in a negative expression and as a specific challenge to a complacent church. Dickens would have enthusiastically concurred with the notion, the phrasing, and the challenge. That is, for Dickens, true Christianity and true Christian discipleship can only be measured by whether or not it is "an effort in the direction of what the New Testament calls Christianity."[58] For Dickens, that was simply taking the life and teaching of Jesus seriously and following that example in concrete and tangible ways.

This sort of Christian worldview and orientation to life undergirded all of his work and always played a major role in his fiction. But Dickens was notorious as the black sheep in the Christian family. His declarations of his faith were often bold and passionate, and his criticisms of the church and pious religiosity were always so. He was merciless in his caricatures of Dissenters and Nonconformists of any sort, and his criticisms of the established church were usually so scathing that they might be considered vitriolic, were they not so penetratingly accurate.

I suspect that at least some of the confusion and misapprehension about Dickens's Christianity stems from the tensions created by his clear declarations of faith on the one hand and his bold denunciations of the church and religionists on the other. Many Dickens enthusiasts and fans with whom I speak typically fall into two camps when it concerns Dickens and religion: they either believe Dickens flagrantly rejected religion, or they are simply unaware of any serious religious aspects of his writing, apart from his criticisms of the clergy and the church and his apparent disapproval of both.

The views and comments of Humphry House and Philip Collins, noted earlier, provide some insight as to why some are surprised to learn that Charles Dickens was a Christian. But their observations also seem to provide some clues, however slight, as to why there seem to be such persistent misconstructions of the religious aspects of Dickens's work. Collins, responding to the observation of Dickens's son, Sir Henry Fielding Dickens, that his father "possessed deep religious convictions," remarked, "'Sincere' would have been an apter word, for if his religion had been 'deep' his novels would have contained more explicit and insistent reference to Christian worship and belief." And House was confident that Dickens's "practical humanist kind of Christianity hardly touched the fringes of what is called religious experience, and his work shows no indication of any powerful feeling connected with the genuinely religious subject." I repeat these comments here, because in both cases, the observations ultimately tell us more about Collins and House than they do about Dickens. That is, they reveal what both Collins and House expected religious expression to look like and precisely how Dickens should have articulated and presented it. In neither man's imagination, according to their comments, do they envision Christianity without religiosity, ceremony, and ritual observance. Nor, by way of extension, do they see that someone with a passionate devotion to Jesus could at the same time criticize the church.

In light of Dickens's express words about Christianity and the life of faith, his criticisms of the church seem to be the voice of an insider, however aloof he may seem, calling for the church to live up to its vocation, rather than the voice of a skeptic outside the church and at enmity with it. Dickens hoped the church would be—no, Dickens *expected* the church to be a community of people who simply imitated Jesus, bringing his teaching and actions to bear on the world around them. Where that was not happening, Dickens called the church to account.

But Dickens's Christian voice is not always a negative one. As I will try to demonstrate, Dickens speaks volumes on the positive expression and joy of Christianity—because that is how he perceived the life of faith. Dickens believed that Christianity, as it has come to us in Christ, is intended to bring strength and courage, encouragement and comfort, peace and joy, and most of all love and hope.

The Christian Voice of Charles Dickens

In the pages that follow, we will hear the Christian voice of Charles Dickens and we will attempt to draw out the implications of what we hear for Christians and for the church today. In most respects, Dickens does not say much that has not already been said. Yet, in the context in which it comes to us and in a way that only the inimitable can say it, Dickens's Christian voice can speak to us in a fresh and transformative way. George Orwell claimed of Dickens, "He is always preaching a sermon."[59] If Orwell is right, and I think he is, it would serve us well to hear Dickens and to hear what he has to say afresh. As we work our way through the chapters of this book, a number of themes will emerge that bolster the claim of Tolstoy and Dostoevsky that Dickens is a "great Christian writer." We have already introduced some of those themes, if indirectly, in our consideration of Arthur Clennam and Esther Summerson. Many of the ideas introduced there will be touched on and some examined in greater detail in the chapters ahead. But brief overviews of two of Dickens's primary themes—ideas that seem to drive his entire understanding of Christianity—can complete this introduction to Dickens's Christian voice and can act as a sort of primer for this book.

The Centrality of Jesus and the New Testament

If there is one thing scholars and critics can agree upon about Dickens's religion, it is that his was a simple faith and Jesus was the central and essential element in it. Naturally, this included an emphasis on and a central place for the New Testament, by which Dickens typically meant the Gospels, although not always exclusively. Dickens never hesitated to make clear in his writing or in his correspondence the importance of the centrality of Jesus and the value of the New Testament for the life of faith. For instance, in *Dombey and Son*, in her final moments, Alice Marwood asks Harriet Carker to read to her.

> Harriet complied and read—read the eternal book for all the weary and the heavy-laden; for all the wretched, fallen, and neglected of this earth—read the blessed history, in which the blind lame palsied beggar, the criminal, the women stained with shame, the shunned of all our dainty clay, has each a portion, that no human pride, indifference or sophistry, through all the ages that this world shall last, can take away, or by the thousandth atom of a grain reduce—read the ministry of Him who, through the round of human life, and all

its hopes and griefs, from birth to death, from infancy to age, had sweet compassion for, and interest in, its every scene and state, its every suffering and sorrow.[60]

It is noteworthy here that Dickens includes an emphasis on both the New Testament and Jesus. For Dickens, the New Testament is the "blessed history," one that is "the most beautiful and affecting history conceivable by man,"[61] and it is precisely so because it is the story of Jesus. Such passages are not uncommon in Dickens's writing or his correspondence.

This same sort of emphasis is clearly evident in his letter to David Macrae cited above, but Dickens would write even more to the point in letters to his sons Edward and Henry concerning "the beauty of the Christian religion as it came from Christ Himself," a deep respect for the New Testament, and a submission to "our Saviour, as separated from the vain constructions and inventions of men."[62]

Even in what would be his final words to his children in his last will and testament, he expressed similar sentiments when he wrote, "I commit my soul to the mercy of God through our Lord and Savior Jesus Christ, and I exhort my dear children humbly to try to guide themselves by the teaching of the New Testament in its broad spirit, and to put no faith in any man's narrow construction of its letter here or there."[63] One final time, Dickens urged his sons and daughters to embrace a Christianity determined by the centrality of Jesus as portrayed to us in the New Testament.

The very fact that Dickens wrote *The Life of Our Lord* speaks to the centrality of Jesus and the importance of the New Testament in his life and thought. As the center of Dickens's faith and the essential element in it, Jesus was the Exemplar. When Dickens referred to what he called "real Christianity," he was referring to the imitation of the life and teaching of Jesus. For Dickens, the imitation of Jesus was the mark of genuine Christianity; indeed, it *was* Christianity. Dickens had little patience with talk about Christianity and Jesus, what he rightly called "mere professions of religion," that was not manifested and lived out in active service to others. In many ways, this was the subject of the sermon that Orwell tells us Dickens was always preaching. Without question, it was at the very heart of Dickens's understanding and practice of the life of faith.

Unobtrusive Christianity

In a letter to Rev. R. H. Davies (see chapter 5), Dickens complains about the "obtrusive professions of and tradings in religion, as one of the main causes why real Christianity has been retarded in this world."[64] And in a letter to J. M. Makeham, Dickens defends the authenticity of his faith, and adds, "But I have never made proclamation of this from the house tops."[65] Dickens was easily rankled by the showy, usually unwelcome, and, more often than not, belligerent expressions of Christianity that were much a part of the religious landscape of the nineteenth century. And so Dickens was one who deliberately avoided such expressions in his own practice of Christianity.

Dickens, of course, never meant to imply that one's faith should be unobtrusive in the sense that it is a purely personal and private matter or that we should try to play it down so as not to be offensive. Dickens wasn't afraid of being identified as a Christian, nor was he reticent to speak passionately of the Christian life. What he wanted to emphasize in this regard was that our Christian faith was not a mere profession of belief or intellectual assent to a body of data but that it was to be woven into the very fabric of our life and character.

For Dickens, Christianity was a deeply rooted orientation by which we perceive, understand, respond to, and order our lives. In his mind, then, Christian faith need not be announced or paraded as public spectacle, but it does need to be lived out. One's faith needs to be demonstrated, Dickens would insist, in a sense of integrity, justice, propriety, common courtesy, and all of those other things that make up what we often refer to today as character. It needs to be demonstrated, too, in our relationships with those whom God has brought into our lives and with whom our paths have crossed. And Dickens would place the highest premium on a faith demonstrated in selfless service to others; in a faith that seeks to be an expression of Christ's love and compassion for the poor, the destitute, and the needy. Dickens speaks to this concern in his singular manner in a piece called "The Short-Timers":

Within so many yards of this Covent-garden lodging of mine, as within so many yards of Westminster Abbey, Saint Paul's Cathedral, the Houses of Parliament, the Prisons, the Courts of Justice, all the

Institutions that govern the land, I can find—*must* find, whether I will or no—in the open streets, shameful instances of neglect of children, intolerable toleration of the engenderment of paupers, idlers, thieves, races of wretched and destructive cripples both in body and mind, a misery to themselves, a misery to the community, a disgrace to civilisation, and an outrage on Christianity.[66]

A passage like this echoes a theme that can be found throughout the Dickens corpus, because for Dickens, Christianity naturally involves relieving the kinds of distresses that he identified here. Such is as much a part of Christian profession, if not more so, than impeccable doctrine or church membership and involvement.

In Dickens's mind, a Christianity demonstrated in selfless service to others stands over and against the religiosity, the false piety, and the churchianity of so much of Christian profession—precisely what Dickens referred to as "obtrusive professions" and what many in the nineteenth century liked to call "cant," which included religious clichés and platitudes, hypocrisy, insincerity, lip service, and sanctimonious jargon. Dickens loathed it and was quite adept at poignantly illustrating it in such characters as the Reverend Mr. Stiggins (*The Pickwick Papers*), Mr. Seth Pecksniff (*Martin Chuzzlewit*) and the Reverend Mr. Chadband (*Bleak House*). In each case, these characters are shining examples of obtrusive profession and the antithesis of genuine and true Christianity.

Obviously, then, Dickens understood Christianity to be far more than subscribing to dogma, agreement with doctrines, devotional exercises, and religious observance. For Dickens, these things paled in comparison with the things that really mattered. Consequently, Dickens's Christian voice makes little mention of religious things. And those characters in his work whom he would claim as exemplars of a genuine Christian faith and as disciples of the Master have no connection with such things. They simply go about the business of imitating Jesus in their service to others. In this way, Dickens was able to provide a clear picture in an emphatic way of what he believed was real Christianity.

2

Charles Dickens's Jesus

The example and the teaching of Jesus, particularly as they come to us in the Gospels, were central to Dickens's understanding of Christianity and the life of faith. For Dickens, Jesus was the definitive element of "real Christianity," and the imitation of Jesus was the definitive mark of the real Christian. Certainly, Dickens believed that the good characters in his novels reflected to some degree the moral-ethical character of Jesus. Consequently, the Dickens corpus contains many references to Jesus, and if we pay attention, we can learn much from Dickens about Christianity, the life of faith, and following Jesus.

Whether in his letters, his novels, or his essays, when his thoughts turned to the things of faith, Dickens ultimately deferred to the teaching of the New Testament—which for him was the Gospels—and the life and lessons of Jesus. Consider, for instance, his response in a 25 March 1847 letter to F. W. H. Layton, who had apparently questioned the orthodoxy of Dickens's concept of Christianity: "As I really do not know what orthodoxy may be, or what it may be supposed to include—a point not exactly settled, I believe, as yet, in the learned or unlearned world—I am not in a condition to say whether I deserve my lax reputation in that wise. But my creed is the creed of Jesus Christ, I believe, and my deepest admiration and respect attend upon his life and teaching, I know."[1] Dickens did not seek to defend himself against his correspondent on any sort of doctrinal grounds or with theological argument. Rather, he simply appealed to his own convictions concerning Jesus and the New Testament. Dickens believed without question that his creed was, indeed, the creed of Jesus Christ, and he certainly believed that a person's best course of action was to humbly and reverently embrace Christianity as it came from Christ himself "as separated from the vain constructions and inventions of men."[2]

Consider, further, his words of affirmation in his essay, "Two Views Of A Cheap Theatre," regarding the sermon he heard by a "preacher" one "damp and muddy Sunday evening." Dickens had been little impressed with the preacher's presence or his particular style of preaching. "But in respect of the large Christianity of his general tone" and "of his renunciation of all priestly authority," Dickens was in agreement. Moreover, "of his earnest and reiterated assurance to the people that the commonest among them could work out their own salvation if they would, by simply, lovingly, and dutifully following Our Saviour, and that they needed the mediation of no erring man; in these particulars this gentleman deserved all praise."[3] Again, it is the centrality of Jesus and following Jesus that draws Dickens's attention and with which he identifies a robust and purposeful Christianity.

With similar emphasis, Dickens wrote to his son Edward (Plorn) on 26 (?) September 1868, the eve of Edward's departure for Australia, "You will therefore understand the better that I now most solemnly impress upon you the truth and beauty of the Christian Religion, as it came from Christ Himself, and the impossibility of your going far wrong if you humbly but heartily respect it."[4] And not too long afterward, he wrote to his son Henry (Harry) on 15 October 1868, "Deeply respecting it [the New Testament] and bowing down before the character of our Saviour, as separated from the vain constructions and inventions of men, you cannot go very wrong, and will always preserve at heart a true spirit of veneration and humility."[5] Obviously, Dickens was not reticent to speak plainly to his sons about a practical Christianity that always situated the Jesus of the Gospels at the center and then sought to imitate Jesus's example.

Perhaps the definitive passage regarding the centrality of Jesus in Dickens's understanding of Christianity and the life of faith is found in *Little Dorrit*. Here, Amy Dorrit addresses Mrs. Clennam in a climactic passage toward the end of the novel:

> O, Mrs. Clennam, Mrs. Clennam . . . angry feelings and unforgiving deeds are no comfort and no guide to you and me. . . . Be guided, only by the healer of the sick, the raiser of the dead, the friend of all who were afflicted and forlorn, the patient Master who shed tears of compassion for our infirmities. We cannot but be right if we put all the rest away, and do everything in remembrance of Him. There is no vengeance and no infliction of suffering in His life, I am sure. There can be no confusion in following Him, and seeking for no other footsteps, I am certain![6]

In all of this, it is certainly understandable then, that Philip Collins calls Dickens a New Testament Christian or a Gospel Christian.[7] That observation is likely more profound than Collins knew. Dickens's singular focus on the life and ministry of Jesus was the heart of his faith, and it was essentially the whole of his faith. In one sense, of course, that makes his faith rather simple. That is not to say, however, that his faith was simplistic and shallow. As his work demonstrates, such a simple faith was carefully reasoned and passionately articulated and found its expression in what Dickens genuinely understood as a practicable Jesus-centered ethic. For Dickens, the entirety of the Christian faith was wrapped up in the teaching and example of Jesus as they come to us in the Gospels. And while he seems to have been aware of many of the current theological, ecclesial, and biblical studies ideas circulating in his day, none of those things seemed to play any substantial or formative role in Dickens's understanding of Christianity compared to the centrality of Jesus and the Gospels.

Still, all of this invites the pertinent questions: Who was this Jesus at the heart and center of Christianity as Dickens understood it? What was the character of this one after whom the Dickensian hero or heroine was modeled and whose example Christians were to imitate? Did Dickens leave us anything resembling a portrait? Or did he, as some insist, leave only a rough sketch much too generic to be informative? Just what did Dickens's Jesus look like?

Jesus and *The Life Of Our Lord*

The fact is, Dickens left us a rather substantial and definitive portrait of Jesus in a small volume we know today as *The Life of Our Lord* (from this point forward, *TLOL*). Actually, *TLOL* was a handwritten manuscript[8] that Dickens would have read—probably dramatically—to his children and a piece that he adamantly refused to have published during his lifetime. This personal, family account of the life of Jesus, written exclusively for the Dickens children, was not seen by the general public[9] until March 1934, when following the death of Sir Henry Fielding Dickens—Dickens's last surviving child—it was published for the first time.[10]

TLOL is a selective juvenile harmony of the Gospels edited and composed by Dickens himself. But it is also a child's life of Jesus. Prior to 1860 in nineteenth-century Great Britain the method of writing a life of Jesus was to write a harmony of the Gospels.[11] A harmony of the Gospels is a rather complex work that weaves together, or harmonizes, the four canonical Gospels into one running narrative.[12] A life of Jesus, on the other hand, is more of an historical task employing the historical-critical method and attempting to go beyond the Gospel records to reveal the historical, and more authentic, Jesus.[13] With *TLOL*, Dickens was, in fact, writing a life of Jesus but, not insignificantly, was employing the method of harmonization.

One of the most fascinating things about *TLOL* is that it provides us with a rather thorough portrayal of Dickens's Jesus. And when we allow *TLOL* to help us navigate the religious landscape of the larger Dickens corpus, the results are informative and enlightening. For in *TLOL* Dickens has given us very clear insight into his understanding of Jesus's person and work as well as a clarifying voice regarding the religious expression throughout his writings. It is certainly one thing for a writer of the stature of Dickens to make use of biblical allusion along with veiled or even overt references to religious themes in his work; it is quite another for that same writer to provide in a self-written piece a clear statement of the Jesus who is so central to his religious thought and who is determinative for his understanding and expression of Christianity and the life of faith. In *TLOL*, Dickens has done precisely that. That is, Dickens has not left scattered fragments of an idea of Jesus spread throughout his work. Rather, he has written a complete and comprehensive composition that articulates, even if in a simple manner, the nature and character of Jesus as Dickens understood him.

Jesus: Saviour, Son of God, Exemplar

Dickens seemed to purposely and purposefully use as many different titles for Jesus as he could imagine to highlight the contours and illumine the nuances of his understanding of Jesus. Jesus is sometimes the Master. Another time, Jesus is the Divinity who walked the earth. Occasionally, Jesus is the Founder of our religion, or the Divine Forgiver. In the end, however, Dickens's Jesus seems most appropriately described by three titles: Our Saviour, the Son of God, and our Exemplar. This last ascription, Exemplar, is not one of which Dickens makes use, but all three, nevertheless, reveal the nature of Jesus as Dickens conceived him. Our course in this chapter will be to view Jesus through the lens Dickens provides in *TLOL*, then consider a few examples to demonstrate how *TLOL* can act as our guide in navigating his larger corpus. In this way, we might come to a clearer vision of the full character of Dickens's Jesus.

I noted above that Dickens left us a rather substantial and definitive portrait of Jesus in *TLOL*. It is a fact that Dickens scholars have never really been much impressed by *TLOL* as a piece of children's literature and even less so as having substantive theological value. Therefore, since the purpose of this chapter is to consider Jesus as Dickens saw and portrayed him, and since *TLOL* plays a major role in that endeavor, it will be worthwhile to offer, briefly, some justification for taking *TLOL* as a serious expression of Dickens's Christian thought and ideas about Jesus.[14]

First, that Dickens wrote *TLOL* exclusively for his children, never intending that it should be published, suggests that, as a father, he was hoping to communicate something substantial to them about the Christian faith and life. Ironically, the fact that Dickens wrote *TLOL* for his children has been used by some to denigrate it and to dismiss any serious intent in its composition. But Dickens was concerned with and involved in most aspects of the lives of his children as they were growing up, certainly not least their moral-religious formation.

Such formation and attendant instruction was not something Dickens would have been comfortable leaving to others, even—and especially—the church. If we accept that Dickens took seriously the moral-religious formation and instruction of his children, we have good reason to suspect that he took the writing of *TLOL* seriously and as a deliberate expression of his religious thought when it came to Jesus and the content of the Gospels. Indeed, *TLOL* played an important role in the moral-religious instruction of his children and, if only for that reason, would have commanded his careful and serious attention.

A second reason for considering *TLOL* a serious expression of Dickens's Christian thought is that it is taken up with the presentation of the life of Jesus. As has been emphasized above, the life and teaching of Jesus as recorded in the Gospels were the defining elements of Dickens's Christian orientation and worldview. Regardless of the audience to whom it was addressed, any extended narrative composed by Dickens that intended to address the life and teaching of Jesus should be given our attention. Even just a bit of careful attention in this wise to *TLOL* will be rewarded.

A third and important reason for taking *TLOL* seriously is that it bears the marks of careful composition and deliberate crafting and appears to have been a project in which Dickens invested no small amount of time or effort.[15] Even a cursory examination suggests that *TLOL* was Dickens's own attempt at composing a selective harmony of the Gospels for his children. Dickens's primary and almost exclusive use of harmonization—a time-consuming and often exacting task—in the formation and composition of *TLOL* suggests that he took some pains with it and that it may well have developed over a period of time. That Dickens would give himself to such a task and such a discipline is not insignificant and speaks to his seriousness of purpose in *TLOL*.

Dickens scholars are right, then, to see little literary value in *TLOL*. Dickens never intended it as a literary piece. He was doing something much different from simply writing a children's story about Jesus. So, it is wrong to attempt to judge *TLOL* from a purely literary standpoint. *TLOL* must be assessed as a biblical-theological composition. To properly understand *TLOL*, it is necessary to approach it for what it is: a selective juvenile harmony of the Gospels, a juvenile life of Jesus.

It is precisely at this point of composition and harmonization that Dickens scholars have failed to recognize the theological value—perhaps, more properly, the spiritual value—of *TLOL*. That Dickens was writing a harmony or a life of Jesus is significant and determinative. That is, *TLOL* is no simple recollection of Gospel stories by Dickens or a collection of hastily assembled Sunday school lessons. It is a reasonably serious attempt by Dickens to write a life of Jesus for his children. As was pointed out above, in Great Britain, especially prior to 1860, the way to write a life of Jesus was to write a harmony of the Gospels. And there was no shortage of nineteenth-century harmonies available in Dickens's day, including a vast number of children's harmonies.[16] So, Dickens chose a very common biblical-theological genre in which to write and in which to seek to communicate the truths of the gospel to his children. In light of Dickens's own words in the letters and passages we have seen above, it makes sense and is certainly telling that Dickens would choose to compose for his children his own life of Jesus in the form of a selective harmony of the Gospels.

Given that Dickens composed his own juvenile life of Jesus, that he was writing in a biblical-theological genre, and that he was deliberate and serious in the planning and composition of *TLOL*, there may be much to learn from it. Surely, there is much to be learned about Dickens's Jesus from it.

Jesus: Our Saviour

It seems that Dickens's favorite designation for Jesus, outside of *TLOL*, was "Our Saviour."[17] This particular designation, employed almost forty times in *TLOL*, is found scattered throughout Dickens's work, both fiction and nonfiction, and is suggestive of Jesus's role in redemption and salvation. It is in *TLOL*, however, that Dickens gives us at least a partial description of the title and in that way helps us to understand what he means by it. He concludes his third chapter in *TLOL*, "But He was always merciful and tender and because He did such good, and taught people how to love God and how to hope to go to Heaven after Death, he was called *Our Saviour*."[18]

Two observations are noteworthy here. First, in Dickens's mind, Jesus is Our Saviour because of three things: (1) Jesus did what is good, (2) Jesus taught people how to love God, and (3) Jesus taught people how to hope to go to heaven after death. Remembering that the audience for *TLOL* consisted of the Dickens children, we should not read into this description what is not there. In fact, we need only take it at face value to get a more substantial understanding of what Dickens might mean by the designation.

Dickens recognized Jesus as Saviour, in the first place because Jesus did what was good. The good that Jesus does in *TLOL* includes that which is salvific: healing the infirm, exorcising demons, raising the dead, teaching and loving people. Biblically speaking, all of this is indicative of the in-breaking of God's new age of salvation in the person of Jesus. And while it is unlikely that Dickens would have been aware of the theological subtleties at work here, that these redemptive deeds were salvific was part of the fabric of a popular lay Anglicanism that would have been taken for granted by Dickens and others like him.

Further, Jesus is Saviour because "He taught people how to love God." Likely, Dickens had in mind here that Jesus taught people how to love God by being an example of loving God in the whole of his life and ministry. While Dickens never used the word, today we might explain what he meant by saying that Jesus taught people how to love God by teaching them to be *obedient*. Rather than the term "obey" or "obedience," however, Dickens uses the term "duty" twice in *TLOL*, both times in reference to our duty toward God.[19] We love God, then, by being obedient or doing our duty toward God. And what constitutes our duty toward God? Displaying the heart of God in mercy, compassion, and love toward others. We do our duty toward God by doing our duty toward other men and women. This is precisely what Jesus did and what Jesus taught in word and deed.

A second pertinent observation here is that chapter 3 of *TLOL*, of which Dickens's description of Saviour is the concluding sentence, is an extended example of Jesus being Saviour in the fullest sense. Prior to the inclusion of this description, Dickens provides four instances of the Saviour "saving": three healings and the raising of Jairus's daughter from the dead. Following the description, Dickens relates four more instances of Jesus "saving": a healing, the raising from the dead of the son of the widow of Nain, the calming of the sea and storm, and an exorcism. In reporting these miraculous events,

Dickens demonstrates Jesus's power over disease, over nature, over demons and demonic forces, and over death. Again, whether or not Dickens was fully aware of the theological subtleties at work here, he illustrates in this full list of miracles in the work of Jesus the saving activity of the redemptive rule and reign of God.

In addition to the clear and deliberate description of Our Saviour, Dickens included two passages in *TLOL* that speak further to the redemptive connotation of that title. One of those passages is Dickens's account of the story of the raising of Lazarus, found only in John 11:1–57. As he relates the response of the people to the raising of Lazarus from the dead and commanding him to come forth, Dickens writes, "At this sight, so awful and affecting many of the people there believed that Christ was indeed the Son of God, come to instruct and save mankind."[20] Clearly, that Jesus came to "save mankind" is suggestive of a redemptive role. Significantly, "that many of the people there believed that Christ was indeed the Son of God, come to instruct and save mankind" is Dickens's own rendering of what John reports in his Gospel simply as, "Many . . . believed on him" (John 11:45 KJV). In the larger Johannine context, that Jesus had come to teach and to accomplish salvation expresses more fully what is meant by John's "Many . . . believed on him." Dickens's rendering in his account speaks not only to his understanding of the Johannine formulation but also to his own perception of the life and ministry of Jesus: Jesus is Our Saviour.

Another significant reference to Jesus as Saviour in a redemptive sense is found in a curious statement in the account of the crucifixion in which Dickens has the crowd taunting Jesus with the words, "He came to save sinners. Let Him save Himself."[21] As with the Lazarus passage above, the taunt was Dickens's own rendering of the synoptic evangelists, who have it, "He saved others; himself he cannot save" (Matt. 27:42; Mark 15.31; cf. Luke 23:35 [KJV], He saved others; let him save himself). Dickens's rendering is conspicuous both because of its presence here and because of its content: Jesus had given people the impression that he had come to save sinners. For Dickens to have introduced the term "sinners" into this context with no scriptural precedent is interesting in itself and is well-suited to represent Dickens's filling out the meaning of the evangelists' "saved" with his own understanding of what that saving entails—salvation from sin.

Clearly, then, Dickens portrays Jesus as Our Saviour in *TLOL* and uses that ascription in a redemptive sense. Jesus is the Redeemer who comes "to save sinners," Jesus is "indeed the Son of God, come to instruct and save mankind." But this understanding of Jesus extends beyond *TLOL* to Dickens's other work. A definitive statement in this regard occurs in a letter Dickens wrote to his good friend Angela Burdett-Coutts on 28 October 1847. In that letter, Dickens enclosed "An Appeal To Fallen Women," which he had written as an open letter and which was to be read to the women of Urania House to encourage them and to impress upon them a sense of accountability and discipline.[22] He writes: "But you must solemnly remember that if you enter this Home without such constant resolutions, you occupy, unworthily and uselessly, the place of some other unhappy girl, now wandering and lost; and that her ruin, no less than your own, will be upon your head, before Almighty God, who knows the secrets of our breasts; and Christ, who died upon the cross to save us."[23] It is noteworthy that Dickens writes almost incidentally of Jesus, "who died upon the cross to save us," and his doing so gave this assertion perhaps even more force with regard to Jesus as Our Saviour. Clearly, here, Our Saviour died upon the cross to accomplish salvation and to redeem us from sin.

Another title which Dickens seems to employ regularly to refer to Jesus's redemptive work and one that can further nuance "Our Saviour" is "Redeemer." In his *Hard Times*, for instance, Dickens provides an intriguing use of both "Our Saviour" and "Redeemer" together. As Stephen Blackpool lay dying from injuries he sustained from his fall into the Old Hell Shaft, a mine shaft, he explains to Rachael his gazing into the sky at a star: "Often as I coom to myseln, and found it shinin on me down there in my trouble, I thowt it were the star as guided to Our Saviour's home. I awmust think it be the very star!" They lift him up, and he is overjoyed to find that they are about to take him in the direction whither the star seemed to him to lead.[24] Dickens closes the account by observing, "The star had shown him where to find the God of the poor; and through humility, and sorrow, and forgiveness, he had gone to his Redeemer's rest."[25] Note in this example that Dickens uses "Our Saviour" almost as simply a proper name. But joined with his use of the ascription "Redeemer" and the further explanation, "through humility, and sorrow, and forgiveness," Dickens seems to be infusing both titles with suggestions of redemptive significance.

Similarly, he employs the term "Redeemer" in his article "Pet Prisoners" from *Household Words*, 27 April 1850: "Now God forbid that we, unworthily believing in the Redeemer, should shut out hope, or even humble trustfulness, from any criminal at the dread pass; but it is not in us to call this state of mind repentance." Here again, Dickens's use of the ascription "Redeemer" seems to carry salvific overtones. Central to Dickens's argument in this particular essay is the eleventh-hour confession of a death-row prisoner that is not so much a confession as it is a self-congratulatory acknowledgment of the crime; it is arrogant, preoccupied with the self, and almost dismissive of the crime committed, the victim, and the victim's family. Dickens does not want to rule out the possibility of salvation here, but he does not see the attitude of such a prisoner as a repentant one.

For Dickens, then, Jesus is the Redeemer, Our Saviour who died on the cross to forgive sins and to save. As such, Dickens's Jesus is Saviour in an orthodox sense. That is, the language Dickens employed to characterize Jesus as Our Saviour indicates that Jesus's work on the cross is redemptive—he died to save sinners. And so, Dickens certainly provided some distinctions in his characterization that present his readers with a nuanced understanding of his Jesus. But Dickens gave even further texture to his characterization of Jesus in using another highly significant ascription—the Son of God.

Jesus: the Son of God

This title, "Son of God," plays a crucial role in bringing even greater clarity to our understanding of Dickens's Jesus. Notably, it is used only in *TLOL* and there only twelve times. Nevertheless, "Son of God" is perhaps the most significant title used for Jesus in *TLOL*. Moreover, Dickens's use of the designation and his choice of episodes in which it is used are of central importance in helping to determine more precisely Dickens's thought concerning Jesus, particularly in terms of the deity of Jesus.

The nineteenth-century orthodox Anglican[26] understanding of the title "Son of God" was informed by two basic ideas: (1) Jesus's deity as God's unique, only begotten Son and (2) Jesus's role as

Messiah.[27] For whatever reasons, Dickens never develops the idea of Jesus's messianic office either in *TLOL* or anywhere else. As such, Dickens's emphasis in using the ascription "Son of God" seems to have been on the deity of Jesus.

This emphasis is clearly seen in Dickens's inclusion in *TLOL* of three of the most christologically charged "Son of God" passages in the Gospels. He included: (1) God's declaration of Jesus as Son at Jesus's Baptism and at the Transfiguration,[28] both recorded in the Synoptics and absent in John; (2) the centurion's declaration at the cross,[29] reported in all three Synoptics, and found in Matthew and Mark as, "Truly this (man) was the Son of God"; and the confession of the disciples after Jesus had walked on water and calmed the sea,[30] reported in Matthew, Mark, and John, and found only in Matthew as, "Of a truth, thou art the Son of God" (KJV). These, of course, are familiar passages and are recognized to provide testimony of Jesus as the Son of God from the very voice of God, from the apostles, and from a representative from among the Gentiles. In terms of Dickens's "Son of God" theology, several observations emerge in considering these passages.

First, the simple fact that Dickens, as sole composer and editor of *TLOL*, chose to include these passages is significant.[31] Second, Dickens did not shy away from using the ascription "Son of God" to describe Jesus in these passages or elsewhere. In both the account of Jesus's Baptism and of the Transfiguration, Dickens clearly reports the words of God verbatim, unforced and unqualified, identifying Jesus as God's Son. Similarly, in his account both of the raising of Jairus's daughter and of Jesus's anointing by the woman at Simon's house, Dickens identifies Jesus as God's Son apart from any Gospel testimony. In his rendering of the raising of Jairus's daughter, Dickens added his own conclusion to the story, "Oh what a sight it must have been to see her parents clasp her in their arms, and kiss her, and thank God, and Jesus Christ His son, for such great mercy!"[32] In his rendering of Jesus's being anointed by the woman at Simon's house,[33] Dickens describes the woman as one "who had led a bad and sinful life, and was ashamed that the Son of God should see her."

A third observation relates to Dickens's account of the Gospel report of the collective declaration by the guard at the crucifixion, "Surely this was the Son of God!"[34] In nineteenth-century Anglican thought, this was considered a central and key affirmation of Christ's divine Sonship. And it is noteworthy that while Dickens might just as easily have rendered his account with Luke's, "Certainly, this was a righteous man" (23:47 KJV), he opted instead for the expression reported by Matthew, "Truly this was the Son of God!"

The passages, incidents, and renderings observed here are undoubtedly conspicuous regarding Dickens's understanding of Jesus as Son of God, and when they are aligned with other material, Dickens's establishing of the deity of Jesus becomes quite compelling. Dickens included, toward the end of *TLOL*, the episode in which the women who had gone to Jesus's tomb early on the day of the Resurrection actually *worshipped* Jesus. His narrative describes Mary Magadalene finding the disciples and telling them that she had seen the risen Christ and that he had spoken to her. When she had found the disciples, with them were the other women who had gone with her to the tomb, of whom Dickens writes: "These women told her and the rest that they had seen at the tomb two men in shining garments, at sight of whom they had been afraid, . . . and also that as they came to tell this, they had seen Christ, on the way, and had held Him by the feet and worshipped Him."[35] The fact that Dickens included this almost incidental reference to the women worshipping Jesus, found only in Matthew 28:9, is powerful and conspicuous. Again, as the sole composer and editor of *TLOL*, he included a definitive and provocative description that could have simply and easily been omitted without being unfaithful to the Gospel accounts.

Perhaps even more significant is the inclusion of the account of Thomas's doubt and subsequent confession in which he declares Jesus "my Lord and my God" (compare *TLOL* 117–118 and John 20:28 KJV). This exclusively Johannine passage was one of the most significant to which nineteenth-century orthodox Anglican commentators turned to confirm the deity of Jesus. Interestingly, Dickens renders the entire episode almost verbatim. Without question, he reports the confrontation and dialogue between Thomas and Jesus word for word from John 20:27–29 (KJV), thus preserving the full force of a central orthodox declaration of the deity of Jesus. It seems clear, then, that for Dickens, Jesus as Son of God was Jesus as God the Son.

While Dickens used the title Son of God only in *TLOL*, he was not reticent to affirm the deity of Jesus elsewhere in his work. For instance, Dickens made repeated use of the words "Divine" and "Divinity" to describe Jesus in his writing using the terms to (1) connote the proper deity of God the Father and (2) to establish a contrast between that which is of humanity and that which is of God. In *David Copperfield*, for instance, Dickens makes a seemingly absolute distinction between what is human and what is divine. Describing Martha's commitment to helping David and Mr. Pegotty find Em'ly, Dickens relates the consequences that Martha would wish come to her if she abandoned this one "object she now had in life": "And then might all help, human and Divine renounce her evermore!"[36]

Similarly, of the obstinate Mrs. Clennam before the rogue Rigaud in *Little Dorrit*, Dickens writes: "Yet gone those more than forty years, and come this Nemesis now looking her in the face, she still abided by her old impiety—still reversed the order of Creation, and breathed her own breath into a clay image of her Creator. Verily, verily, travellers have seen many monstrous idols in many countries; but no human eyes have ever seen more daring, gross, and shocking images of the Divine nature than we creatures of the dust make in our own likenesses, of our own bad passions."[37]

The significance of these examples lies in the fact that Dickens employed the term "divine" as an equivalent of deity. And they become all the more significant when it is recognized that Dickens used the same language in reference to Jesus. Dickens referred to Jesus as "the Divine Master,"[38] "the Divine friend of children,"[39] and "the Divine preacher."[40] And a most significant use of such descriptors in reference to Jesus is found in a letter concerning capital punishment that Dickens wrote to the *Daily News* on 16 March 1846,[41] in which he refers to Jesus as "the Divinity who walked the earth." Granted, these ascriptions in themselves are by no means conclusive in establishing Dickens's thought on the deity of Jesus. Given the collective weight, however, of what we have observed to this point, it seems fair to conclude that Dickens understood the proper deity of Jesus as God the Son.

A clear affirmation of Jesus's deity in this same language is found in an intriguing passage in *Dombey and Son*.[42] When Paul Dombey sees in his deathbed vision two figures standing on a shore apparently to greet him and welcome him to heaven, we learn from Dickens's explanation and description that one of the figures is Paul's mother.

The other figure, it becomes clear, is Jesus. "Mama is like you Floy. I know her by the face!" Paul says to Florence, his sister. Then, by the same sense of familiarity, Paul recognizes Jesus, and his impression of Jesus is one of deity. He bids Florence, "But tell them that the print upon the stairs at school is not Divine enough."[43] Having come face to face with Jesus in his vision, Paul recognizes something lacking in the earthly representations of Jesus. It seems that Dickens would have us understand that human representations of Jesus, while they may capture Jesus's humanity and compassion and, perhaps, even self-sacrificing love, they cannot do justice to Jesus's deity.

By means, then, of his use and development of the title "Son of God," his portrayal of Jesus as the object of worship, and his use of deity/divinity language, Dickens brought his understanding of Jesus into clearer focus for his audience. Most significantly, Dickens's portrait of Jesus emerges not from any formal theological speculation about Jesus, but rather from Dickens's own impressions of Jesus as they emerge from his reading of the Gospels and as they are expressed in *TLOL* and his larger corpus. In the end, Dickens's Jesus is the divine Son of God, the second person of the triune Godhead. He performs miracles, raises the dead, is the object of worship, and is expressly declared God.

In all of this, it is important to remember that Dickens's goal was never to formulate pristine christological dogma. His intent rather was to portray a Jesus who, in Dickens's mind at least, emerged from the Gospels unsullied by denominational or sectarian bias and who, most importantly, provided the example of real Christianity.

Jesus: Our Exemplar

In February of 1850, Dickens corresponded with Miss Emmely Gotschalk, a young Danish woman, who sought his wisdom as she worried over certain personal spiritual concerns. Dickens was attempting in the letter he wrote to speak to her immediate need and her concerns. Not surprisingly, however, Dickens advice soon turned to an exhortation to "doing duty." He writes to her, "Our Saviour did not sit down in this world and muse, but labored and did good."[44] Dickens was speaking to her, of course, according to his fundamental understanding of the essence of the life of faith: the imitation of the example of Jesus. And the imitation of the example of Jesus meant, in a word, "duty," or laboring and doing good. Whatever we may gather from Dickens's portrait of Jesus in his work, we have missed the point if we miss the fact that as Christians, we are first of all to imitate the example of Jesus.

This obvious emphasis in Dickens is expressed quite clearly in *TLOL*. Dickens begins his concluding paragraph of *TLOL*, "Remember!—it is Christianity to do good always—even to those who do evil to us."[45] This conclusion should not be unexpected, for Dickens's moral-ethical portrayal of Jesus, which the Christian is to imitate, is grounded squarely upon the goodness of Jesus. The sinful woman at the house of Simon the Pharisee "trusted so much in his goodness."[46] Jesus was feared and hated by the religious leaders "because of his goodness,"[47] but in spite of that, he continued "to do good"[48] and the people followed him "because they knew He did nothing but good."[49] Clearly, Dickens saw this goodness as the fundamental basis on which the imitation of Jesus could be pursued. And for Dickens, Jesus's goodness seems to have consisted of three particular qualities.

One such quality of Jesus's goodness in *TLOL* is compassion. Dickens chose to include in *TLOL* no fewer than six episodes in which Jesus's pity and compassion are expressly highlighted. Significantly, in each of the episodes Dickens included in *TLOL*, there is no parallel mention in the Gospel sources of Jesus's compassion and pity. For instance, Dickens closes his account of the raising of Jairus's daughter with the gloss, "Oh what a sight it must have been to see her parents clasp her in their arms, and kiss her, and thank God and Jesus Christ, His Son, for such great mercy! But He was always merciful and tender."[50] In the Gospel accounts (Matt. 9:18–26; Mark 5:22–43; Luke 8:41–56), the only emotion associated with the raising of this girl is astonishment. But as Dickens read the story, he saw a compassionate and merciful Saviour.

Likewise, neither Jesus's healing of the paralytic in the Synoptic accounts (Matt. 9:2–8; Mark 2:1–12; Luke 5:18–26) nor the account of Jesus healing the man at the pool of Bethesda (John 5:1–16) contains any reference to Jesus's compassion. Yet, in Dickens's rendering of these episodes in *TLOL*, Jesus "took pity" on the man at the pool of Bethesda, healing him,[51] and being "full of pity" for the paralytic, healed him also.[52] It seems clear that as Dickens read the Gospels, he saw compassion and mercy as one of Jesus's most conspicuous traits.[53]

Another quality of Jesus's goodness which Dickens highlights in *TLOL* is his character as the servant of others, that is, as one who constantly thought of the needs of others and sought to meet them. The entire narrative of *TLOL* is focused in this direction and is captured most clearly in Dickens's rendering of the preparation of Jesus for his public ministry. Following his Baptism, Jesus "went into a wild and lonely country called the wilderness, and stayed there forty days and forty nights, praying that He might be of use to men and women."[54] For Dickens, Jesus's sojourn and temptation in the wilderness was preparation for His public ministry of which "to be of use to men and women" in humility and servanthood was a central component.

In *TLOL*, for Jesus "to be of use to men and women" meant, for one, that he wanted to help them be better people. And so, Jesus taught them "to be better."[55] Dickens places great emphasis on the teaching ministry of Jesus in *TLOL* and often remarks, without reference to any specific content, that Jesus taught or instructed people. For Dickens, whatever Jesus taught men and women made them better and closer to the kind of people God wanted them to be.

"To be of use to men and women" also meant that Jesus wanted to teach them how to love and serve and know God. In perhaps the most important passage in *TLOL*, at least in Dickens's mind, he includes the account of Jesus declaring what is the Greatest Commandment. Dickens renders it: "The first of all the commandments is, the Lord our God is one Lord: and thou shalt love the Lord thy God with all thy heart, and with all thy soul, and with all thy mind, and with all thy strength."[56] What is especially significant here is that in the original manuscript of *TLOL*, Dickens underlined this entire passage—something that occurs nowhere else in the entirety of *TLOL*.[57] Obviously, Dickens wanted to place great emphasis on loving God with our entire being. From this declaration by Jesus, an entire thread runs throughout *TLOL* concerning loving God, doing our duty toward God, and knowing God.

Probably the most significant way in which Jesus was "of use to men and women" in *TLOL* was his merciful and compassionate care for the sick, infirm, and needy. "No one ever lived," Dickens writes of Jesus, "who was so good, so kind, so gentle, and so sorry for all people who did wrong, or were in any way ill or miserable as He was,"[58] and "No one ever loved all people so well and so truly as He did."[59] In everything Jesus does in *TLOL*, he serves others. He heals, he teaches, he forgives, he exorcises, he loves, he dies. Indeed, the story of *TLOL* is the story of Jesus being "of use to men and women."

The third quality of Jesus's goodness was his forgiveness. In *TLOL*, Dickens portrays Jesus as not only offering forgiveness for sin but also as teaching the responsibility of forgiving others. Dickens keeps the two bound rather tightly together, never letting the one overshadow the other. For Dickens, these are, to all intents and purposes, two sides of one coin. This is seen most readily in Dickens's rendering of Jesus's teaching the forgiveness of others seventy times seven and the parable of the unmerciful servant (Matt. 18:21–35; *TLOL* 61–63), to which pair Dickens conjoins the parable of the workers in the vineyard (Matt. 20:1–16). Dickens uses this section of *TLOL* not only to teach both God's grace in the forgiveness of sin and the responsibility to forgive others but to try to show the close relationship between the two.

Consider in this regard Dickens's account of Jesus offering forgiveness to the sinful woman at the home of Simon the Pharisee. Dickens renders the conclusion of the narrative: "And He [Jesus] said to her, 'God forgives you!' The company who were present wondered that Jesus Christ had power to forgive sins, but God had given it to Him. And the woman, thanking Him for all His mercy, went away."[60] Dickens immediately follows this account with: "We learn from this that we must always forgive those who have done us any harm, when they come to us and say they are truly sorry for it. Even if they do not come and say so, we must still forgive them, and never hate them or be unkind to them, if we would hope that God will forgive us."[61] Not surprisingly, Dickens blends Jesus's offering a forgiveness of sins with his teaching on forgiving others. Accordingly, it seems clear that Dickens understood Jesus as the forgiver of sins and, as such, the Exemplar of forgiving others.

In Dickens's mind, then, Jesus is the Exemplar of the life of faith with his goodness the primary characteristic to be imitated. And this goodness finds specific expression in the qualities of compassion, service, and forgiveness. It should not be supposed, however, that these three virtues constitute a comprehensive or exhaustive list. While they are the ones most readily singled out in *TLOL*, and while they do represent a major expression of the imitation of the example of Jesus, there is certainly more to which to give attention in this regard. Specifically, there is more to be learned from considering, if even just briefly, Jesus's teaching and lessons in *TLOL*.

The Teaching of Jesus

The day before his death, and in the last letter he would compose, Dickens wrote to J. M. Makeham, "I have always striven in my writings to express veneration for the life and lessons of our Saviour; because I feel it; and because I rewrote that history for my children."[62] The "history" that Dickens wrote for his children to which he refers here is *TLOL*. And here, Dickens suggests that *TLOL* is comprised of "the life and lessons of our Saviour." Having considered the life of Jesus as example, it follows that the lessons in the teaching of Jesus in *TLOL* might add further clarity to just how Jesus is Exemplar for the Christian life.

Dickens includes at least eight parables[63] in *TLOL* and no fewer than eleven other episodes from the Gospels[64] in which Jesus expressly or implicitly teaches. These "lessons of Our Saviour" are revealing. As has already been pointed out, Dickens placed a special emphasis on Jesus's teaching on forgiveness, particularly on the importance of having a forgiving spirit toward others. In fact, Jesus teaches more on this topic in *TLOL* than on any other. Likewise, Jesus calls attention to God's readiness to forgive those who would come to God in humility and repentance. The lesson that Jesus teaches in the parable of the prodigal Son, for Dickens, is "that those who have done wrong and forgotten God, are always welcome to Him and will always receive His mercy, if they will only return to Him in sorrow for the sin of which they have been guilty."[65] And the parable of the workers in the vineyard teaches that "people who have been wicked, because of their being miserable or not having parents and friends to take care of them when young, and who are truly sorry for it, however late in their lives, and pray God to forgive them, will be forgiven and will go to Heaven too."[66]

Jesus further teaches the importance of remembering God, loving God with our whole being, and being humble before God. Such humility was also to characterize our relationships with men and women, intending to result in a compassionate heart that considers the needs of others and seeks to do good to others. In the parable in which Jesus urges his hearers to always avoid taking the best seat, Dickens renders the lesson as "that we are never to be proud, or think ourselves very good, before God, but are always to be humble."[67] And, of course, Dickens includes in *TLOL* Jesus's parable of the publican and the Pharisee, which teaches that God would be merciful to the publican "because he made [his prayer] with a humble and a lowly heart."[68] Similarly, Dickens reminds his hearers, "Never be proud or unkind, my dears, to any poor man, woman or child."[69]

Finally, Jesus teaches generosity of spirit and guarding our affections against the love of money. Dickens includes in *TLOL* the episode that recounts Jesus and the disciples observing the widow giving her two mites at the temple, which is used as an opportunity to teach on generosity.[70] Dickens also makes use of a series of parables in *TLOL* to teach against covetousness and the love of money. The seventh chapter of *TLOL* notably includes six of the eight parables found in *TLOL*. In some ways these six parables seem to collectively contribute to Dickens's rendering of the introduction to the parable of the rich man and Lazarus. Dickens writes, "Now the Pharisees received these lessons [the previous parables] from Our Saviour scornfully; for they were rich and covetousness and thought themselves superior to all mankind."[71] As a warning to them, Dickens says, Jesus related the parable of the rich man and Lazarus. The lessons on generosity, covetousness, and the love of money that Dickens hoped to teach by his inclusion of this parable are certainly there—Dickens was so confident of this that he let the parable stand by itself with only his introductory words of explanation. Nevertheless, the parable's lessons find much of their power from the collective force of the six parables that precede it.

In this brief summary of the "lessons of Our Saviour" in *TLOL*, I have attempted to unpack those lessons and to broaden both our understanding of Dickens's representation of the imitation of the example of Jesus as well as the horizons of the life of faith. As becomes apparent, the imitation of the example of Jesus involves attention to the life of Jesus as he teaches us how to respond to God and how to respond to our fellow human beings. But we learn further that, for Dickens, this concept of the imitation of the example of Jesus goes beyond a superficial copying of actions, penetrating to attitudes, dispositions, values, and aspirations. That is, the imitation of the example of Jesus will include both the life and the lessons of Jesus.

Hearing Dickens and Listening to Him

While Dickens doesn't get it all right all the time and while there are points at which we can and should argue with him or take exception to his assertions or omissions, he can certainly remind us of—or even teach us afresh—some important facets of the life of faith. Certainly, there are in his portrait of Jesus some pertinent reminders, if not central lessons, we would do well to consider.

The Preeminence of Jesus

Perhaps the most obvious reminder that Dickens provides is that Jesus is Lord, Savior, and Example. Certainly, that has been the thrust of this chapter and perhaps seems to go without saying. But Dickens is in good company with this reminder. The apostle Paul reminds us in Colossians 1:13–23 that preeminence in all things belongs to Jesus precisely because Jesus is Lord and Saviour. It is, of course, no small thing to affirm Jesus's preeminence in all things. Paul is not simply arguing that Jesus is to have first place on a list of priorities. Rather, he is insisting on the more radical, far-reaching notion that Jesus is to have the first place in all things: our marriage, our vocation, our relationships, our pocketbook, our sex life, our leisure, our values, our aspirations—you complete the list. And that is not to mention, of course, that Jesus is to have first place in our prayer, our worship, our theology, our church activity, and whatever else you care to add. As Lord and Saviour, Jesus has earned that preeminence.

The Centrality of Jesus

That Jesus is to have first place in all things introduces a second reminder from Dickens that is merely an extension of that preeminence:

the centrality of Jesus in the life of faith. I use the expression "the centrality of Jesus in the life of faith" to place an emphasis on the role of the very *fact* of Jesus in spiritual formation. Granted, the centrality of Jesus in the life of faith is suggestive of the preeminence that was just mentioned, but it focuses that preeminence more specifically on the centrality of the role of Jesus in shaping and determining the Christian life.

So, to speak of the centrality of Jesus in the life of faith is to say that as we live the Christian life, Jesus must remain at the center of our endeavor. Our center is not the church, it is not Christian activity (or activism), it is not Bible study, it is not theology or doctrine, it is not programs, paradigms, or models—the center is Jesus. Please hear this properly and carefully. These things are not bad things. They are good and constructive things—but they are simply not the center of the Christian life and have no place there. Yet, sometimes, inadvertently and when we are practically unaware of it, these things can slip to the center and push Jesus to the periphery. That is why a stiff reminder from the likes of Dickens can be a wake-up call, clearing our thinking and our pursuits.

The Imitation of Jesus

Probably the most important thing we can learn from Dickens in this chapter comes from his conviction that the demonstration and practice of "real Christianity" was expressed in the imitation of the character and example of Jesus. As emphasized throughout this chapter, the imitation of the example of Jesus is the very heart of Christianity as Dickens understood it. Significantly, it seems also to be at the heart of what the New Testament recognizes as Christianity. So, once again, Dickens is in good company with his emphasis on following the example of Jesus in imitation.

Certainly, the New Testament writers explicitly employ the concept of imitation. Paul writes in Ephesians 5:1, "Therefore be imitators (μιμηταὶ = mimetai) of God as beloved children", and in 1 Corinthians 11:1, "Be imitators (μιμηταὶ = mimetai) of me, just as I also am of Christ." Using the same terminology, Paul writes to the church at Thessalonica, "You also became imitators of us and of the Lord" (1 Thess. 1:6). The writer of the book of Hebrews, again, using the same terminology, urges his audience to be "imitators of those who through faith and patience inherit the promises" (6:12) and to "remember your leaders, . . . and imitate their faith" (13:7). So, the idea of imitation is not a concept forced on the New Testament from the outside.

Moreover, the language of Jesus as example is conspicuous in the New Testament. In 1 Peter 2:21, Peter writes to his audience that Jesus "also suffered for you, leaving you an example (ὑπογραμμὸν = hupogrammon) for you to follow in His steps." And in John 13:15 Jesus says to his disciples, after having washed their feet, "I gave you an example (ὑπόδειγμα = hupodeigma) that you also should do as I did to you." But the passage that really seems to capture the essence of the imitation of the example of Jesus, and one that has a most interesting affinity with John 13:1–15,[72] is the Christ-hymn in Philippians 2:5–11. The apostle Paul says plainly in Philippians 2:5, "Have this attitude in yourselves which was also in Christ Jesus." That this implies an imitation of the example of Jesus is made clear by the fact that this statement follows directly from the moral-ethical teaching of Philippians 2:1–4. There, Paul exhorts the Philippians to be "of the same mind, maintaining the same love, united in spirit, intent on one purpose" (2:2). He continues this exhortation, "Do nothing from selfishness or empty conceit, but with humility of mind regard one another as more important than yourselves; do not *merely* look out for your own personal interests, but also for the interests of others" (2:3–4). In all of this, says Paul, your attitude should be the same as that of Jesus—that is, Jesus is your example and you need to imitate Him.

Just as we saw in this idea of the imitation of Jesus in Dickens's *TLOL*, this imitation is obviously no simple copying of selective activities. Nor is it mere moralism for its own sake or a superficial religious facade propped up by pious-looking activities. Rather, it is the deeper, more profound sense of having our lives and minds transformed by an encounter with Jesus resulting in our being conformed more and more to the mind of Christ. Note what Paul says regarding this same attitude "which was also in Christ Jesus": (1) he did not regard equality with God a thing to be grasped, and (2) he emptied himself. In simple terms Paul says, even though Jesus was God—or better, precisely *because* Jesus was God—he didn't stake a claim as God but instead poured himself out, spending his life on others, serving them and dying for them.

This, then, is the example Paul extends to the Philippians, and to us, to imitate. Moreover, Philippians 2:5–11 gets at the very heart of the transformation of one's attitudes and behaviors; it exemplifies the very essence of this idea of the imitation of the example of Jesus. Certainly, it would be more palatable, not to mention a lot easier, if the imitation of the example of Jesus could be reduced simply to the mindless and artificial copying of some "religious" activity. But then, it would never be the transformative power that it is to change lives and to change our world.

None of this was lost on Dickens, of course. That's not to say that he approached the whole idea as a churchman, Bible scholar, or theologian. He did not. But he did grasp, to some degree at least, the radical and transformative nature of the concept of the imitation of Jesus. Indeed, his understanding, to whatever degree, of the profound nature of the imitation of Jesus was surely one of the driving forces behind his composing *A Christmas Carol.*

Wes Standiford, borrowing from Byron Rogers,[73] refers to Dickens as the man who invented Christmas. While Dickens's *A Christmas Carol* had a hand in shaping Christmas as we know it, Standiford has playfully and intentionally overstated the case. Nevertheless, it certainly can be said that, while Dickens did not exactly invent Christmas, he certainly understood the Christmas spirit. That is, Dickens understood that the Christmas spirit is not simply a facade of kindness, goodwill, and warm feeling that we don during the Christmas season. Rather, he understood that the Christmas spirit is a posture we assume, an orientation we embrace the year round. He understood that it must be part of the person we are—and part of the person we are as Christians. Dickens understood it as part and parcel of the imitation of Jesus.

In Stave 1 of *A Christmas Carol*, the ghost of Jacob Marley visits Scrooge and they engage in a crucial conversation central to the theme of the book. At the heart of the dialogue is Marley's ghost informing Scrooge of the reason why he is visiting Scrooge from the afterlife: "It is required of everyman . . . that the spirit within him should walk abroad among his fellow-men and travel far and wide; and if that spirit goes not forth in life, it is condemned to do so after death. It is doomed to wander through the world . . . and witness what it cannot share, but might have shared on earth and turned to happiness."[74]

Early on, then, Dickens is hinting at the theme of the book and setting the stage for the transformation of Scrooge, not so much a covetous old miser as a thoughtless and self-absorbed businessman who remained isolated in his own private world, oblivious to the pain and needs of others. This becomes clear as Marley continues his soliloquy, lamenting,

> Oh! Captive, bound, and double ironed, . . . not to know, that ages of incessant labour by immortal creatures, for this earth must pass into eternity before the good of which it is susceptible is all developed. Not to know that any Christian spirit working kindly in its little sphere, whatever it may be, will find its mortal life too short for its vast means of usefulness. Not to know that no space of regret can make amends for one life's opportunity misused! Yet such was I! Oh! Such was I![75]

It becomes increasingly clearer as the conversation between Marley's ghost and Scrooge develops that Marley's ghost's purpose is to provide Scrooge with the opportunity to participate in a life of doing good and caring for others, to pour himself out in service to the poor and needy, to concern himself with the interests and the needs of others. In other words, Scrooge has the opportunity to secure a chance to imitate Jesus in the concrete realities of life.

This seems to be the primary reason why Scrooge responds as he does to the realization that his is the name on the tombstone shown to him by the Ghost of Christmas yet to come. Scrooge is not arrested by the fear of death. Rather, he is filled with the misgivings and remorse that had gripped Marley's ghost for "one life's opportunity misused."

Dickens's insistence on the imitation of Jesus being the distinguishing mark of genuine Christianity is certainly a clarion call to the church today. The church's job is to make disciples—learners or followers; more properly, apprentices—and in simple terms a disciple is one who imitates the master or the teacher. The disciple is not one who simply sits in the classroom and takes notes while the teacher dispenses information. The disciple anxiously desires to be like the teacher. The disciple purposes to imitate the master. In this way, discipleship is apprenticeship. For just as the apprentice works under but alongside of the craftsman to learn by practice, so the disciple observes and imitates the master in order to learn the skill of living, right thinking, and good decision making.

An important aspect of this concept is that, in terms of the idea of the disciple in the New Testament, all believers are to be disciples. That is, discipleship is not for a select group of qualified or elite Christians. Neither is it the result of participation in a program or a series of studies or talks. It is, instead, the vocation of all Christians and it is incumbent upon all Christians to be who they are—that is, disciples—and to take that call seriously. And so, our concern in the practice of an unobtrusive faith is primarily to find in Jesus the exemplar of that faith and to humbly go about the business of imitating him.

As Dickens saw things, life was full of opportunities to imitate the life and lessons of Jesus. He might say, "Just look around you. Look at the people God has brought into your sphere of influence. Consider your spouse, your children, your parents. Consider your neighbors, your coworkers, your fellow students. Consider the needy, the homeless, the broken in your community." It is after this manner, then, that Dickens understood the imitation of Jesus. And he reminds us in no uncertain terms of the responsibility and the privilege of doing our duty to God and to our fellow creatures in this way.

3

Charles Dickens

THEOLOGIAN?

Charles Dickens was not a theologian. He did not want to be one.
But he was interested in things theological. He was not a Bible
scholar. But he knew his Bible—probably better than most twenty-
first century churchgoers—and he believed it. Dickens was not a
churchman. But he was certainly an informed and engaged layperson.
And that is what is so interesting about Dickens. He took the life
of faith seriously and he thought carefully about those things that
might come to bear upon it in significant ways. And while he was not
given to speculative theology or theological formulation, he seems
to have kept himself abreast of contemporary issues in theology or
things of a theological or biblical interest. Moreover, contrary to
what some have alleged about Dickens, he held some definite and
clear notions about his faith and his Christian beliefs.

Establishing a Context

In a letter written to his good friend, W. M. de Cerjat, 28 May 1863,
Dickens addresses Cerjat's questions concerning certain religious

controversies that "were agitating men's thoughts" at the time. According to the letter, Cerjat was particularly curious about academic biblical and theological controversies that involved Bishop J. W. Colenso (Anglican Bishop of Natal, South Africa), Benjamin Jowett (Regius Professor of Greek at Oxford), and *Essays and Reviews*, a controversial and pioneering volume of seven essays that championed the historical-critical method of academic Bible study.

Essays and Reviews, written by six Anglican churchmen and an Anglican layman and published in 1860, created a furor for almost a decade and radically changed the method and study of the Scriptures in Great Britain almost overnight. Compared to *Essays and Reviews*, Darwin's *On the Origin of Species* (1859) was a nonevent in Great Britain. Jowett's essay, "On the Interpretation of Scripture," considered by many the most influential and provocative of the bunch, not only argues strongly for the adoption of the historical-critical method for academic study of the Bible but also insists that revelation was a dynamic process that demanded reinterpretation of the Scriptures by each succeeding generation. Jowett's essay was consistent with his Broad Church alignment, his desire to challenge the establishment with historical-critical study of the Bible, and with his earlier commentary, *Romans* (1855). Colenso had stirred controversy with his *The Pentateuch and the Book of Joshua Critically Examined* (1862–63) and his commentary *St. Paul's Epistle to the Romans* (1861).

In his letter to Cerjat, Dickens shows clearly that he was familiar with the Colenso controversy, Jowett, and *Essays and Reviews* (Dickens's Gadshill library contained a copy).

> The Colenso and Jowett matter is a more difficult question, but here again I don't go with you. The position of the writers of "Essays and Reviews" is, that certain parts of the Old Testament have done their intended function in the education of the world *as it was;* but that mankind, like the individual man, is designed by the Almighty to have an infancy and a maturity, and that as it advances, the machinery of its education must advance too. . . . Again, it is contended that the science of geology is quite as much a revelation to man, as books of an immense age and of (at the best) doubtful origin, and that your consideration of the latter must reasonably be influenced by the former. As I understand the importance of timely suggestions such as these, it is, that the Church should not gradually shock and

lose the more thoughtful and logical of human minds; but should be so gently and considerately yielding as to retain them, and, through them, hundreds of thousands. This seems to me, as I understand the temper and tendency of the time, whether for good or evil, to be a very wise and necessary position. And as I understand the danger, it is not chargeable on those who take this ground, but on those who in reply call names and argue nothing. What these bishops and such-like say about revelation, in assuming it to be finished and done with, I can't in the least understand. Nothing is discovered without God's intention and assistance, and I suppose every new knowledge of His works that is conceded to man to be distinctly a revelation by which men are to guide themselves. Lastly, in the mere matter of religious doctrine and dogmas, these men (Protestants—protestors—successors of the men who protested against human judgment being set aside) talk and write as if they were all settled by the direct act of Heaven; not as if they had been, as we know they were, a matter of temporary accommodation and adjustment among disputing mortals as fallible as you or I.[1]

Four pertinent observations pertaining to Dickens's engagement and knowledge should be made here. First, because he seemed to consider them as a group, it appears that Dickens was more than popularly familiar with Colenso, Jowett, and *Essays and Reviews*. His grouping them together as he does suggests, at least, that he recognized that all three controversies concerned a new turn toward the historical-critical method in the academic study of the Bible. Furthermore, he seemed to have understood what each was arguing and why they were arguing it. Second, from his comments, it appears he had read *Essays and Reviews*—almost exclusively an academic work—and more specifically, he seems to have been familiar not only with Jowett's essay but also with the essay of Frederick Temple ("The Education of the World") as well. While he does not seem to agree entirely with Jowett, his comments about revelation nevertheless suggest more than a superficial understanding of Jowett's concept of dynamic revelation. Third, his statement "that the Church should not gradually shock and lose the more thoughtful and logical of human minds" points to the thought of Colenso and *Essays and Reviews* collectively and goes back to Thomas Arnold and the Broad Church call for greater "comprehension," which included the idea that the established church needed to be more receptive and less restrictive in its doctrinal demands on clergymen in order that it might retain some of its younger and perhaps more progressive thinkers. Dickens's fourth and final observation in this excerpt of the letter hints at his disdain for what he saw as the arrogance of the church to pronounce as dogmatically as it did on various issues of doctrine. This suggests why Dickens was given to the more pragmatic or practical concerns of the Christian life. He was quite sure that a wise person was not able to be dogmatic on very much concerning things theological. Note his comment—actually rather astute—pointing out that Protestants, who originally led the way in calling for the exercise of human judgment in the study of the Bible, were now, in his mind, trying to stifle that judgment.

The issues swirling around Colenso, Jowett, and *Essays and Reviews* were almost exclusively academic. While *Essays and Reviews* sold well, it would have been relatively unknown outside the academy and intellectual circles and among men of letters. The controversy that Jowett stirred raged primarily within the academy. And Colenso was actually a rather controversial character (as was Jowett), but his biblical and theological eccentricities were largely academic as well. The point is, Dickens's familiarity with Colenso, Jowett, and *Essays and Reviews* suggests alertness to, knowledge of, and thoughtful engagement with, even if limited, some of the major controversies of academic theology of his time.

Of course, Dickens didn't make a habit of discussing academic theology or writing about it. Neither did he use his writing to grind a theological axe. Nevertheless, he did weigh in through the course of his writing on several general theological topics that were important to him and that occupied his mind and his Christian reflection. And it is here that his Christian voice is heard often at its most passionate and in its most revealing tones. As Dickens was neither a theologian nor a Christian novelist, his theological or Christian writing is not overt and is rarely forced. Instead, it seems to come as part and parcel of the texture of his thematic and narrative interests. And so, it comes to the reader not only more naturally but also more passionately and simply more interestingly.

It should not be surprising that Dickens revealed quite a bit about his concept of God in his writing. For Dickens, like so many other nineteenth-century Anglicans, God was unquestionably the sovereign Lord and Creator of the universe. Neither should it come as a surprise that Dickens dealt with what the Victorians referred to as the Four Last Things—death, judgment, heaven, and hell. These Four Last Things were a major preoccupation with Victorian clerics, laypersons, and academics alike. Dickens was no exception. What may come as a surprise to some, especially those who might be somewhat familiar with Dickens and Dickens criticism, are his views on judgment, hell, and the unseen spiritual world. Dickens was clearer in this area than most critics have claimed and his views a bit different from their typical assessments. Dickens also expressed his views on sin and salvation, and again, he did so in a way that runs against the grain of typical Dickens scholarship. In this chapter, we will consider Dickens's thought on God and on The Four Last Things. In chapter 4, we will look at Dickens's ideas about sin and salvation.

God: Great Creator and Supreme Beneficence

The Victorians should be singled out for their extravagant yet revealing names for God. In academic and popular literature alike, it would take little time or trouble to accumulate a list of literally dozens of titles for God. Consider, for instance: the God of Truth, the God of Nature, the Great Architect of Nature, Providence, the Divine Wisdom, the Divine Mind, All-Gracious God, Stupendous Creator, and the wise Disposer of all things. These are just a handful of titles for God found in family devotional books, published sermons, and academic essays from the nineteenth century. Dickens alone seems to try to refer to God using different titles without ever repeating himself: the Great Creator of mankind, the Creator of Heaven and Earth, the Supreme Beneficence, the Infinite Benevolence, or the Eternal Majesty of Heaven. In each case, Dickens and the Victorians seem to be attempting to capture in this variety of titles not only the glory and majesty and grandeur of God but also something of God's character and fundamental nature.

In Dickens's conspicuous use of such titles, he revealed a rather majestic concept of God. In all that is revealed about God by the titles Dickens uses, those that come to the fore are: (1) God is the

Creator of the universe and humankind and (2) God is active in the present, ordering history and the lives of men and women according to God's will. That is, God is the sovereign Lord of the universe.

The Providence of God

As the Lord of the universe, God is the God of Providence, the God who orders the events of the world according to a benevolent will, and who invades history on behalf of humankind for its good. Victorian theologian Edward Parsons provided a definition of Providence that expressed what was commonly understood by the term in Dickens's day. Parsons wrote that Providence "is the superintending care of the Great Creator, exercised over all events, all beings and all worlds."[2] Providence, Parsons remarked further, was the "right direction" of all things that occur in the universe by a good and beneficent Creator and functioned on both the global and individual levels. This, quite naturally, is how Dickens understood the idea, and it appears that Providence understood in this way was a natural element of Dickens's worldview.

In *Bleak House*, John Jarndyce offers some advice to his young ward, Richard Carstone, "Trust in nothing but Providence and your own efforts."[3] Here, Dickens affirms a common two-fold understanding of Providence. First, of course, is the obvious acknowledgment of Providence as God's superintending care over life's events. Second, Dickens affirms there is a natural compatibility between Providence and "your own efforts." Dickens would not countenance a view of Providence that made it merely an oppressive and distorted Calvinistic predestination. Dickens, and many like him—laypersons, churchmen, and scholars—agreed with the anonymous pamphlet "On God's Providence," which emphasizes that trusting a thing "to Providence" should not be, as it had become for some individuals, an excuse for idleness, carelessness, or inattention. Some, the pamphleteer remarks, "would have God take their share as well as his own."[4] Like Dickens, many felt that there must be a synergy between human effort and God's providential workings on behalf of humankind, and so the advice of John Jarndyce is more than sentimental rhetoric. It is likely a subtle but deliberate reminder of the nature of Providence.

A most poignant acknowledgment of God's Providence occurs in an autobiographical passage in *David Copperfield* in which Dickens recognizes God's Providence in God's merciful care. Young David reflects, "I know that but for the mercy of God, I might easily have been, for any care that was taken of me, a little robber or a little vagabond."[5] Later in the same novel, Betsy Trotwood, David's aunt and guardian, wonders about "the mysterious dispensations of Providence" that brought about the meeting of Mr. Murdstone and David's mother, conceding that their meeting is "more than humanity can comprehend."[6]

Both of these examples reflect a common understanding of Providence and one with which Dickens was in total agreement: that God directs things according to God's own good pleasure and for our good, but not according to our whims or our personal preferences. So, in *Oliver Twist*, when Oliver and Mrs. Maylie consider the possibility that Rose might die, Mrs. Maylie affirms: "I have seen enough, too, to know that it is not always the youngest and best who are spared to those that love them; but this should give us comfort in our sorrow; for Heaven is just; and such things teach us, impressively, that there is a brighter world than this; and that the passage to it is speedy. God's will be done! I love her; and He knows how well!"[7]

Dickens expresses a similar understanding in *Bleak House* when "the Eternal Wisdom" helps and comforts Ada in a most unexpected manner and when Esther recognizes God's hand at work, even in the scarring effects of her bout with smallpox. Recalling when Lady Dedlock looked to her for forgiveness, Esther says: "I felt, through all my tumult of emotion, a burst of gratitude to the providence of God that I was so changed as that I never could disgrace her by any trace of likeness; as that nobody could ever now look at me, and look at her, and remotely think of any near tie between us."[8]

Dickens was confident that "Heaven is just" and God's will is done for good, even when it might not appear that way to human beings. Sometimes, as in Esther's case, the providential working of God appears evident; other times, as in the case of Betsy Trotwood, Providence is inscrutable. In any case, Providence is irresistible and it is good.

God: The Divine Artificer

Dickens's concept of God as the All-Wise Orchestrator of life's events is really rather unremarkable. That is, Dickens was no different in his views this way than most nineteenth-century Anglican laypersons. Likewise, Dickens's concept of God as Creator was a common one. Dickens referred to God as the wise Creator, the Great Creator of mankind, the Creator of heaven and earth, the Almighty Hand, and the Divine artificer. His concept of God as Creator was derived clearly from Scripture and exhibited his very lofty view of God. In a speech before an audience at the Manchester Athenaeum, 5 October 1843, Dickens extolled the social, educational, and personal benefits to those who would avail themselves of the opportunities of the Athenaeum. Like many of the educators of his day, Dickens firmly believed that there was spiritual benefit to be had in knowledge and education, particularly in the form of a greater understanding and perception of God as Creator. Dickens remarked in his speech: "Something of what he hears or reads within such walls can scarcely fail to become at times a topic of discourse by his own fireside, nor can it ever fail to lead to larger sympathies with man, and to a higher veneration for the great Creator of all the wonders of the universe."[9] For Dickens, the more one could learn about the world, the greater appreciation and veneration one could bring to "the great Creator of all the wonders of the universe."

Dickens speaks directly not only to this veneration and appreciation but also "the wonders of the universe" in a noteworthy passage from his *American Notes*. On his first visit to America, Dickens experienced a sublime moment during a visit to Niagara Falls. He writes:

> Then, when I felt how near to my Creator I was standing, the first effect, and the enduring one—instant and lasting—of the tremendous spectacle, was Peace. . . . But always does the mighty stream appear to die as it comes down, and always from its unfathomable grave arises that tremendous ghost of spray and mist which is never laid: which has haunted this place with the same dread solemnity since Darkness brooded on the deep, and that first flood before the Deluge—Light—came rushing on Creation at the word of God.[10]

Dickens's concept of God as Creator was not limited to the creation of the physical universe but included, of course, the creation of humankind. Like the references above, Dickens's mention of God as Creator is typically brief but conspicuous. That is, Dickens is not trying to theologize about God, yet he does want to make a point. At the conclusion of his Christmas Book of 1844, *The Chimes*, Dickens prays:

> So may each year be happier than the last, and not the meanest of our brethren or sisterhood debarred their rightful share, in what our Great Creator formed them to enjoy.[11]

In an especially graphic passage of *A Child's History of England*, Dickens writes of the atrocities of the armies of Richard II in collusion with the general populace at York in the twelfth century. His description is telling:

> When the populace broke in, they found (except the trembling few, cowering in corners, whom they soon killed) only heaps of greasy cinder, with there and there something like part of the blackened trunk of a burnt tree, but which had lately been a human creature, formed by the beneficent hand of the Creator as they were.[12]

And in *Barnaby Rudge*, speaking of the cognitively challenged Barnaby, whose name is given to the novel, Dickens remarks,

> It is something to know that Heaven has left the capacity of gladness in such a creature's breast; it is something to be assured that, however lightly men may crush that faculty in their fellows, the Great Creator of mankind imparts it even to his despised and slighted work.[13]

From each of these last three quotes, it is clear that Dickens saw humankind as the direct creation of God possessing a majesty and a dignity derived from God's hand, by virtue of that creation. Undoubtedly, it was this fundamental understanding of the inherent dignity of humankind from which Dickens developed his high view of the human being. Consequently, Dickens believed that, regardless of their station in life, all human beings should be able to enjoy a quality of life corresponding to this inherent dignity and free from neglect, want, disease, oppression, ignorance, and injustice. Moreover, Dickens's conviction that human beings have a moral responsibility to one another most certainly emerged from this same understanding of God's direct and purposeful creation of humankind.

Again, Dickens's concept of God as Creator, whether of the physical universe or of humankind, situated him squarely within the popular lay Anglicanism that carried the day among early to mid-nineteenth-century Anglican laypersons. Just so, Dickens and Victorians like him, were able to make a seemingly natural and easy accommodation to the new findings of science and the influence such findings were beginning to exert in the early decades of the nineteenth century, particularly on the traditional concept of God as Creator.

Behind the impetus of landmark discoveries and remarkable advances, the science of geology began to establish its preeminence in scientific circles as well as in the popular mind. Scriptural cosmogony was being rethought and redefined in works like Charles Lyell's *Principles of Geology* (1830–33) and Robert Chambers's *Vestiges of the Natural World* (1844). As a result of the publication of Darwin's *On the Origin of Species* in 1859, the scientific upheaval that was incipient in the 1830s and 1840s, along with its attending intellectual and cultural shifts would come to fruition in the 1860s. Walter Houghton has commented, "The assumptions of the old order had been bred into young minds of almost all mid-Victorians; and now in the nineteenth century, . . . [those assumptions] suddenly began to crumble."[14] The reconfiguring of the basic mid-Victorian worldview included challenging not only the unquestioned appeal to the Mosaic creation account in the Scriptures but also the traditional methods and beliefs of the sciences at large.

Notwithstanding, the commonly held view in the first half of the nineteenth century that science and religion were loyal partners remained, for the most part, steadfast. Certainly, the winds of change were in the air, but many—scientists, clergymen, and laypersons alike—continued to maintain well into the 1850s and even into the 1860s the natural compatibility between science and faith. "Science was not generally seen as in opposition to religion before the publication of *Origin of Species*," T. W. Heyck observes, "but as part of a widely accepted natural theology."[15]

Dickens's views on theological and biblical ideas, like many of his day, were informed by the new work in science. And his views developed according to popular thinking and the growing preeminence of science as it was developing in the 1830s and 1840s. In fact, it appears that the views Dickens developed during this period were the views he held well into the 1860s and most probably until his death in 1870.

It is noteworthy, for instance, that Dickens's library in his home at Gadshill contained no fewer than seventeen titles (some multivolume) concerned with natural history and natural theology. Among these titles were five of the eight *Bridgewater Treatises*,[16] Darwin's *On the Origin of Species*, Lyell's *Geological Evidence of the Antiquity of Man*, and Hugh Miller's *Testimony of the Rocks*. The presence of these volumes suggests that Dickens may have been at least familiar, and perhaps even conversant, with the issues circulating around science and theology in the thirties, forties, fifties, and beyond. And it seems reasonable to believe that Dickens embraced a popular natural theology that was held to be common knowledge, which affirmed both a scriptural view of God as Creator and the discoveries and evidences of science. Apparently, Dickens was one who, like many of his contemporaries, believed that the natural sciences confirmed God's agency in creation; that the discoveries of science merely served to allow us to appreciate all the more God's creative activity.

The letter to Cerjat (cited above) seems to confirm as much. In fact, Dickens makes specific mention there of "the science of geology" and remarks, "Nothing is discovered without God's intention and assistance, and I suppose every new knowledge of His works that is conceded to man to be distinctly a revelation by which men are to guide themselves."[17]

At first glance, Dickens's comments appear to reflect a rather progressive view of the relationship between science and religion, but his choice of words and his argument actually suggest a more traditional view, especially considering those comments were made in 1863. By insisting that scientific discoveries are "revelation" given by God's "assistance" and according to God's "intention" and that these discoveries are "new knowledge of His works," Dickens was simply voicing the popular view of the 1830s and 1840s. Significantly, he was affirming that same view in 1863, four years after the publication of Darwin's *On the Origin of Species* and three years after the publication of *Essays and Reviews*. Dickens's views, then, had not changed from the 1830s to the 1860s in any substantial way.

Neither were they especially progressive nor any more noteworthy than popular Christian thought. To be sure, he appeared to exemplify a rather common understanding of how the new scientific methods might come to bear on the Scriptures, but again, this was in keeping with popular lay-Anglican thought.

It could be suggested, of course, that Dickens was progressive in his thinking by the very fact that he accepted the new trends in science and sought to bring them into harmony with a biblical cosmogony. Still, while that may be true, he was not prepared to concede that new scientific discovery had called into question the biblical affirmations of God's creative agency, as some were willing to do. Rather, Dickens continued to accept a ready harmony between natural science and revealed religion—a stance that, although already being challenged by some, remained a framework of stability well into the 1860s.

Dickens's concept of God, then, is not expressed or formulated in terms of a systematic theology, but it is solidly scriptural, at least according to the popular scriptural understanding of his day, and it appears to have emerged from the thoughtful reflection of an engaged and serious layperson. Dickens was not given to theological formulation or speculative theologizing and, as will become evident in the pages that follow, believed that such formulation and theologizing were destructive, eventually leading to sectarian squabbles and divisiveness. Still, he thought carefully about biblical and theological issues because they were important to him and because he was certain they were definitive issues that shaped and influenced the world in which he lived.

The Four Last Things

The spirituality of popular lay Anglicanism in the early nineteenth century was shaped to a large degree by an almost superstitious preoccupation with death, judgment, heaven, and hell—The Four Last Things. The common belief, which transcended denominational and partisan divisions but was largely influenced by Evangelicalism, was that at one's death, a final judgment was passed and one's eternal destiny—heaven or hell—was assigned. As a result, Christian thought in the first half of the nineteenth century was often taken up with these Four Last Things.

Death

Dickens, of course, was no stranger to the experience of the death of loved ones. He felt keenly the loss of his beloved sister-in-law, Mary Hogarth (1836); when he was eleven years old, his sister Harriet Ellen died of smallpox; and in his adult life, Dickens's sister Fanny died of tuberculosis (1848); he lost his eight-month-old infant daughter Dora (1851); and his nephew, Fanny's son, died just three months after Fanny's death.[18] Dickens's understanding of death and his response to it once again situated him well within the confines of popular Christian spirituality in the nineteenth century. In fact, Margarete Holubetz has pointed out that Dickens's treatment of deathbed scenes in his novels and other fiction "are indeed largely typical of general Victorian attitudes."[19] Certainly, Nell's death in *The Old Curiosity Shop* is a classic treatment reflecting Victorian practices, attitudes, and social rites surrounding death. The deaths of Paul Dombey (*D & S*) and Richard Carstone (*BH*) are treated less dramatically and extensively than Nell's death but, nevertheless, exhibit many of the same social features important to the Victorians.[20] Certainly, Dickens's fictional accounts of death and the events surrounding it can reveal a great deal about his ideas and views concerning death, but death had touched his life directly, and it is in these personal experiences that we hear Dickens's Christian voice about death and the afterlife most clearly.

The death of his beloved sister-in-law, Mary Hogarth, was a defining moment in Dickens's life. Dickens thought the world of Mary, who died in his arms, and her death left an indelible impression on him. Dickens relates the details of Mary's death in a letter, most likely to one of Mary's relatives:

Why should I say more than that she was taken ill without an instant's warning on the night of Saturday the 7th of May, almost immediately after she retired to bed—that although every effort was made to save her, and no danger apprehended until nearly the very last, she sank under the attack and died—died in such a calm and gentle sleep, that although I had held her in my arms for some time before, when she was certainly living (for she swallowed a little brandy from my hand), I continued to support her lifeless form, long after her soul had fled to Heaven.[21]

Dickens took it upon himself to write a chain of letters—the equivalent of phone calls today—all of much the same character, to various recipients announcing Mary's death.[22] Significant in these letters are the expressions that bear witness to his understanding of death. In the letter cited above, Dickens remarks that Mary died in "such a calm and gentle sleep" and that "I continued to support her lifeless form, long after her soul had fled to Heaven." Similarly, he writes to Richard Johns, 31 May 1837, that Mary is now "in that happy World for which God adapted her better than for this" and in the above letter sent to the unnamed relative he points out, "that before a single care of life had wounded her pure heart, she had passed quietly away to an immortality of happiness and joy."

Two simple and straightforward observations can be made here. First, while death was the harsh reality of this life, there was for Dickens the sure and steadfast hope of joy and happiness in the life to come. When Dickens dealt with death, whether in his fiction or in his own life, he approached it with the certainty of an afterlife and the hope of heaven. Second, Dickens seems to make a gesture toward the popular notion of his day that God in his mercy would take a child or youth (Mary was seventeen when she died) in death to protect that child or youth from a sinful world and any future grief or harm.[23] James Hervey, a popular devotional writer in Dickens's day, muses in his popular *Meditations and Contemplations*:

> Consider this, ye mourning parents, and dry your tears. Why should you lament, that your little ones are crowned with victory, before the sword is drawn, or the conflict begun?—Perhaps, the supreme Disposer of events foresaw some inevitable snare of temptations forming, or some dreadful storm of adversity impending. And why should you be so dissatisfied, with that kind precaution, which housed your pleasant plant, and removed into shelter a tender flower, before the thunders roared: before the lightnings flew: before the tempest poured its rage?—O remember! They are not lost, but *taken away from the evil to come*.[24]

What Dickens tells us elsewhere about the death of Mary reveals that he experienced the inevitable grief that comes with such a loss. But while Dickens's grief could be at times almost overwhelming, it was never ultimately defeating because he held on to God's bright promise of a joyful and happy afterlife in heaven.

With such resolve, Dickens responded to the death of his eight-month-old daughter Dora, his ninth child, who died on 14 April 1851. Dickens wrote to Angela Burdette Coutts, a close friend of the family, concerning the circumstances of Dora's death, adding: "We laid the child in her grave today. And it is part of the goodness and mercy of God that if we could call her back to life, now, with a wish, would not do it."[25] To F. M. Evans he wrote similarly,[26] and to Mrs. Henry Austin, he wrote, "We have buried our poor little pet, and can quite quietly (I hope) entrust her to God."[27] It makes sense, then, that this same language is reflected in the inscription Dickens wrote for Mary's gravestone:

> Young Beautiful and Good
> God in His Mercy
> Numbered Her With His Angels
> At the Early Age Of
> Seventeen.[28]

Nothing really is very remarkable in Dickens's views concerning death. His views are the views of the popular Christianity of his day. They are neither academic nor deeply theological. Yet they do suggest sober reflection, however simple. Neither are the written words and expressions Dickens employed in facing the reality of the death of a loved one those of mere convention or platitude. Rather, they suggest that Dickens faced that reality with the authentic and substantial conviction of the hope of heaven.

Heaven

Heaven certainly provided for rich and varied discourse especially among devotional writers and clergymen of the nineteenth century. That is not to say, however, that theologians did not weigh in as well. Nineteenth-century conceptions of heaven generally fell within one of two categories, which Michael Wheeler succinctly describes as "heaven as worship and heaven as community."[29] That is, heaven was understood in one view as a place (or state) of eternal worship; in the other, as an eternal community in which earthly relationships were continued and perfected—in Wheeler's words, "often more like a middle-class suburb in the sky."[30] A third view, which circulated primarily in academic discussion, conceived of heaven as a metaphysical state of being, transcendent and impenetrable. Not unexpectedly, this third view commanded little or no attention in popular Christian thinking or in the pastoral mind.

Although the view of heaven as a place or state of eternal worship was certainly widespread and was a part of most any conception of heaven, it was the view of heaven as community that carried the day. Francis Knight identifies the trend as beginning in the late 1830s and being reflected in popular devotional literature "that emphasized heaven as the eternal home of Christians"[31] and that loved ones who had died would be "reunited with other relatives, and would continue family life in a perfected form."[32] Wheeler supports Knight's observations when he suggests, "Perhaps the most characteristic Victorian ideas of heaven are of a place in which family reunions and the recognition of friends are to be achieved after death, and (more radically Romantic) of a site in which lovers are reunited as couples."[33] It is not difficult to find in these descriptions or ideas the understanding of heaven to which Dickens subscribed.

Dickens's concept of heaven was quite straightforward. Nothing in his thought could be construed as even hinting that heaven was a state of being, and we find there virtually nothing suggesting that worship was the exclusive activity in heaven. For Dickens, the two things that mattered most about heaven were, first, that he would be there after death and, second, that he would enjoy reunion with loved ones there, especially family members. It should be noted, however, that in Dickens's mind, heaven was not profaned by its character as community, as some of his contemporaries might have been inclined to argue, nor was it any less holy or pure for being the locale of family reunion. Dickens recognized heaven as the source from which the holiness and purity of domestic affection and familial love was derived, sanctified as it were by God. Indeed, home and family were two things that for Dickens derived their essential quality from heavenly resources.

To suggest, then, as Dickens does, that home and family bear a heavenly stamp implies a subtle but crucial distinction. That is, earthly ideas of home and family do not establish and determine their heavenly nature. Rather, heaven infuses its character and quality into home and family, imparting to them value and sanctity. More often than not, Dickens only implies this distinction. On occasion, however, he articulates it explicitly. Just over midway through *The Old Curiosity Shop*, Dickens pauses to "linger . . . for an instant to remark that if ever household affections and loves are graceful things, they are graceful in the poor." As Dickens begins to clarify Kit's affection for his old home over Abel Cottage, Finchley, he insists that Kit's love of home and family "are of the true metal and bear the true stamp of Heaven." Kit "has his love of home from God."[34] Here, Dickens points to Kit's affection for his home as born in heaven where it derives its nature and quality from God. It is not Kit's natural affection and instinctive love that give substance to these ideas in heaven. Rather, it is the love and affection born of God and bearing the stamp of heaven that sanctifies his love of home and family with heavenly substance and character.

Even Dickens's most fundamental observations of heaven appear to reflect not only the popular notions of heaven but also a bit of its sacred character. Writing for his children in *TLOL* he remarks, "what a good place Heaven is" and that it is a place "where we hope to go, and all to meet each other after we are dead, and there be happy always together." Dickens hints at the sacred character of heaven here in that all of this is observed in the context of Jesus's presence in heaven. That is, because Jesus "is now in Heaven . . . you never can think what a good place Heaven, is without knowing who he was and what he did."[35] Moreover, Dickens's direct and simple words to the Reverend James White at the death of White's child surely captured a bit of this sacred character: "Our blessed Christian hopes do not shut out the belief of love and remembrance still enduring [in heaven] but irradiate it and make it sacred."[36]

Continuing to reflect some of the more popular notions of heaven, Dickens further characterizes heaven in *TLOL* as a place where God's mercy and forgiveness will welcome all who seek them; that it is a place of comfort, happiness, and peace; that it is the hope of which all those who suffer hardship and sorrow in this life may be confident. Heaven is "The world that sets this [world] right."[37] This, for Dickens, was heaven and this heaven was the hope to which he turned in the face of death and loss.

What are perhaps some of Dickens's most profound words on heaven come amid his reflections on Mary's death in a short-lived attempt at a diary began on 1 January 1838. In his entry of 14 January, he writes concerning Mary and the afterlife borrowing from the words of Sir Walter Scott as Scott mused on the death of his own wife. Dickens writes, "She is sentient and conscious of my emotions somewhere—where, we cannot tell, how, we cannot tell; yet would I not at this moment renounce the mysterious yet certain hope that I shall see her in a better world, for all that this world can give me."[38] Dickens's reflections on death are never words of passive resignation to the cruel twists of fate. For Dickens, heaven and the afterlife may have been mysteries, yet they were mysteries he embraced with confidence and hope.

Judgment and Hell

What might cautiously be referred to as the more negative aspects of nineteenth-century Christian thought—judgment, hell, evil, God's wrath, and the like—have not always been considered as carefully in Dickens studies as they should be or with the attention they deserve. Some even have argued that Dickens paid little attention to these things, that he rejected some of the ideas outright, and that he ignored others. In fact, God's judgment on sin, hell, God's wrath, evil, and an unseen world of malevolent spirits are all very much a part of Dickens's Christian worldview. What is more, the way Dickens writes and thinks about these subjects and issues is telling.

In the previous chapter, I suggested that *TLOL* can be instructive in helping us navigate the religious landscape of the larger Dickens corpus. This is especially true in the case of judgment and hell and the like. Dickens included three passages in *TLOL* that are significant, first, by their very presence there and, second, by how they inform certain ideas in Dickens's fiction. Dickens selected for inclusion in *TLOL* (1) the account of the rich man and Lazarus, (2) the account of the Gerasene demoniac, and 3) the account of the ascension of Jesus. All three of these become important indicators as we consider what Dickens has to say about God's judgment on sin, hell, God's wrath, evil, and an unseen world of malevolent spirits.

Dickens is really quite clear on eschatological judgment both in *TLOL* and in the larger corpus of his work. In *TLOL*, Dickens brings what is essentially the basic narrative of his life of Jesus to a close—he included what might be called an epilogue—with his account of the ascension of Jesus. For this account, Dickens harmonizes 1 Corinthians 15:6; Acts 1:1–11 and the corresponding Synoptic material. From Luke, Dickens writes that Jesus led "his disciples . . . as far as to Bethany" (KJV) and from Mark that Jesus "was received up into heaven, and sat on the right hand of God" (KJV). Naturally, Dickens depends upon Acts for the account of the ascension itself. What is peculiarly conspicuous in Dickens's rendering of the account is that the angels declare that Jesus would one day return "to judge the world." For one thing, the declaration clearly implies an eschatological judgment at which Jesus is judge. The more significant issue, however, is that the phrase "judge the world" is Dickens's own gloss and is found in neither the book of Acts nor the Synoptic Gospels. Theology may suggest the implication, but the phrase itself is not there. Apparently, Dickens wanted to provide clarity for what is only implied. This would be a bold stroke and quite unexplainable if such a notion was not part of his Christian understanding and worldview.

This concept of judgment finds expression in Dickens's other work as well. In 1846, Dickens wrote a series of letters to the *Daily News* (England) in which he expressed his views on capital punishment. On 16 March 1846, he writes of final judgment as inevitable and as an event in which all meet on level ground: "When the judge's faltering voice delivers sentence, how awfully the prisoner and he confront each other; two men, destined one day, however far removed from one another at this time, to stand alike as suppliants at the bar of God."[39] Compare the following excerpt, written some fifteen years later, from *Great Expectations* in which Dickens describes the death sentence of Magwitch: "The sun was striking in at the great windows of the court, through the glittering drops of rain upon the glass, and it made a broad shaft of light between the two-and-thirty and the Judge, linking both together, and perhaps reminding some among the audience, how both were passing on, with absolute equality, to the greater Judgment that knoweth all things and cannot err."[40] And this same idea of final judgment finds expression in *David Copperfield* as David chides Martha: "In the name of the great Judge . . . before whom you and all of us must stand at His dread time, dismiss the terrible idea! We can all do some good, if we will."[41]

To posit the idea of a final judgment, of course, requires that there is some basis on which judgment stands and that there are distinct outcomes of the resulting verdict. Certainly, this was true in the nineteenth century. And, of course, the idea of final judgment, particularly from the negative side, naturally suggested the associated idea of God's wrath. Interestingly, Dickens was not reticent to broach the topic of the wrath of God in his work. On 25 July 1839, he responded in a letter to a Mrs. Godfrey, an author of children's books. The letter is often cited for Dickens's stern language on misrepresenting God almost exclusively as a God of wrath. "I think it monstrous," he writes in part, "to hold the source of inconceivable mercy and goodness perpetually up to them [children] as an avenging and wrathful God."[42] This particular topic was one that Dickens revisited often, for he would not countenance the view that portrayed God only as Judge and not first as Father, especially when such a view was used as some sort of coercive measure to manipulate children toward either right behavior or conversion.

Notwithstanding, Dickens did not ignore the idea of God's wrath. He was just not fond of bantering the idea about to coerce conversions or to try to elicit what would become less than genuine expressions of morality. Dickens was quite opposed to the idea of the wrath of God in the distorted form of Calvinism that seemed to hold the wrath of God as a central and defining tenet and make the majority of humanity the object of that wrath, excluding or ignoring God's love and grace. As a result, Dickens developed an understanding of the wrath of God as limited in its exercise and specific in its application. That is, God's wrath is not poured out on humanity universally or in a blanket manner. Rather, it is directed toward specific individuals for their particularly flagrant defiance of God's order in the universe and for their willful, and often heinous, disobedience of God's moral Law.

Dickens was always clear and seldom detached when he introduced the idea of the wrath of God into his work. In the narrative thread of the Haredale murder in *Barnaby Rudge*, for instance, God's wrath becomes a thematic element. Dickens observes of Barnaby Rudge Sr., "His double crime, the circumstances under which it had been committed, the length of time that had elapsed, and its discovery in spite of all, made him, as it were, the visible object of the Almighty's wrath."[43] Earlier, in the same novel, as Rudge attempts to find refuge from the inexorable tolling of a phantom bell proclaiming his guilt, Dickens asserts, "A hundred walls and roofs of brass would not shut out that bell, for in it spoke the wrathful voice of God, and from that voice, the whole wide universe could not afford refuge!"[44] And in *A Tale of Two Cities*, the wife of the Marquis St. Evrémonde hopes to "avert the wrath of Heaven from a House that had long been hateful to the suffering of many."[45] But according to Dr. Mannette, the House of Evrémonde had been abandoned by God and was to "have no part in His mercies."[46]

The idea of the wrath of God, then, is not foreign to Dickens and he is more than comfortable appealing to it and its retributive justice especially against sin or crime that was particularly loathsome and destructive. For Dickens, that included any type of inhumanity, prejudice, hatred, or cruelty perpetrated by one human being against another. Likely, part of the reason for his including in *TLOL* the account of the rich man and Lazarus was to speak to this kind of sin.

Dickens introduces the account of the rich man and Lazarus by paraphrasing Luke 16:14, "Now the Pharisees received these lessons from our Saviour, scornfully; for they were rich, and covetous, and thought themselves superior to all mankind." In Luke's account, the story immediately follows Jesus's statement "No man can serve two masters; . . . [You] cannot serve God and mammon" (Luke 16:13 KJV) and is formally introduced by a stern reprimand by Jesus. Dickens's editing seems to indicate that he saw this story's teaching along these same lines. Perhaps most telling in Dickens's rendering is that he expressly remarks in the final words of his introduction, "As a warning to [the Pharisees], he related this story."

In the context of a discussion on final judgment and the wrath of God, and as a warning, Dickens's account of this episode is significant in several ways. First, as was pointed out above, the very fact that Dickens chose to include the story is significant. At the point in the narrative that Dickens situated the story, there are no narrative constraints that make its inclusion necessary. It is present simply because Dickens wanted it included in his life of Jesus. Second, its inclusion is significant because it relates the judgment of two men after death. Third, it includes the idea of punishment in hell and retributive justice. Fourth, it serves as a warning to those who are more concerned about worldly goods and their own prosperity than about the well-being of others and their moral responsibility to them. Fifth, it identifies this self-absorbed moral indifference with sin, the sort of flagrant violation of God's order which brings the retributive justice of God's wrath.

Dickens was a bit more measured when it came to the use of the idea and imagery of hell. Granted, in the story of the rich man and Lazarus, Dickens says explicitly that the rich man was suffering torments in hell, but this is the only place Dickens touches on the subject in *TLOL*. Dickens does not ignore hell in his other work, but it is not as prevalent as one might suppose considering his clear voice on judgment and the wrath of God. In *Barnaby Rudge*, in which these eschatological ideas seem most frequently employed, Rudge, resigned to his own fate, offers, "Did I go forth that night, abjured of God and man, and anchored deep in hell, to wander at my cable's length about the earth, and surely be drawn down at last?"[47] The allusion to Satan in Revelation 20:1–10 speaks to Rudge's ultimate destiny.

Similarly, Fagin's last hours in *Oliver Twist* elicit from Dennis Walder the statement: "There can be little doubt of his ultimate destination."[48] Dickens describes Fagin in his cell: "He started up every minute, . . . with gasping mouth and burning skin . . . ; his unwashed flesh crackled with the fever that burnt him up."[49] Dickens treats Bill Sikes similarly, and Dennis Walder makes a similar statement. "Let no man talk of murderers escaping justice," Dickens declares, "and hint that Providence must sleep."[50] In the denouement Sikes attempts to elude his captors, with Walder commenting: "Sikes is followed by a ruthless conscience, which takes on a cosmic significance. . . . The next sight to meet his eyes is a huge fire: there can be little doubt of his ultimate destination."[51]

If the idea of hell gave Dickens pause, the idea of genuine spiritual evil and an unseen world of malevolent spirits surely did not. A. E. Dyson has remarked on Dickens's profound sense of evil in the world. "He saw [the world] almost as Hell at times," says Dyson, "a place of exile threatened by evil and dæmonic powers."[52] Even Humphry House agreed that Dickens had a profound sense of evil, although he rejected the idea that this might be attributable to Dickens's Christian worldview. "Evil is always terrifyingly real," says House, "but the source of it is obscure."[53]

It is not surprising, then, that in the larger body of his work we should find the presence of this unseen world of spiritual evil. In his sober "A December Vision" essay from *Household Words* (14 December 1850), Dickens attempts to expose certain evils at the social and institutional levels that, in his mind, threatened society with its demise. Singling out "Disease" and "Pestilence" borne on the "poisoned air" and "charged with heavy retribution," he writes: "I saw, wheresoever I looked, cunning preparation made for defacing the Creator's Image, from the moment of its appearance here on earth, and stamping over it the image of the Devil. I saw, from those reeking and pernicious stews, the avenging consequences of such Sin issuing forth, and penetrating to the highest places."[54] It is significant here that Dickens employs the language of supernatural evil in this essay, drawing a contrast between "the Creator" and "the Devil" that seems to acknowledge the reality of both. The essay is obviously about social and institutional evil, but Dickens clearly sees these evils in a moral-religious context through the lens of his Christian worldview as "a low dull howl of Ignorance [rose] up to the Eternal Heavens." He was indignant that "all the gifts of God" in thousands of children were "perverted in their breast or trampled out." And he was prophetic as the "wicked, selfish men" who apathetically dismissed such evils were admonished that they shall bear their "portion of that wrong through ALL TIME." It seems reasonable to suggest that the evil Dickens observed around him and that he condemned so roundly was in some way connected to the unseen world of spiritual evil.

To some degree, a similar orientation seems to have informed Dickens's comments in a letter to the Reverend Thomas Robinson, 8 April 1841. The same kinds of evil that Dickens observed in "A December Vision" he describes to Robinson as "cruelty and oppression" and insists that his own efforts will be given to identifying and denouncing such evil: "While you teach in your walk of life the lessons of tenderness you have learnt in sorrow, trust me that in mine, I will pursue cruelty and oppression, the Enemies of all God's creatures of all codes and creeds, so long as I have the energy of thought and power of giving it utterance."[55]

Apparently, this exchange of correspondence was not unrelated to the subject matter of *Oliver Twist*, specifically as it was discussed in the 1841 preface, in which Dickens writes, "I confess I have yet to learn that a lesson of the purest good may not be drawn from the vilest evil."[56] It is clear from this preface that Dickens's intent in *Oliver Twist* is not merely to expose the dark underbelly of London's backstreets and slums. He hopes, rather, to reach beyond crime and its symptoms to "pursue cruelty and oppression" and to present the conflict between "the purest good" and "the vilest evil" that lay beneath the surface. In his preface, it is Sikes whom Dickens characterizes as having become "utterly and irredeemably bad."[57] In the novel it is Fagin, who with "every evil thought and blackest purpose . . . working at his heart"[58] has Oliver "in his toils" and is "slowly instilling into his soul the poison which he hoped would blacken it, and change its hue forever."[59] This language suggests it was not enough that Fagin simply turn Oliver into a thief; Fagin's intent, as Dickens depicts it, is to taint Oliver's soul. Sikes and Fagin, as well as Nancy, are used in *Oliver Twist*, as Dickens points out in his preface, "to serve the purpose of a moral."[60]

Surely, Barnaby Rudge Sr. is one of Dickens's most diabolical characters, and his characterization as evil is explicit. His confrontations with his estranged wife, Mary, are of particular significance in his characterization. He describes himself to her in one of these confrontations as "a thing from which all creatures shrink, save those curst beings of another world, who will not leave me."[61] And other words of his, when understood in the context of genuine and present supernatural evil, carry the diabolical force of a curse in keeping with his character. "The blood with which I sprinkle it," he invokes, "be on you and yours, in the name of the Evil Spirit that tempts men to their ruin!"[62] In the context of a worldview in which supernatural evil is present, these words help to express not only the hateful and odious nature of Rudge but also a realization of a connection to such evil.

In all of this, Dickens is appealing to the moral-religious language and imagery of supernatural evil. This is apparent in the broader scope and context of his use of such language as well as in the Christian moral textures of his worldview. Dickens is preaching a sermon and the evil with which he grapples in that sermon is not simply of human origin. It is genuine supernatural evil that plays in a cosmic scheme of malevolent spirits.

Additionally, Dickens included two definitive passages in *TLOL* that play a significant role in establishing the reality of this unseen spiritual world in his worldview. He included there the account of the demon-possessed man in the country of the Gerasenes [Gadarenes in Matthew] (Matt. 8:28–34; Mark 5:1–20; Luke 8:26–39; *TLOL* 44–45) and Jesus's healing of the boy with an evil spirit just after descending the mount of Transfiguration (Matt. 17:14–21; Mark 9:14–29; Luke 9:37–43; *TLOL* 59–60). The fact that Dickens included both of these accounts is telling.

In the first place, both stories involve the unseen world of malevolent spirits. Second, in much of nineteenth-century biblical commentary, these two stories were often handled rather differently from one another. That is, typically the account of the demon-possessed man in the country of the Gerasenes was approached quite straightforwardly as the account of an exorcism. The other, the account of the healing of the boy with an evil spirit, however, often was understood as Jesus's curing a disease rather than casting out an evil spirit. In the third place, Dickens included both stories and relates them along the lines of contemporary biblical commentary.

Dickens relates the first account, the story of the demon-possessed man, by explicitly stating that Jesus "perceived that he was torn by an evil spirit."[63] Dickens relates the second account by describing the boy as "mad" and by remarking that Jesus "cured" him.[64] Dickens does refer to the man in the country of the Gerasenes as a "dreadful madman," but he nevertheless includes the idea of the evil spirit involved. In including both of these episodes, Dickens may have been attempting to strike the balance that a number of nineteenth-century commentators attempted when dealing with scriptural passages that included the notion of an unseen world of evil spirits and demon posssession.

It was common in Dickens's day for some commentators to consider the biblical writers rather primitive and superstitious, understanding what was, in fact, mental illness, epilepsy, or other infirmity as demon possession. Other commentators attempted to nuance the biblical data to try to offer a reasonable balance. That is, some agreed that what was named demon possession by biblical writers may have been disease or infirmity, but, they insisted, the biblical writers were seeing below the surface and providing the reader with deeper insight.

Hermann Olshausen, a nineteenth-century commentator and biblical scholar points out in this regard: "Hence, the common opinion, which pronounces the demoniacs to be sick people, is true in one aspect; but it takes a partial view, embracing only what is outward, while the representation of Scripture regards the phenomena in their moral origin."[65] In a sermon, Thomas Arnold also notes: "Yet in that good man [Jesus], endowed with such mighty power, there dwelt, we know amidst all the perfection of the human nature, the fullness of the Godhead also; and in those madmen, with all the symptoms of what we call common and natural madness. The Scripture has revealed to us that there dwelt an author of that madness, of whom, without such revelation, we could have known nothing."[66]

Just as some, then, sought to accommodate findings in medicine, psychology, and science to their belief in the Scriptures, so may have Dickens been inclined.[67] In any case, he chose to relate the story of the demon-possessed man in the country of the Gerasenes "torn by an evil spirit" along with the story of the boy with the evil spirit. As sole compiler and editor of *TLOL*, had he not believed in an unseen world of malevolent spirits, he had every option available to him to omit the former. He did not. And that is telling.

As Dickens did not theologize about his concept of God, likewise, nowhere did he theologize about the Four Last Things. But whether in regard to heaven or hell, death or God's wrath, or an unseen world of spiritual evil, Dickens clearly saw these things through the lens of a biblical and a Christian worldview. Apart from such a context, much of what he said in this regard would have little narrative force and less meaning. That Dickens's Christian voice is heard and is brought to bear on his work becomes increasingly necessary, then. Otherwise, we might miss much of the power and the impact of his work. And we might miss, as well, something valuable he has to teach us.

Learning from and Thinking with Dickens

What Dickens has to teach us about theology has, I think, very little to do with the content of theology and theological inquiry. Instead, Dickens's most valuable lessons concerning theology have to do with how he handled and thought about theology and doctrine. And that comes to us as a caution. As Dickens was no theologian, I am not referring to methodology or approach. It is unlikely that Dickens was even vaguely aware of such concepts. What I have in mind is how he viewed the theological enterprise—his basic attitude toward theology and doing theology. In short, Dickens was convinced that theology and doctrine should be taken with a grain of salt. And if we take a moment to catch our breath, what we can draw from him in this regard is rather remarkable and can be transformative.

Theology in Dickens's Hands

In *Listening to Your Life*, Frederick Buechner observes: "Theology is the study of God and his ways. For all we know dung beetles may study man and his ways and call it humanology. If so, we would probably be more touched and amused than irritated. One hopes that God feels likewise."[68] There is so much to think about in this definition, but let me focus on one particular idea for our purposes, and that is this: Theology is a human enterprise. It is an idea conceived by human beings and developed by human beings, and because of that, it will be flawed. Dickens grasped this idea firmly. And while he may not have couched it in this language, he understood it clearly. His entire approach to Christianity was shaped to a large degree by this particular take on theology and doctrine.

Years ago, I used Henry Thiessen's *Lectures in Systematic Theology* as an undergraduate textbook for a theology course. In his introductory chapter, Thiessen writes: "God has not seen fit to write the Bible in the form of a systematic theology; it remains for us, therefore, to gather together the scattered facts and to build them up into a logical system."[69] There is good reason to suspect that Thiessen meant that as an endorsement for the doing of theology, what he refers to as the "Necessity of Theology." And it is as good an endorsement for doing theology as any. But it also affirms—almost glaringly—what Buechner said more poetically. Theology is our human attempt to think clearly and correctly about God and God's ways, and so we must take it with a grain of salt.

When Dickens wrote to F. W. H. Layton, "As I really do not know what orthodoxy may be, or what it may be supposed to include—a point not exactly settled, I believe, as yet, in the learned or unlearned world" (see above, chapter 2), he was touching on the idea of the limits of human theologizing in his recognition of the fact that there were many theological systems vying for ascendancy in the nineteenth century, just as there are today. And there was little agreement or consensus to be found among them, just as today. Significantly, it is not Dickens's point that one is right and the others wrong. It is simply that the systems and those defending them are engaged in the human enterprise of doing theology. And there are some mysteries in that enterprise that cannot and will not be penetrated by the human mind. What is left, then, is speculation. It may be sanctified speculation, but it is speculation nonetheless.

In spite of all of this, theology is no less a noble and, I think, necessary enterprise. I have no personal axe to grind against the study of theology and doctrine. Indeed, I am fully convinced that they are important and relevant—especially at this transitional postmodern turn in the life of the church. Perhaps Dickens takes a much too glib approach on a serious matter. But his caution is no less a vitally important one and can bring some necessary perspective to the church on a matter of some consequence.

Granted that these observations have some validity, there is a related caution that Dickens offers the church. As we have seen, Dickens placed Jesus squarely at the heart of Christianity and the life of faith while also maintaining a concomitant emphasis on the New Testament. And he was always careful to add qualifiers, such as giving no credence to "man's narrow construction of [the New Testament's] letter here or there,"[70] and understanding the character of Jesus "as separated from the vain constructions and inventions of men."[71] Such qualifications as these reveal, at least in part, Dickens's concerns about a misplaced emphasis on doctrine that can inadvertently, or sometimes almost brazenly, challenge Jesus's place at the heart of the life of faith and the church. That is, Jesus sometimes has to compete with theology or doctrine to maintain his place of preeminence and centrality in the church.

If we are not careful, our theological systems and concern for doctrinal precision can easily slip into the center, because it is easy for theology and doctrine to be mistaken for the object of its focus. In theology, we are seeking to think clearly and correctly about God, about Christ, about the Holy Spirit, so that they remain central and clearly before us. And we employ the Scriptures to direct us toward this clarity and accuracy. Because of these close connections, it becomes easy for the thinking and the process by which we develop our understanding of God, Christ, and the Holy Spirit to stand in place of that which we ultimately want to think clearly and correctly about—God and God's ways. So, there is a fine line separating the tools and the means from the object and the end. And without the conscientious examination to which Paul calls Timothy in 1 Timothy 4:16, "Pay close attention to yourself and to your teaching [or doctrine]," the concern for doctrinal purity, however well-intentioned, can sometimes unknowingly usurp Jesus's place at the center of the life of faith. This is precisely why Dickens's cautious attitude toward theology is so important. Theology, like everything else connected to the church, has become dislocated when it becomes an end itself. Theology is simply a tool to the end that we think clearly and correctly about God and God's ways. It is not the end in itself. When it becomes an end, it is no longer a means, it is no longer a tool, and it has become dangerous and deadly. Thus, it is imperative that we remain ever vigilant that our concern for clarity of doctrine never drifts to the center to take the place of Jesus there.

The Lay Theologian

There is one more lesson that Dickens offers to the church on the subject of theology. On the one hand, it is clear that Dickens was no theologian. He didn't theologize and he didn't speculate. Often, he simply accepted the popular thought of the day. Yet, it seems he never did so passively. If he accepted the popular thought of the day, he did so because he was convinced the popular view was correct or was at least the better option. On the other hand, it is clear also that Dickens did think seriously and carefully about theological subjects. In fact, he seems to have developed informed and knowledgeable views of his own, and he did have clear notions and certain convictions about his faith. The lesson here is that the church needs and benefits from the theologically informed and engaged layperson. Dickens was one of them.

Just as there are those who are informed and knowledgeable about politics or economics but would never pretend to be politicians or economists, so there are those who are informed and knowledgeable about theology and biblical studies yet are not professors or pastors. And the church needs these people. In fact, informed and knowledgeable laypersons will likely play a major role in the church in the days ahead. These will be laypersons who are not just knowledgeable in a popular sense but in an academic sense as well. That is, like Dickens, they will not be formally and professionally trained in the academy, but they will be informed, well-read, and engaged with the central issues and ideas that are shaping the church and its theology.

The major distinction between the pastoral or professional theologian and the informed and engaged layperson is that the layperson, while informed and engaged, thinks like a layperson. And that is the attraction and advantage of having such persons in the church. That they think differently than do the pastors and teachers—the professionals—offers a perspective otherwise unavailable to the church. Their perspective on the implications of the theological trends and ideas shaping the thinking of the church comes from the pew side of the pulpit. As a result, a fuller, more integrated understanding of formative theological trends is made available to the church, giving it greater means by which to accommodate, challenge, ignore, reimagine, or reject the various ideas that present themselves.

The idea here is not to suggest the creation of a new office in the church or the establishment of a formal group or collective body. Rather, the focus is on individuals. That is, the idea must be taken up by individuals who are convinced of the need and the value of such persons in the church. They will see their role as a ministry, one to which they are called. Dickens was certainly an informed and knowledgeable layperson. And Dickens was engaged—but not in any conventional manner. While Dickens would not think in terms of playing a role, or of ministry or vocation, his voice in the church was necessary and valuable. Later, chapter 6 will speak to Dickens's unique and almost subversive contribution to the church as an informed and knowledgeable layperson.

4

Charles Dickens

RESURRECTIONIST

On 10 May 1843, Dickens wrote to David Dickson, apparently in response to Dickson's criticism of references to the doctrine of the new birth in *The Pickwick Papers* (266–67). With some notion, seemingly, of conversion in mind, Dickens writes: "That every man who seeks heaven must be born again, in good thoughts of his Maker, I sincerely believe. That it is expedient for every hound to say so in a certain snuffling form of words, to which he attaches no good meaning, I do not believe. I take it there is no difference between us."[1]

Dickens was seldom given to using the cant of the "snuffling" Evangelicals[2] in a serious manner. In fact, Dickens's dislike for Evangelicals[3]—and a reason for his parodies in *The Pickwick Papers* and so many other places—was likely more cultural than theological. That is, Dickens was put off by the ostentatious, boisterous, and "snuffling" posturing of many Evangelicals. Dickens preferred propriety, order, and discretion, especially in things religious. He was of the opinion Evangelicals were neither proper, orderly, nor discreet. Notwithstanding, in this letter to David Dickson, he was willing to affirm his belief in the necessity of being "born again" to make his point. He does qualify his use of the term "born again" with the phrase, "in good thoughts of his Maker," but that does not dilute this affirmation or otherwise render his words hollow. Rather, it seems to suggest, at least, a little of his own understanding of spiritual rebirth or conversion, and as such, it is an invitation to consider Dickens's understanding of salvation.

In many respects, Dickens's idea of salvation falls in line rather comfortably with early to mid-nineteenth-century popular lay Anglicanism. But the finer contours of his concept of salvation provide an interesting study. Not only will a consideration of Dickens's idea of salvation further clarify his Christian voice, it will also provide an additional glimpse of the nineteenth-century religious landscape in Great Britain.

Dickens's reference to being "born again in good thoughts of his Maker" in the letter to Dickson may well express an idea that was common currency in the mid-nineteenth century. This idea seems to be at the heart of an Edward Bouverie Pusey[4] sermon that describes conversion: "In its widest sense 'conversion' is turning towards God . . . [it] is a course of being conformed to God, a learning to have Him more simply in our minds, to be turned wholly to Him, solely to Him, . . . opening our hearts to Him, to have their warmth, their health, their life, from Him."[5] This, Dickens, might say, is being "born again, in good thoughts of his Maker."

Dickens certainly would have been wary of using the term "born again" in the precise sense that the nineteenth-century Evangelical would have, so it is peculiarly noteworthy here that he affirmed, with rather familiar words, the idea of conversion or regeneration and the concomitant notion of salvation. And such familiar terms are used elsewhere by Dickens. For instance, in chapter 2, I demonstrated that for Dickens, Jesus is indeed "Our Saviour" and that the designation in his writing carried with it a redemptive significance. And in an open letter sent to Angela Burdett-Coutts—discussed in chapter 2—Dickens declares unequivocally that Christ "died upon the cross to save us." Further, *TLOL* establishes that Jesus died to save sinners. Notwithstanding, while Dickens may at times seem to express his concept of salvation in familiar terms, Dickens's concept itself is marked, as I have suggested above, by finer contours that indicate it is not as conventional as we might like it to be or as it might at first appear. Indeed, as it is considered more extensively, it becomes clear that Dickens's concept of salvation has more facets than appear at first glance. This is not to say that Dickens is undecided or confused, nor is it to say that Dickens's views will in the end resemble those of a twenty-first-century conservative Evangelical. It is only to suggest that Dickens's understanding of salvation is a bit more subtle than either his detractors or allies in this particular area have typically allowed.

Dickens's view of salvation was shaped by several factors. First, of course, was the fundamental idea in popular lay Anglicanism that Francis Knight referred to as "a composite but undefined view of salvation by works and by faith." (See chapter 1.) As far as that description goes, Dickens seems to have been quite comfortable with such an idea, but his precise understanding of salvation was slightly more nuanced, as we will see. Second, the nature of atonement was a topic of some scholarly debate in Dickens's day, and that debate resonated, at least to some degree, with Dickens. Combined with other factors and concerns, Dickens's understanding of atonement naturally shaped his view of salvation in unique ways. A third factor was his understanding of sin and human sinfulness, or more accurately, human depravity. Dickens always wanted to think the best of human beings, but, as we will see, his experience demonstrated that human beings were not always good or what they should be and that human sin and evil were profound human problems. A fourth factor, and one that colored all three of those just mentioned, was the pervasive influence in popular thought of a rather harsh Calvinistic soteriology. In Dickens's mind, at least, this Calvinism was a negative influence that misrepresented God and beat people up with their own sinfulness. In reality, it seems to have been a distorted view of Calvinism that was the brunt of Dickens's sharp criticisms, but for good or bad, it was Calvinism as Dickens understood it, and that perception of Calvinism was one more factor in shaping his idea of salvation. These four factors, then, provide a formative dynamic that helped to shape Dickens's idea of salvation and to nuance that idea into a less conventional form.

Sin and Forgiveness

Any discussion of salvation must naturally include a discussion of human sin and God's forgiveness. It has been common to suggest that Dickens had no real concept of personal sin and evil, at least in any religious or theological sense. In a paper prepared for a BBC radio broadcast talk, Humphry House speaks briefly on the topic of sin and evil in Dickens. Citing the familiar Lord Acton quote from a review of *Great Expectations*, that Dickens "knows nothing of sin when it is not crime," House comments: "Within the narrow limits of theological pigeon-holes this is true; the word 'sin' hardly occurs in the novels; wickedness is not regarded as an offence against a personal God. But if the judgment is that Dickens knows nothing of evil unless it is recognized and punishable by law, it is quite false."[6] House also adds, "It is clear from the evidence of the novels alone that Dickens's acquaintance with evil was not just acquired *ab extra* [Latin, "from without"] . . . ; it was acquired also by introspection."[7] So, House argues, Dickens knew evil and sin from his own inherent experience of it—that Dickens, like all of us, knew the evil in his own heart and of which he was capable. House is not ready to allow, however, that Dickens wrote about human sin and evil from a Christian orientation, or that his thinking about sin and evil was the result of a Christian worldview.

While it must be granted that House's view is one of very early Dickens criticism, it is certainly a view that influenced the direction of Dickens scholarship and has been carried over and built upon so that it figures into current thought on Dickens, especially in popular discourse. The fact is, the Christian ideas of sin, repentance, and forgiveness are, contrary to House's assessment, quite basic to Dickens. In a letter that he wrote to his wife, Catherine, 14 April 1851, Dickens includes his own "A Prayer at Night."[8] Early in what is actually a rather long prayer reflecting the language of the Bible and the Book of Common Prayer, Dickens prays, "Sanctify and improve to us any good thought that has been presented to us in any form during this day; forgive us the sins we have committed during its progress and in our past lives; all the wrong we have done; and all the negligences and ignorances of which we have been guilty."[9] This prayer, which Dickens wrote for and offered to his family, is one that expressly acknowledges human sin and failure and the need of God's forgiveness and is characteristic of Dickens's worldview and his work.

To find the elements of sin, repentance, and forgiveness in Dickens's fiction, then, should come as no surprise. In *Dombey and Son*, for instance, when Harriet Carker reads to Alice Marwood from "the blessed history," or the Gospels, Dickens's use of words such as "fallen," "shame," and "error" in that context speaks to more than just crime or social deviance.[10] Dickens's narrative of the meeting between David, Mr. Peggotty, and Martha is colored throughout with the ideas of divine judgment and repentance,[11] and the charged exchanges between Mary Rudge and Barnaby, her estranged husband, center on sin, prayer, repentance, and forgiveness.[12] Each of these episodes consists of the unmistakable content and language of sin, repentance, and forgiveness, in a conspicuous Christian sense.

References to sin, repentance, and forgiveness are frequent in *TLOL* as well. For example, Dickens relates the parable of the laborers in the vineyard and then explains the parable's meaning, "People who have been wicked . . . and who are truly sorry for it, however late in their lives, and pray God to forgive them, will be forgiven and will go to Heaven too."[13] Likewise, Dickens relates the parable of the prodigal son and then explains, "Those who have done wrong and forgotten God, are always welcome to Him and will always receive his mercy, if they will only return to Him in sorrow for the sin of which they have been guilty."[14] In both of these examples, the ideas of returning to God, repentance, and God's mercy and grace in forgiveness are clearly present.

A more subtle, but especially poignant, example of sin and forgiveness is found in chapter 51 of *David Copperfield*. There, in a scene in which Mr. Peggotty's long and relentless search for Em'ly finally comes to an end, Dickens employs the biblical imagery of repentance and forgiveness as Em'ly falls before the feet of Mr. Peggotty "humbled, as it might be in the dust our Saviour wrote in with his blessed hand."[15] Clearly, Dickens wants the reader to see and consider the allusion here to John 8:1–11,[16] in which the woman caught in the act of adultery is brought before Jesus. Dickens seems to deliberately set the scene of Em'ly before her uncle—the only father she ever knew—in the context of sin, repentance, and forgiveness. It is Mr. Peggotty who offers grace, mercy, and forgiveness to a sinful, yet humbled and repentant Em'ly.

Both in his fiction and in *TLOL*, Dickens clearly recognizes sin and the need for God's forgiveness in a theological and Christian sense. And these were ideas that were constituent of Dickens's understanding of salvation. Moreover, what he has to say on sin and forgiveness is simple, straightforward, and familiar. That is, it is not difficult to determine what he means by these terms. So, once more, such views as Dickens held regarding sin and forgiveness were not remarkable in themselves and were part and parcel of an orthodox view of salvation.

For Dickens, the intended end of salvation was, of course, arriving in heaven after death. Sin was an obstacle in the way of that final destination and had to be removed. Approaching God in genuine humility and sincere repentance, and thereby receiving God's forgiveness, was the means by which that obstacle was removed. But, it may be argued, Dickens also indicated that getting to heaven was conditioned by the performance of good works as well. His closing words in *TLOL* seem to suggest as much: "Remember!—It is Christianity to do good, always—even to those who do evil to us. It is Christianity to love our neighbours as ourself, and to do to all men as we would have them do to us. It is Christianity to be gentle, merciful, and forgiving. . . . If we do this, and remember the life and lessons of Our Lord Jesus Christ, and try to act up to them, we may confidently hope that God will forgive us our sins and mistakes, and enable us to live and die in peace."[17] These words exemplify Knight's "composite but undefined view of salvation by works and by faith" in popular lay Anglicanism. And while that represents a fair understanding of Dickens's view of salvation as far as it goes, it does not go far enough, for Dickens's understanding of salvation is further nuanced by his reflections and musing on the nature of atonement and its related debate.

Dickens and Atonement

Not unlike our own day, in the early to mid-nineteenth century, the nature of atonement was a point of contention and debate. The idea of atonement, of course, is that the death and resurrection of Jesus dealt with the problem of human sin and provided the means by which a relationship with God might be established. The exact nature of just how those results were brought about provided the grounds for controversy and debate. What made atonement such an integral factor in shaping Dickens's view of salvation was that a concept of atonement necessarily involves the basic preliminary concerns of the need for atonement—namely, the issue of human sinfulness, or more precisely, the issues of human depravity and original sin. Dickens had serious questions concerning both of these issues. Further, whatever one's view, two fundamental questions lay at the heart of formulating a doctrine of atonement: (1) Was Jesus a propitiatory sacrifice for sins assuaging the wrath of God or not? (2) Did Jesus die on the cross in place of men and women as a substitute?[18]

In one sense, the various parties of the church were fundamentally agreed on the nature of atonement. Evangelicals, along with many Dissenters and Nonconformists, subscribed, often quite passionately, to vicarious or substitutionary atonement, stressing Christ's death as a propitiation for sins. Orthodox high churchmen also typically held to the doctrine of vicarious atonement, although they deliberately sought to distance themselves from the dogmatic Evangelical expression of the doctrine that sometimes was so emphasized that it appeared to be the only doctrine of Evangelical faith. Even Broad Churchmen, in general, seemed to hold to a doctrine of vicarious atonement. W. J. Conybeare, in his classic article on church parties (1853), comments, "The doctrines taught by this party [i.e., the Broad Church] are the same in which both High and Low Church are agreed. The Incarnation and the Atonement, conversion by Grace, and Justification by Faith, are fundamental articles of their creed."[19] According to Conybeare, then, atonement was one of the doctrines upon which there seemed to be agreement, or at least a sort of consensus, across the parties of the church.

Notwithstanding, it was not difficult to find dissenting voices against this consensus view. Nineteenth-century Unitarians, for example, were especially hostile to the notion of vicarious atonement in that such a theory denigrated the character of God and undermined his free and independent forgiveness of sin.[20] Benjamin Jowett, a Broad Churchman (discussed in chapter 3), was also one of the dissenting voices—one that commanded attention. Jowett was adamantly opposed to the idea of vicarious atonement and Christ's death as a propitiatory sacrifice. He understood such a doctrine as primitive and barbaric, an artifact of the old dispensation. And, of course, Jowett and those who agreed with him spoke from within the established church, while the Unitarian did not.

Dickens was one with whom a dissenting opinion resonated, but for different reasons than it did for the Unitarians or for those who held Jowett's views or ones similar to his. Dickens's problem with vicarious atonement was, in one sense, rather involved. For him, vicarious atonement was identified with and characterized by an extreme and distorted form of Calvinism—a Calvinism that was more than ready to relentlessly assault people with reminders of their sinfulness; that seemed to take a delight in pronouncing the judgment of God's wrath on others; that emphasized God as Law-giver and Judge almost to the exclusion of God's Fatherhood; and that taught an exclusivist form of election. Central to this form of Calvinism was its emphasis, too, on vicarious atonement and the necessity of Jesus's suffering to appease the wrath of a vengeful God. Dickens unequivocally rejected this Calvinism and with it any of the doctrines it espoused, vicarious atonement included.

What especially unsettled Dickens in this form of Calvinism was its portrayal of God the Father as vengeful Judge. For Dickens, this was a misrepresentation, and one that accounts for his passionate opposition to this extreme Calvinism and its version of vicarious atonement. Dickens's starting point for any of his Christian thought was the Fatherhood of God. That is, he started with the idea of God as a loving Father, a beneficent Father who seeks always and only for the good and well-being of his children. In Dickens's mind, to hold a view of God as Lawgiver and Judge was to establish a flawed point of reference that could only result in a distorted and problematic understanding of Christianity and the life of faith, not to mention faulty notions of atonement.

Dickens was not the only one who had serious misgivings about the results of this pervasive Calvinistic Evangelicalism on his generation's understanding of the Fatherhood of God and thus atonement. Two Scottish pastors, Thomas Erskine of Linlathen and John McLeod Campbell, working independently of one another, were rethinking and reimagining the nature of atonement in light of the perceived inimical effects of a distorted Calvinism. It is not possible here to delineate fully the nonpenal, nonvicarious nature of these reimaginings of atonement, but some observations can be made.[21]

First, both were seeking to address the anxiety of many nineteenth-century believers caused by the uncertainty of their eternal destiny. Both Erskine and Campbell emphasized that God's pardon had been secured in Christ's work on the cross before human beings ever thought about the need for it and that it was already operative for those who would simply believe. All that was necessary to receive pardon for sin was for the person to believe that their pardon had already been secured.[22] The assurance of forgiveness, then, was founded in the character of God—not the activity of the person. At the heart of their recasting of the atonement was a bold—and ultimately costly—challenge to the idea of the limited atonement demanded by Calvinism and included among its five major tenets. (Campbell, in fact, would eventually be brought up on charges of heresy and stripped of his ministerial license for preaching against limited atonement.) Second, both rejected the idea of penal suffering by Jesus. Here, Campbell's view was similar to Erskine's, but he developed the idea more distinctly. For Campbell, Jesus was not appeasing the wrath of God or enduring penal suffering. Instead, Jesus offered vicarious repentance and vicarious sorrow for sin on behalf of humanity as its representative head. Third, and perhaps most important, was Campbell's conviction that a proper understanding of atonement must be formulated squarely upon the foundation of God as loving and merciful Father—as opposed to Lawgiver and Judge—who desires fellowship and relationship with humanity more than humanity desires fellowship and relationship with God, and that this filial or relational purpose was accomplished in the Christ event. Indeed, this was the very purpose of the Christ event.

The point of this very brief outline is not to suggest that Dickens was engaged with or even necessarily familiar with the work of either Erskine or Campbell. Rather, the point is that there were alternative views to the vicarious atonement model circulating in Dickens's day and which came from those who embraced the triunity of God. These views were not Unitarian, nor were they academic—both Erskine and Campbell were pastors and both spoke not for the academy but in and for the church. Surely, with such an emphasis on the Fatherhood of God and such a comfortable distance from the vicarious atonement of a distorted Calvinism, Dickens could have found within such ideas as represented by Erskine and Campbell a view of the atonement that made sense to him and that was fitted to his Christian worldview.

Dickens and Human Sinfulness

One more factor that comes in to play in Dickens's idea of salvation is the idea of human sinfulness, particularly as it is understood in terms of the companion notions of original sin and human depravity. Original sin refers to the sin of Adam imputed to his posterity from generation to generation such that all human beings are polluted by sin and are fallen creatures by virtue of being human. Total depravity, most often associated with Calvinism, maintains that sin has reached to and corrupted every aspect of the human being—the physical, the emotional, the volitional, the intellectual, the spiritual. Together, these companion doctrines—original sin and human depravity—characterize human beings as enemies of God, hostile to and alienated from God. Dickens rejected both doctrines—or so it is alleged.

In his clever essay, "Two Views of a Cheap Theatre," Dickens takes exception to a description of human beings as "sinners" by a preacher and poses the questions:

> Is it necessary or advisable to address such an audience continually as "fellow-sinners"? Is it not enough to be fellow-creatures, born yesterday, suffering and striving to-day, dying to-morrow? By our common humanity, my brothers and sisters, by our common capacities for pain and pleasure, by our common laughter and our common tears, by our common aspiration to reach something better than ourselves, by our common tendency to believe in something good, and to invest whatever we love or whatever we lose with some qualities that are superior to our own failings and weaknesses as we know them in our own poor hearts—by these, Hear me!—Surely, it is enough to be fellow-creatures. Surely, it includes the other designation, and some touching meanings over and above.[23]

Clearly, this is exemplary of what is typically accepted as Dickens's almost Romantic notions of humanity: the inherent goodness of humanity, our common personhood, our aspirations to seek "something better," the tendency toward the good, and the exception taken to a designation such as "fellow-sinners."

With healthy doses of sometimes scathing sarcasm and irony, Dickens would apparently seek out any opportunity to challenge the notions of human depravity and original sin. He does so in *Bleak House* with his caricature of the self-proclaimed Reverend Chadband. In context, Dickens's sarcasm is thick as Chadband preaches to Jo:

> O running stream of sparkling joy
> To be a soaring human boy!

> And do you cool yourself in that stream now, my young friend? No. Why do you not cool yourself in that stream now? Because you are in a state of darkness, because you are in a state of obscurity, because you are in a state of sinfulness, because you are in a state of bondage.[24]

Dickens was especially repulsed by the imposition of these doctrines upon children. In Jo's case, Dickens maintains that he was not "in a state of darkness . . . of sinfulness"; instead, Dickens says that he lacked proper upbringing and opportunity. Later, in this same novel, Dickens tells Chadband to sit down, shut up, and get out of the way in order that Jo might at least have some opportunity to see Jesus in the Gospels apart from the assault of the cheap opinion of bloated, self-absorbed preachers.

Again, Dickens articulates in sardonic tones his perceptions of the doctrines of total depravity and original sin in *Little Dorrit* as Mrs. Clennam described her upbringing in "wholesome repression, punishment and fear. The corruption of our hearts the evil of our ways, the curse that is upon us, the terrors that surround us—these were the themes of my childhood."[25] Dickens employs Mrs. Clennam's son, Arthur, to a more humorous, if even greater, effect when Arthur recalls from his youth "a horrible tract" in Sunday school, "which commenced the business with the poor child by asking him in its title, why he was going to Perdition?"[26]

Finally, Dickens's letter to Mrs. Godfrey, 25 July 1839, communicates with as much intensity as his fiction his distaste for the doctrines of original sin and total depravity. He writes,

I do most decidedly object, and have almost invincible and powerful repugnance to that frequent reference to the Almighty in small matters, which so many excellent persons consider necessary in the education of children. . . . I object decidedly to endeavouring to impress them with a fear of death, before they can be rationally supposed to become accountable creatures, and so great a horror do I feel at the thought of imbuing with strict doctrines those who have just reflection enough to know that if God be as rigid and just as they are told he is, their fathers and mothers and three fourths of their relations and friends must be doomed to Eternal Perdition, and if I were left to choose between the two evils, I would far rather that my children acquired their first principle of religion from a contemplation of nature and all the goodness and beneficence of the Great Being Who created it, than I would suffer them with such a strict construction ever to open a Bible or a Prayer Book, or enter a place of Worship.[27]

In light of the above examples, there does seem to be justification for asserting that Dickens categorically rejected the doctrines of original sin and total depravity. The caricatures, the irony, and the bold categorical denouncements by Dickens have more often than not been taken in just this way. Nevertheless, we need not take Dickens's reasonably positive outlook on life and his passionate belief that we can be better as indicating his theological anthropology. It is one thing to say that Dickens was incensed by the smug and self-righteous spiritual indictments of presumptuous religionists stemming from the doctrines of total depravity and original sin. He was. It is quite another thing entirely, however, to suggest that Dickens embraced a Romantic view of human nature and a Pelagian view of Christianity. Dickens was not so naïve. Indeed, Dickens understood well the human inclination toward sin and evil and, contrary to popular thought, had no grand illusions of the inherent goodness of humanity.

One of Dickens's clearest narrative observations of human nature comes in *Little Dorrit* as a group of patrons at the Break of Day Inn are deliberating over the villain Rigaud. In the course of their discussion, the landlady of the Break of Day comments,

And I tell you this, my friend, that there are people (men and women both, unfortunately) who have no good in them—none. That there are people whom it is necessary to detest without compromise. That there are people who must be dealt with as enemies of the human race. That there are people who have no human heart, and who must be crushed like savage beasts and cleared out of the way. They are but few, I hope; but I have seen (in this world here where I find myself, and even at the little Break of Day) that there are such people. And I do not doubt that this man—whatever they call him, I forget his name—is one of them.[28]

These words, significantly, comprise the landlady's response to "the tall Swiss who belonged to the church" and had ventured to observe about Rigaud: "It may have been his unfortunate destiny. He may have been the child of circumstances. It is always possible that he had, and has, good in himself if one did but know how to find it. Philosophical philanthropy teaches—."[29] The landlady, abruptly cutting the Swiss off, is not interested, in this case, with philosophizing or theologizing. For her, facts are facts—some people are just no good.

In his *Dickens and Crime*, Philip Collins maintains that what the landlady presumes is, in fact, the view of Dickens himself.[30] Basing his conclusion on Dickens's journalism and selected correspondence, Collins remarks, "For all his gaiety and high spirits, Dickens was not at bottom very optimistic about human nature."[31] Because Collins recognized that such a comment flies in the face of what is typically believed about Dickens, he adds, "His reputation has often blinded his readers to the implications of what he actually wrote."[32] What Dickens actually did write is instructive and seems to provide an interesting counterpoint to the allegations that Dickens is soft on human sinfulness.

Consider the following passage from *Barnaby Rudge* in which Dickens speaks to the human condition:

In the exhaustless catalogue of Heaven's mercies to mankind, the power we have of finding some germs of comfort in the hardest trials must ever occupy the foremost place; not only because it supports and uphold us when we most require to be sustained, but because in this source of consolation there is something, we have reason to believe, of the divine spirit; something of that goodness which detects amidst *our own evil doings* [my italics], a redeeming quality; something which even in *our fallen nature* [my italics], we possess in common with the angels; which had its being in the old time when they trod the earth and lingers on it, yet, in pity.[33]

A similar idea is expressed in *The Old Curiosity Shop*:

Why were the eyes of little Nell wet, that night, with tears like those of the two sisters? Why did she bear a grateful heart because they had met, and feel it pain to think that they would shortly part? Let us not believe that any selfish reference—unconscious though it might have been—to her own trials awoke this sympathy, but thank God that the innocent joys of others can strongly move us, and that we, even in *our fallen nature* [my italics], have one source of pure emotion which must be prized in Heaven![34]

Passages like these seem to provide at least some insight into Dickens's opinion of the human condition and must be brought to bear on the conclusions that are drawn concerning his views on human depravity and original sin. It would seem that he had in some way come to terms with the doctrine of human depravity or had reimagined it to his own satisfaction. That he was put off by the almost flippant applications of the doctrine by certain self-righteous Nonconformists and dissenting Evangelicals must be held in tension with his observations that we are "fellow-sinners" with a "fallen nature" and that there are some people who are "enemies of mankind."[35] That Dickens would, on the one hand, highlight human goodness in his characters—Oliver Twist wants to do right, Nell is innocent and good, Florence Dombey is humble and the giver of selfless love, Amy Dorrit is the steadying servant of all—surely recalls his words in his letter to Macrae of his intent "to exhibit in all my good people some reflections of the teachings of our great Master." That he would, on the other hand, recognize human depravity and corruption in others—Jonas Chuzzlewit is Cain, Daniel Quilp is the devil, Barnaby Rudge is the essence of evil, James Carker is diabolically self-serving, Bill Sikes is a murderer and irredeemably bad strongly suggests that Dickens actually held to some degree a concept of human depravity and corruption, as compartmentalized as it may have been.

What adds a unique twist to all of this is that Dickens attributed such sin or evil as might be found in children to the failure of society or the negligence of parents or guardians. But in the case of sin and evil in adults, Dickens's view became a bit more nuanced. In the introduction to the 1841 edition of *Oliver Twist*, Dickens offers the following comments on Bill Sikes: "I fear there are in the world some insensible and callous natures that do become, at last, utterly and irredeemably bad. But whether this be so or not, of one thing I am certain: that there are such men as Sikes, who being closely followed through the same space of time, and through the same current circumstances, would not give, by one look or action of a moment, the faintest indication of a better nature."[36] Such men as Sikes have "become" bad. In fact, because of an "insensible and callous nature," they have become "utterly and irredeemably bad." Others, like Rigaud, "have no good in them—none." Either way, Dickens seems to have little sympathy for them.

Then, there are others, like Nancy in *Oliver Twist*, in whom Dickens seems to recognize certain "redeeming traits" and who seem to exemplify the tension in human nature that Dickens obviously felt: the tension between a recognition of the reality of human sin and evil on the one hand and his hope that there might be some goodness even in the most "depraved and miserable" individuals, on the other. Dickens is willing to allow this to be "a contradiction, an anomaly, an apparent impossibility; but it is a truth," he insists. In fact, "It is emphatically God's truth, for it is the truth He leaves in such depraved and miserable breasts; the hope yet lingering behind; the last fair drop of water at the bottom of the dried-up, weed-choked well."[37]

In all of this, what seems to emerge in Dickens's thought is what I will call a doctrine or notion of "particular corruption." This is the idea that certain individuals exhibit human sinfulness practically to the point of total depravity, or worse, total evil. While this notion is rather clumsy and contrived, even compartmentalized, it seems to have worked for Dickens. Specifically, it allowed Dickens to hold in tension what he would have liked to believe about the human condition together with what his experience and observations of the human condition yielded. That he held this view consciously or deliberately is not likely. Collins's observation in *Dickens and Crime* above is apropos here: "His reputation has often blinded his readers to the implications of what he actually wrote." It is quite possible that Dickens himself was not always aware of the collective implications of what he wrote, particularly as it related to human nature, sin, and salvation—and not because of his own reputation, of course, but because he struggled with these tensions that would give rise to the idea of particular corruption.

In any case, such an idea was, for Dickens, a formative element in a sort of loose pattern or idea of atonement shaped by the several factors considered here. And while it might be wise to think of Dickens as an atonement minimalist, it is not likely that his views would place him outside the Christian tradition. True, Dickens would not have embraced the doctrine of total depravity as it was understood in the most stringent form of the Calvinism of his day, but he did recognize human sinfulness, our fallen nature, and the need for the grace of God in forgiveness. His concept of Jesus, too, as Saviour-Redeemer points to a traditional Christian understanding of salvation and certainly must be brought to bear on his pattern or idea of atonement. And, surely, Dickens's words about the cross contribute to a clearly Christian sense of salvation and a pattern of atonement.

Dickens and the Cross

In his article "The Murdered Person," in *Household Words*, 11 October 1856, Dickens writes of a particular judicial case that had arrested his attention and seems to have raised his ire considerably. William Dove was convicted of murdering his wife by strychnine poisoning and was executed on 10 August 1856. What seems to have been especially disconcerting to Dickens was Dove's statement that God "had adopted this plan to save me." Dickens, indignant at such callous presumption, writes that Dove had taken "the special express-train to Paradise called the gallows," and adds later in the article, "Thus, the New Drop [gallows] usurps the place of the Cross."[38] The article is a scathing attack on the idea of "pattern penitents"[39] and in part, speaks to the manner in which God brings about redemption. And it is clear that Dickens is connecting the cross to redemption and salvation.

Consider, too, the words of Mr. Redlaw in *The Haunted Man*, Dickens's last Christmas Book (1848). This story is one of remembrance, grace, and forgiveness, and in the end when Redlaw has been reclaimed, he prays: "O Thou, . . . who through the teaching of pure love, has graciously restored me to the memory which was the memory of Christ upon the cross, and of all the good who perished in His cause, receive my thanks."[40] In the context of *The Haunted Man*, the restored memory of Redlaw and the memory of Christ are both integrally connected to forgiveness and "Christ upon the cross." Likewise, in Dickens's "A Christmas Tree," in *Household Words*, 21 December 1850, pardon for sin is directly connected to the cross. Dickens describes Jesus, "A Solemn figure . . . dying upon a Cross, watched by armed soldiers, a thick darkness coming on, the earth beginning to shake, and only one voice heard, 'Forgive them, for they know not what they do.'"[41]

Perhaps some of Dickens's most significant observations concerning the cross were made as a result of his fondness for the idea of resurrection. Dickens seems to have possessed an obvious affection for Jesus's words in the story of the raising of Lazarus in John 11:1–57, particularly 11:25: "I am the resurrection, and the life: he that believeth in me, though he were dead, yet shall he live" (KJV). Dickens's abbreviated use of the verse in *TLOL* is fascinating and important. There, he seems to use it with the same eschatological significance that it possesses in Johannine theology, an interpretation also found in some nineteenth-century commentators. For instance, R. C. Trench comments that Jesus's words in John 11:25 involve the idea, "In me is victory over the grave, in me is life eternal: by faith in me that becomes yours which makes death not to be death, but only the transition to an higher life."[42]

In *TLOL*, it appears that Dickens hoped his account of the episode would point to Jesus as the Resurrection and the Life in the fullest sense of that phrase. The raising of Lazarus was not just the resuscitation of a corpse—although it certainly was that; it was also a foreshadowing of the eschatological resurrection. Dickens was careful to relate the conversation between Jesus and Martha faithfully along the lines of John's Gospel, juxtaposing Martha's stated belief that her brother will rise again "in the resurrection at the Last Day" with Jesus's claim to be "the resurrection, and the life." In John, Martha's response to Jesus's query as to whether or not she believes his claim is that she believes that he is "the Christ, the Son of God, which should come into the world." In *TLOL*, her response is a simple, "Yes, Lord," that is, that Jesus is, in fact, the Resurrection and the Life. Commenting on this exchange between Jesus and Martha, Olshausen writes, "He [Jesus] leads her thoughts from the *departed* brother to the *present* Saviour, the Saviour both for Lazarus and for herself, and shews her, that in him alone she may obtain the perfect remedy against death corporeal and spiritual."[43] Likewise, for Dickens, Jesus's words possess the broader eschatological significance.

This particular take on Dickens's understanding of these words from John 11:25 seems to be confirmed in *A Tale of Two Cities*, in which these words seem to become the credo of Sydney Carton. They are words that he chooses finally to live by and then to die by. In "The Game Made" (Book 3 chapter 9), a compelling argument can be made that Sydney Carton experiences a genuine conversion, which is abetted and sustained by the words from John 11:25, "I am the resurrection, and the life." It is not within the scope of this work to pursue that argument, but that the words are understood and used by Dickens in a salvific sense seems clear. "The prayer that had broken up out of his heart for a merciful consideration of all his poor blindnesses and errors," Dickens writes, "ended in the words, 'I am the resurrection and the life.'"[44] These words invigorate Carton and enliven him as his boldness and resolve stiffen throughout the chapter and, in the end, make it possible for his young companion in death to say that because of Carton, "I have been able to raise my thoughts to Him who was put to death, that we might have hope and comfort here today"[45]

In light of such material in the larger Dickens corpus, it seems reasonable to conclude that Dickens recognized a redemptive significance in Jesus's work on the cross. Moreover, ideas of salvation and redemption are central to *TLOL*. As has already been noted, salvation, both in *TLOL* and in Dickens's larger Christian thought, consists primarily in securing a place in heaven after death. To do so, the individual must be saved or redeemed. Put simply, sins must be forgiven. For Dickens, sin is a moral and religious phenomenon and must be dealt with as such. Obviously, Dickens saw sin as an offense against God. Note in Dickens's characters, then, how Florence pleads with Edith, "Oh, pray to Heaven, pray to Heaven, Mama, to forgive you all this sin and shame";[46] or how Nancy is entreated by

Rose that she "might be yet reclaimed," for "it is never too late for penitence and atonement."[47] Dickens regularly maintains a connection between sin, repentance, and forgiveness, and while his language is rarely liturgical or even "religious," it is nevertheless the language of the human heart going out to God seeking forgiveness of sins.

When all has been heard, then, it appears, once more, that Dickens's Christian thought, particularly his understanding of salvation, falls in line quite comfortably with the popular lay Anglicanism of his day. The person who seeks forgiveness in humble repentance can be confident that God is ready to extend merciful forgiveness. In theory, and according to *TLOL*, even those who are "utterly and irredeemably bad" are welcome to come to God in humble repentance to receive ready forgiveness. In practice, however, Dickens did not expect that such a thing would happen. An extended quotation from his "Pet Prisoners," in *Household Words*, 27 April 1850, is an example of this very conviction:

A strange absorbing, selfishness—a spiritual egotism and vanity, real or assumed—is the first result. It is most remarkable to observe, in the cases of murderers who become this kind of object of interest, when they are at last consigned to the condemned cell, how the rule is (of course there are exceptions) that the murdered person disappears from the stage of their thoughts, except as a part of their own important story; and how they occupy the whole scene. *I* did this, *I* feel that, *I* confide in the mercy of Heaven being extended to *me*; this is the autograph of *me*, the unfortunate and unhappy; in my childhood I was so and so; in my youth I did such a thing, to which I attribute my downfall—not this thing of basely and barbarously defacing the image of my Creator, and sending an immortal soul into eternity without a moment's warning, but something else of a venial kind that many unpunished people do. I don't want the forgiveness of this foully murdered person's bereaved wife, husband, brother, sister, child, friend; I don't ask for it, I don't care for it. I make no enquiry of the clergyman concerning the salvation of that murdered person's soul; mine is the matter; and I am almost happy that I came here, as to the gate of Paradise. "I never liked him," said the repentant Mr. Manning, false of heart to the last, calling a crowbar by a milder name to lessen the cowardly horror of it, "and I beat in his skull with the ripping chisel." I am going to bliss, exclaims the same authority, in effect. Where my victim went to is not my business at all.[48]

That Dickens is unwilling to deny to anyone the opportunity for repentance and pardon is clear from his concluding remarks on this subject, but so, too, is his suggestion that such repentance would unlikely be forthcoming from such an individual: "Now, God forbid that we, unworthily believing in the Redeemer, should shut out hope, or even human trustfulness, from any criminal at the dread pass; but it is not in us to call this state of mind repentance."[49]

Dickens's comments about the incident above and about the William Dove murder case, his remarks in his 1841 Introduction to *Oliver Twist,* and the observations of the landlady at the Break of Day Inn in *Little Dorrit* strongly indicate that, for him, human sin and evil are real but are anomalous in the world as God intended it to be. Yet, God has acted in the world to provide hope, the hope in "Our Saviour" and the redemptive work on the cross. It was just this lively hope to which Dickens was drawn and which bolstered his positive view of humanity even in a broken and sinful world. In the end, for Dickens, it was this very hope that could alone make human beings what they were intended to be and thereby make our world what it was intended to be.

Hearing Dickens and Listening to Him

While Dickens's understanding of salvation, human sin, and atonement seems to be subtly nuanced, complex, and idiosyncratic, I want to suggest that in its uniqueness there is a sense of logical consistency. That is, contrary to what is typically maintained about Dickens's thought on these topics, his understanding of human sin, salvation, and atonement are consistently developed throughout his work. His idea of particular corruption, his pattern of atonement, and his anthropology may be idiosyncratic, but they are idiosyncratically consistent. And in the end, even with the apparent idiosyncrasies, his views are easily accommodated within the popular lay Anglicanism of his day.

In one sense, we do Dickens a disservice by trying to systematize his theological thought in this particular area. He did not provide us with a theological primer on soteriology, nor is he here to comment upon, challenge, or reject the theological vocabulary that I have imposed upon him. Moreover, as I discussed in the previous chapter, Dickens was not given to theological speculation, particularly of the sort I have introduced here. It would be difficult to imagine Dickens going where we have gone here or even wanting to. Notwithstanding, my purpose is to give Dickens's Christian voice a hearing, and in this case, that has involved some theologizing.

Obviously, Jesus was central to Dickens's understanding of Christianity, but we have seen, too, that Dickens held clear notions of God as the beneficent and sovereign Creator and Sustainer of the universe. And if there is one thing that characterized Dickens's understanding of God, it was God's Fatherhood. For Dickens, God was first and foremost Father. Any other attribute of God was secondary and derivative, so to speak, of that Fatherhood. It is precisely this concept of the radical Fatherhood of God that Dickens offers as a lesson to the church.

As I have noted, Dickens took extreme exception to the concept of God as Lawgiver and Judge, especially as it was conceived in the Calvinism of his day. Significantly, however, it does not appear that Dickens's concept of God as Father was simply a reaction against Calvinism; rather, radical Fatherhood was a concept of God that Dickens already held and was, thus, just one more reinforcement for his rejection of Calvinistic ideas of theology and the Christian life.

It goes without saying, certainly, that there is a marked contrast between Dickens's concept of God as Father and the concept of God derived from a staunch Calvinistic view of God as Lawgiver and Judge. Nevertheless, the recognition of this contrast is essential to understanding Dickens's passionate denunciations of such a view. When he denounces such views—and he rarely misses the opportunity—he is not simply targeting an understanding of God or a particular theological system to which he takes exception. Rather, he is taking aim at an approach and a theological premise that shapes a conception of the character of God that, for him, is both erroneous and destructive.

Dickens began with God as Father not arbitrarily, but because of the message of Scripture and because in his own experience, the message of Scripture rang true. It is not surprising, then, to find this theme of the radical Fatherhood of God articulated in his work.

Some of Dickens's most poignant observations about the Fatherhood of God have to do with God as the Father of the fatherless and the orphan. Throughout *Oliver Twist*, for instance, Dickens hints at this notion of the Fatherhood of God in God's providential care for Oliver. Dickens gives voice to this notion as his narrator recollects "how the two orphans, tried by adversity, remembered its lessons in mercy to others, and mutual love, and fervent thanks to Him who had protected and preserved them—these are all matters which need not be told. I have said that they were truly happy; and without strong affection and humanity of heart, and gratitude to that Being whose code is Mercy, and whose great attribute is Benevolence to all things that breathe, happiness can never be attained."[50]

In *Little Dorrit*, Dickens is brief in his observations, but more direct. Tattycoram, the attendant to Pet Meagles, had been an orphan in the Foundling Hospital in London.[51] When Mrs. Meagles recounts taking in Tattycoram, she remembers having seen "all those dear children ranged tier above tier, and appealing from the father none of them has ever known on earth, to the great Father of us all in Heaven."[52] That Dickens was involved in the work of the hospital and a patron suggests that these words of Mrs. Meagles reflect his own thoughts. And while this is one of Dickens's more simple instances of drawing attention to the Fatherhood of God, it is representative of the notion that recurs throughout his work.

It is perhaps in *Dombey and Son*, in which Florence is adopted by the Father of the fatherless, that Dickens develops this idea most fully. In the novel, Dickens makes the point on more than one occasion that God steps into the breach, becoming for Florence the father that Mr. Dombey, her earthly father, refuses to be. Quite early in the novel, Mrs. Chick observes, almost prophetically, "Florence will never, never, never be a Dombey, not if she lives to be a thousand years old."[53] As the story unfolds, we watch as Florence desperately tries, without success, to win the love of Mr. Dombey and her place as his daughter, but Dombey has closed his hardened and hardening heart to her. Climactically, at the point in the narrative where Dombey strikes Florence, "She saw that she had no father on earth."[54] The observation by Dickens that follows is hardly necessary thematically, for the implication is clear in the turn of the phrase. Nevertheless, when Florence has finally resigned herself to the fact that she is "homeless and fatherless," Dickens observes, "She only knew that she had no Father upon earth, and she said so, many times, with her suppliant head hidden from all, but her Father who was in Heaven."[55]

What is significant in Dickens's shaping of this theme and its related ideas is that he develops it in such a way that he places as much emphasis on the Godward perspective as he does on the earthbound. In other words, Dickens deliberately highlights God's active engagement in pouring out compassion and lovingkindness in being Father to Florence, even when Florence may not recognize it. And it is precisely in this way that Dickens could refer to God in *Dombey and Son* as "that higher Father who does not reject his children's love, or spurn their tried and broken hearts."[56]

For Dickens, shaping a proper concept of the character and being of God was determined by one's fundamental starting point. If, on the one hand, that starting point is God as Lawgiver and Judge, then what follows is a God whose character and being is exemplified by wrath against sin and sinners. If, on the other hand, the starting point is God as Father, what follows is a God whose character and being is exemplified in goodness, grace, and love for his creatures and creation. In theological terms, the contrast is between a forensic theological starting point that sees God as the Lawgiver whose law has been broken and whose penalty must be paid, or a familial theological starting point that sees God as a Father whose desire is to restore and enjoy a relationship with his children.[57]

Intimately connected to Dickens's understanding of God as Father is his understanding of God as the Supreme Beneficence. For Dickens, the concomitant expression of God's Fatherhood is goodness; the simple child's prayer that "God is great and God is good" is a central theological premise. God is indeed Father, and because God is Father, God is good. In Dickens's mind, God does only what is good and always seeks the best for his children. Dickens had plenty to say about God's goodness.

Speaking to the Birmingham and Midland Institute, 27 September 1869, Dickens took exception to the insistence by some of his era that theirs was a material one. In his speech, Dickens expresses his conviction that even the harnessing of electricity for humanity's benefit and the invention of the steam locomotive for the improvement of travel is to be attributed to the gracious activity of God. He attributes such advancements to "the good providence of God" and the hand of the "Supreme Beneficence."[58] The gesture toward God's Providence is clear and he hints at God's creative activity in the way he turns his phrases, but Dickens's point in all of it is that God provides good things for God's creatures. Such advancements are, in Dickens's mind, extraordinary benefits for humankind, and anything that benefited humanity in such a way must be from the hand of God, the gracious and loving Father.

As Dickens recounts in *TLOL* the episode of Jesus as a young boy in the temple, Jesus's parents "found him, sitting in the temple, talking about the goodness of God, and how we should all pray to him, with some learned men who were called Doctors."[59] Dickens's rendering of the account here is noteworthy because the account in Luke's Gospel mentions nothing about the goodness of God as a subject of Jesus's conversation with the religious leaders, and there is nothing in the account to suggest such a reading. This is Dickens's own gloss identifying goodness as one of God's most conspicuous attributes. And for Dickens, God's goodness is an essential aspect of his Fatherhood.

Dickens was always quick to remind those who saw God as Law-giver and Judge and whose idea of justice was wrought in God's wrath and vengeance—the Murdstones, the Clennams, the Barbarys, for instance—that God the Father is good and that goodness dare not be slighted or suppressed. Whether it is "Youth and Beauty work-ing out the ends of your Beneficent Creator,"[60] or "the beneficent design of Heaven" being overthrown by "man's indifference" or "man's presumption,"[61] or Esther's sense of "the goodness and the tenderness of God" in Ada's newborn infant "to bless and restore his mother,"[62] it is clear that, for Dickens, God is not only intrinsically good in being and character but also good in both willing and activity. That is precisely how Dickens could see even in such ordinary things as electricity and train travel "the good providence of God," "the Supreme Beneficence," from whom alone such good things come.

For Dickens, these twin ideas of the Fatherhood of God and the goodness of God can be transforming, for they provide a starting place for the Christian that is at once liberating, hopeful, and encour-aging. When God is understood as a loving and gracious Father, we respond to him quite differently than we would if we understood God as Lawgiver and Judge. For one thing, we see ourselves under God's loving instruction, Fatherly advice, and careful direction rather than under a set of prohibitions, restrictions, and penalties. It might be argued, "Well, that's just a matter of perspective, isn't it?" Exactly. It *is* a matter of perspective—a perspective that makes an enormous difference.

When God is understood as a gracious Father, we are confident that God will be there to pick us up after a fall and that God will be intimately involved in getting us going in the right direction and will be there to guide us along the right way. Make no mistake. God, like a loving Father, is never indifferent to the sin and the fall, nor is God willing that we are. Nevertheless, we can be assured that as Father, God is going to be involved in restoration, healing, and prevention—and not as Judge, but as Father—because that's what fathers do.

When God is understood as Father, we at one time or another will be struck by the incredible idea that it is the Father who initiates a relationship with us because he desires a relationship with us more than we desire a relationship with him. When God is understood as Lawgiver and Judge, if there is a relationship at all, it is normally of an official or formal sort, with little intimacy to speak of, and no familial bond to rest in.

In this light, the simple prayer, "God is great, God is good" is indeed transformative. Perhaps the simple lessons spoke by Dickens's Christian voice are too.

5

Real Christianity

I have made several references to the phrase "real Christianity," a phrase Dickens uses in a letter dated 24 December 1857, to the Rev. R. H. Davies, who had written a letter to Dickens concerning the child's hymn in "The Wreck of the Golden Mary," a Christmas story.[1] Dickens writes in part:

> There cannot be many men, I believe, who have a more humble veneration for the New Testament, or a more profound conviction of its all-sufficiency, than I have. If I am ever (as you tell me I am) mistaken on this subject, it is because I discountenance all obtrusive professions of and tradings in religion, as one of the main causes why real Christianity has been retarded in this world; and because my observation of life induces me to hold in unspeakable dread and horror, those unseemly squabbles about the letter which drive the spirit out of hundreds of thousands.[2]

Precisely what Dickens means by the designation "real Christianity," he does not spell out in his reply to Davies. But his letter to David Macrae, which I have already quoted (see chapter 1), provides a good beginning to understanding just what Dickens meant by the phrase. Some additional background will be beneficial in considering

Macrae's letter and in understanding how it helps to give clarity to Dickens's thoughts on "real Christianity."

Macrae had written an article that speaks of Dickens's novels and the positive impact they had had on Christian morality. But the article also criticizes Dickens's work and, in fact, his representations of Christianity. Putting Dickens's correspondence and comments to him in context, Macrae writes, "I had taken occasion to criticise his treatment of professing Christians—expressing the opinion that, while he had dealt with hypocrites as they deserved, he had not, on the other side, given us, amongst his good people, any specimens of earnest Christianity to show that Christian profession may be marked and yet sincere; and that, so far, his representations of Christianity were gravely defective."[3] Macrae actually expresses here a notion that some before him and many after him have held about Dickens's work: that Dickens's Christianity was anemic and less than substantive; that it was little more than general moralism wrapped up in social action; that there was in actuality nothing very Christian about it. To this criticism by Macrae, Dickens replies, "I have so strong an objection to mere professions of religion, and to the audacious interposition of vain and ignorant men between the sublime simplicity of the New Testament and the general human mind to which our Saviour addressed it, that I urge that objection as strongly and as positively as I can. In my experience, true practical Christianity has been very much obstructed by the conceit against which I protest."[4] The contrast expressed here is unmistakable: a practical Christianity grounded in the sublime simplicity of the New Testament versus mere professions of religion and the audacious interposition of vain and ignorant men. In other words, Dickens's specimens of earnest Christianity are intentionally devoid of the characteristic and the posturing that Macrae hoped to see.

In this way, Dickens does give a reasonably clear picture of what real Christianity is *not*. When Dickens says "mere professions," he is not speaking primarily to the insincere or even hypocritical profession of religion—although he does understand "mere professions" as hypocritical in one sense. What he means is *just* profession and not much else, the person whose Christianity is only profession and intellectual assent to a body of data. For Dickens, one may know the content of the Bible inside and out, one may attend church regularly, and one's doctrine may be pristine, but that is simply window-dressing, merely intellectual assent—"mere profession." As such, Dickens considers it hypocritical. And it is hypocritical in the sense in which Jesus used the term to dress down the religious leaders of his day—that they were play actors, or hypocrites, not merely deceiving others but deceiving themselves, and not by being deliberately deceitful or conspiratorial, but by being ignorant of their own folly and misdirected piety.

Dickens also speaks to this negative aspect of what "real Christianity" is *not* when he refers to the "the audacious interposition of vain and ignorant men between the sublime simplicity of the New Testament and the general human mind to which our Saviour addressed it."[5] Dickens was adamantly opposed to preachers who loved to hear themselves speak and got in the way of God's Word. Dickens saw a "sublime simplicity" in the New Testament, particularly the Gospels, and felt that it could stand on its own without the endorsement or embellishment of "vain and ignorant" preachers.

But Dickens mentions, too, in his letter to Davies, "obtrusive professions of and tradings in religion."[6] These are not "mere professions." Rather, this is showmanship and using Christianity to take advantage of others in whatever way the perpetrator is seeking to take advantage. As I've pointed out regarding mere professions, "obtrusive professions and tradings in religion" can be intentional and devious, and sometimes for Dickens they are—but usually not. Usually, they are, again, from ignorance, born of arrogance and a preoccupation with the self.

These are not the only examples of Dickens's negative approach to religion or Christianity, but they tend to be representative of the types of criticisms and misgivings Dickens had about religion that is *not* "real Christianity." And they do provide, when combined with Dickens's positive affirmations, a nice profile of "real Christianity."

As to such positive affirmations, Dickens does go on in his letter to Macrae to provide at least a brief indication of real Christianity. Dickens points out, contrary to Macrae's opinion, that all of his good characters reflect at least some of the teaching of Jesus and that they do so by the author's intent. Furthermore, in deliberately demonstrating the teaching of Jesus in his good characters, Dickens was attempting to encourage the reader to practice the teachings of

Jesus. Plainly, Dickens saw his good characters as biblical examples. Consequently, and perhaps most importantly, Dickens claims, "All my good people are humble, charitable, faithful, and forgiving. Over and over again, I claim them in express words as disciples of the Founder of our religion." Thus, Dickens provides an orientation and a starting point for the understanding of what he called "real Christianity." The exemplar of real Christianity is a disciple of Jesus and demonstrates, at least, humility, charity, faithfulness, and forgiveness.

In chapter 2, I outlined the idea of the imitation of Jesus. For Dickens, the imitation of Jesus constitutes discipleship. That is, the disciple of Jesus is simply one who imitates him. Here in his letters to Davies and Macrae, Dickens begins to delineate what that imitation would involve, at least in terms of basic character. Obviously, the virtues that he lists here are integrally connected to being a disciple of Jesus and are reflected in the life of the disciple as the disciple imitates Jesus. The list of virtues is not an exhaustive one, nor is it intended to be. But it does provide a place to begin the practice of the imitation of Jesus. Clearly, that place is in his fiction. In other words, if one wants to know what Dickens understands as "real Christianity," one should read his work and observe the character and behavior of his heroes and heroines.

Obviously, the character trait of humility is an extremely important one in Dickens's concept of "real Christianity." It is especially noteworthy in his reply to Macrae that he, obviously alluding to Jesus's teaching on the practice of Christian righteousness in Matthew 6 (particularly 6:16–18), points out that all of his noble characters "arise and wash their faces, and do not appear unto men to fast." For Dickens, the inconspicuous practice of Christianity—that is, humility—is of the highest order of Christian virtue and spiritual depth. And he looked with suspicion upon anything that smacked of religiosity or pharisaical pretense. At the end of *TLOL*, though he uses a different list of virtues, he reiterates the same sentiments: "It is Christianity to be gentle, merciful, and forgiving, and to keep those qualities quiet in our own hearts and never make a boast of them or of our prayers or of our love of God, but always to show that we love Him by humbly trying to do right in everything."[7]

In his letter to J. M. Makeham (see chapter 2), Dickens writes: "I have always striven in my writings to express veneration for the life and lessons of our Saviour; because I feel it; and because I rewrote that history for my children . . . *But I have never made proclamation of this from the house tops* [my italics]."[8] And Dickens's son, Sir Henry Fielding Dickens, would later write of his father, "He made no parade of religion, but he was at heart possessed of deep religious convictions. . . . What he did hate and despise was the cant of religion. "[9] This is the sort of humility of which Dickens speaks and which plays such a central role in his understanding of the practice of real Christianity.

Moreover, this sort of humility and unobtrusive presence speaks to a fundamental element of Dickens's understanding of the imitation of Jesus and so suggests why Dickens never felt the need—indeed, refused—to make his characters overtly Christian. That is, he avoided portraying practitioners of "real Christianity" in terms of conspicuous piety and religiosity because those who practiced Christian spirituality in such a way, he believed, were violating the very instruction that Jesus gave concerning the unobtrusive and humble practice of righteousness. It is no wonder that when we examine Dickens's work, it is precisely this unassuming and self-effacing Christian spirituality that we see.

Dickens believed the virtue of charity was just as fundamental as humility. Dickens seems to use this term to refer to the idea of a self-giving and self-sacrificing love that is long-suffering and not easily provoked or diminished. It is everything the apostle Paul said it should be in 1 Corinthians 13. It is a genuine love for people and a genuine desire to see people be what God intends them to be. Dickens's "good people" are ready to do whatever is necessary to serve others, to love them unconditionally without end, and to lead them up to what God wants them to be. Charity in this sense is almost always costly, requiring selflessness and sacrifice. In this respect, Dickens understands charity as it is articulated by Paul and as it is seen in Jesus.

Dickens mentions, too, in his letter to Macrae, the idea of faithfulness. It is likely that he is using this word in the sense of the Old Testament's common use of "righteous."[10] The righteous person is one who is faithful; who is dependable, reliable, trustworthy; and who is diligent to be so. For Dickens, this is exemplified in his characters as they remain uncompromised in their righteous convictions and in their noble purposes even and especially when to be so committed is costly or demands sacrifice. For Dickens, the resolve to remain steadfast in conviction and purpose plays a key role in the nature of such faithfulness. His heroes and heroines are strong in this regard. They know what is right and they do what is right, not for advantage, recognition, or benefit, but because doing the right thing is an end in itself.

Finally, Dickens makes mention of his "good people" being forgiving. In the previous chapter I spoke to the idea in Dickens's writing of God's willingness to forgive sins. Just as important to Dickens is the forgiveness people should extend one to another. In fact, Dickens's work might contain more of the latter than the former. For Dickens, one sure sign of real Christianity is a forgiving spirit manifested in the readiness to forgive others. This is captured in the "Prayer at Night," when Dickens petitions, "That we may be honest and true in all our dealings, and gentle and merciful to the faults of others: remembering of how much gentleness and mercy we stand in need ourselves."[11]

Forgiveness, one for another, is a dominant theme in *TLOL*. Consider, for instance, the lesson Dickens draws from the account of the sinful woman who had anointed Jesus's feet in the home of Simon the Pharisee: "We learn from this that we must always forgive those who have done us any harm, when they come to us and say they are truly sorry for it. Even if they do not come and say so, we must still forgive them and never hate them or be unkind to them, if we would hope that God will forgive us."[12] And later in *TLOL*, Dickens recounts the parable of the unforgiving servant and concludes: "'So,' said Our Saviour, 'how can you expect God to forgive you, if you do not forgive others!' This is the meaning of that part of the Lord's Prayer, where we say 'Forgive us our trespasses'—that word means faults—'as we forgive them that trespass against us.'"[13]

Undoubtedly this theme of forgiveness is one that runs throughout Dickens's larger body of fiction as well. It is the main theme of *The Haunted Man*, as well as "The Story of Richard Doubledick" segment of "The Seven Poor Travellers," a Christmas story.[14] The frequency with which this theme appears in the novels indicates that forgiveness is indeed a distinguishing mark of real Christianity for Dickens. Whether it is Miss Havisham seeking forgiveness from Pip,

Pip seeking forgiveness from Joe, Em'ly from Mr. Pegotty, Bella from her father, Lady Deadlock from Esther, or Mrs. Clennam from Amy, the seeking of forgiveness and the free offer of forgiveness is replete in his fiction. And it is the free offer of forgiveness that exemplifies that which Dickens saw as a virtue of the genuine Christian.

Joe's offer of forgiveness to Pip is a classic example in this sense. Joe's response to Pip's request for forgiveness is characteristic of Dickens's "good people." "'O dear old Pip, old chap,' says Joe, 'God knows as I forgive you, if I have anythink to forgive.'"[15] This spirit of forgiveness, which Dickens counts as so central to real Christianity, is a spirit of grace that holds no grudge and bears no ill will. The offense of the offender has already been absorbed by the grace of the forgiving spirit, so that all that is left is for the one seeking forgiveness to know they have been forgiven. Perhaps it is especially noteworthy that Pip, in learning that it had been Joe who had taken care of him throughout his illness, prayerfully whispers of Joe, "O God bless him! O God bless this gentle Christian man!"[16]

With the same grace and forgiving spirit, Florence Dombey offers forgiveness to her father despite the fact that he has not yet sought out her forgiveness. "Homeless and fatherless, she forgave him everything; hardly thought that she had need to forgive, or that she did."[17] Once again, and consistent with Dickens's characterization of his "good people," Florence has such a gracious and forgiving spirit that she sees little, if anything, to forgive, but she initiates forgiveness nonetheless. Late in this same novel, the irony in the denouement situates Florence beseeching her father for forgiveness. Dickens's simple observation that Florence is "asking *his* forgiveness!" points first, of course, to the characteristic unconditional love and forgiving grace of Florence; more importantly, perhaps, it gives a focused voice to the arrogance and hardness of heart that closes the heart off to love and to the ability to ask forgiveness and receive it.

A scene with obvious affinity to that of the reconciliation between Florence and her father is the one in which Mrs. Clennam seeks forgiveness from Amy. Dickens portrays Mrs. Clennam's arrogance and hardness of heart early in the novel: "Forgive us our debts as we forgive our debtors, was a prayer too poor in spirit for her. Smite thou my debtors, Lord, wither them, crush them; do Thou as I would do, and Thou shalt have my worship: this was the impious tower of stone she built up to scale Heaven."[18] Mrs. Clennam's inability to forgive, of course, is the antithesis to Amy's gracious spirit of forgiveness. Yet, when Mrs. Clennam eventually seeks Amy's forgiveness for the wrong she has done her family, she entreats her simply: "Forgive me. Can you forgive me?" Amy replies: "I can, and Heaven knows I do! Do not kiss my dress and kneel to me; . . . I forgive you freely, without that."[19]

The scenes are short ones, but they present in bold relief the forgiving spirit of the real Christian. As with Amy, Florence, and Joe especially, the forgiveness is freely given from a sincere heart and a gracious spirit that has already released any sense of offense. It is given readily and unconditionally and with the largesse of the spirit of Christ. And it is in this forgiving spirit, indicative of real Christianity, that humility, charity, and faithfulness are intertwined and become a dynamic force in Christian character.

While it is certainly fair to associate the virtues of humility, charity, faithfulness, and forgiveness with his "real Christianity," it would be wrong to suppose that these virtues comprise the whole of "real Christianity." For Dickens also makes clear in his letter to David Macrae that all his "good people" are "disciples of the Founder of our religion." And so, while it is certainly informative to identify the virtues Dickens names and then look for them in his characters, it is informative, too, to take a look at his good people and let them demonstrate other virtues of real Christianity.

Esther Summerson, the heroine and main character in Dickens's *Bleak House*, unassumingly and quite sincerely aspires "to be industrious, contented, and kind-hearted [or, true-hearted], and to do some good to some one."[20] Esther expresses this aspiration toward servanthood three times in *Bleak House*. In this form, the expression connects her aspiration toward servanthood to the servant attitude of Jesus. In *TLOL*, just before Jesus enters into his public ministry, his simple prayer in the wilderness is "that He might be of use to men and women."[21] Esther's prayer is of this same character and is indicative of her intent to imitate Jesus as a true disciple by sharing this attitude of servanthood.

The "real Christianity" of Florence Dombey is conspicuous in her unrelenting and unconditional love for her father, a father who will have nothing to do with her and whose anger and resentment over the death of his young son falls squarely on Florence for no reason other than she is not her brother. Undaunted, her determination to express her undying love and to win his love becomes for her "a sacred purpose" in life and is evident throughout the duration of the narrative.[22] Paul Dombey, Florence's brother, offers "voluntary service" and like Esther, hopes to be "gentle and useful" at Doctor Blimber's academy.[23] The charitable nature of "real Christianity"—that is, a selfless and sacrificial love—is demonstrated in Harriet Carker's steadfast devotion to her brother, John, and her genuine interest in and compassion toward Alice.[24] In both instances, Harriet exhibits the selfless and sacrificial love that established her in Dickens's mind as a true disciple of the Master.

Esther, Florence, Paul, and Harriet are intended by Dickens to be examples of the "real Christianity" and the Christian character of which Dickens spoke in his letters to Davies and Macrae, and all are intended by Dickens to be disciples of Jesus by virtue of their imitation of him. In Dickens's mind, they find their counterpart in Jesus, for "No one ever lived," Dickens writes of Jesus in *TLOL*, "who was so good, so kind, so gentle, and so sorry of all people who did wrong or were in any way ill or miserable, as He was."[25] Esther, Florence, Paul, and Harriet, in their respective ways, reflect the character of the Saviour.

It is Amy Dorrit, however, the heroine and main character in *Little Dorrit*, who may be Dickens's finest example of "real Christianity" and the character of Jesus. In the early pages of *Little Dorrit*, Dickens describes her: "She was inspired to be something which was not what the rest were, and to be that something, different and laborious, for the sake of the rest. Inspired? Yes. Shall we speak of the inspiration of a poet or a priest, and not of the heart impelled by love and self-devotion to the lowliest work in the lowliest way of life!"[26] "She took the place of eldest of the three [Dorrit children]," Dickens adds, "in all things but precedence; was the head of the fallen family; and bore, in her own heart, its anxieties and shames."[27] Amy accepts the responsibility, willingly and with no motives other than love, to care for her family as well as for Maggy. She is diligent to make sure that Fanny and Tip (her sister and brother) have what they need and that their clothes are "mended and made up," and she often sacrifices the meager meals that Mrs. Clennam provides for her, giving them to her father instead. Amy's life and attitude are indicative of Dickens's "real Christianity" in that she possesses the mind of Christ in serving, helping others, and doing good.

Nell, in *The Old Curiosity Shop*, like those already mentioned, is an exemplary specimen of "real Christianity" in humility, charity, and selflessness. Nell's grandfather threatens the well-being both of his life and Nell's by his uncontrollable gambling habit. Nell takes it upon herself, then, to care for her grandfather. Not only does she take responsibility for both of their lives but she also does all she can and whatever is necessary for his rescue and reclamation without sacrificing her selfless and affectionate care. In what amounts to a tribute to Nell, Mr. Marton, the schoolmaster, observes, "Has this child heroically persevered under all doubts and dangers, struggled with poverty and suffering, upheld and sustained by strong affection and the consciousness of rectitude alone! . . . Have I yet to learn that the hardest and best-borne trials are those which are never chronicled in any earthly record and are suffered every day!"[28] Nell is, once more, the exemplar of Dickens's real Christianity in her selfless devotion to her grandfather, her sacrificial love, and her desire always to do what is right.

Clearly Dickens's work seems to bear out his claim in the letter to Macrae that he attempts "to exhibit in all my good people some faint reflections of the teachings of our great Master, and unostentatiously to lead the reader up to those teachings as the great source of all moral goodness" and that, "All my good people are humble, charitable, faithful, and forgiving. Over and over again, I claim them in express words as disciple of the Founder of our religion; but I must admit that to a man (or woman) they all arise and wash their faces, and do not appear unto men to fast."[29] Without question, the list of characters who exemplify "real Christianity" in Dickens could be expanded considerably to include, for instance, Mr. Brownlow in *Oliver Twist*, the Cherryble Brothers in *Nicholas Nickleby*, Gabriel Varden in *Barnaby Rudge*, Agnes Wickfield in *David Copperfield*, and John Jarndyce in *Bleak House*. Dickens, conspicuously, never identifies the characters in this short list and the ones considered above as "Christian" (he does identify Joe Gargery as a Christian in *Great Expectations*) or as disciples of Jesus. Consistent with his convictions, Dickens never allows these characters to indulge in "obtrusive professions of and tradings in religion" or in those attitudes and behaviors that, to him, resembled false piety and pretentious religiosity. Indeed, he makes certain that "they all arise and wash their faces, and do not appear unto men to fast."[30] They simply exhibit in their character and in their relationships with others the teaching and the example of Jesus.

And that, of course, is crucial to understanding Dickens's concept of Christianity and the life of faith. It is not, as some would argue, that Dickens was a mere moralist, for his sense of morality was firmly grounded in the New Testament and the teaching of Jesus. Dickens did not uphold morality simply for morality's sake. Rather, he believed that if what was affirmed in our Christian profession did not come to bear on the common everyday affairs of life, then such a profession must be suspect. Dickens was convinced that Christianity was not simply to be professed but that it must be practiced, and it must be lived out in one's relationships and community. For Dickens, Christianity is not simply about embracing right doctrine. Rather, those who embrace "real Christianity" involve themselves in the lives of the needy, the poor, the destitute, and the downtrodden; they are ready to forgive, to show mercy, grace, and compassion in tangible and concrete ways; they are ready to serve selflessly and sacrificially in order to bring about change in the lives of others and to contribute to cultural transformation.

Dickens's brilliant *A Christmas Carol* contains one of his most profound and most telling passages. When Ebenezer Scrooge is confronted by the ghost of his deceased partner, Jacob Marley, Scrooge finds himself a bit detached from the gravity and significance of their exchange. And at a crucial juncture when Scrooge is beginning to catch just a glimpse of Marley's purpose with him, Scrooge attempts to comfort Marley by reassuring him with the accolade, "But you were always a good man of business, Jacob."[31] At this, Marley's ghost is filled with both outrage and regret, and almost chastising Scrooge, he cries, "Business! Mankind was my business. The common welfare was my business; charity, mercy, forbearance, and benevolence, were, all my business. The dealings of my trade were but a drop of water in the comprehensive ocean of my business!"[32] This passage articulates like few others the essence of Dickens's worldview and the basic foundation of his Christian conviction: the willingness to give oneself away in service to others.

That Dickens was a novelist by vocation should never be over-looked. And as a novelist, he was an entertainer. Had Dickens lived in the twenty-first century, he could have been an actor or a stand-up comedian and maybe both. But Dickens was not simply an entertainer. He always wrote with a message and from a Christian orientation directed by a passionately held Christian worldview. Indeed, Dickens wrote in order to awaken the Christian conscience and to call Christians to their responsibilities as followers of their great Master. For Dickens, that means imitating Jesus and constantly learning from him apart from, and perhaps in spite of, the church, its doctrinal minutiae, its sectarian agendas, and its conspicuous religiosity. For Dickens, it is the unobtrusive practice of Christian character and virtue that is the mark of true Christianity. This is precisely why Dickens portrays his "Christian" characters as he does. They are simply people who go about being who and what they are. Dickens felt no compulsion to include their Christian testimony or to describe their conversion and their spiritual journey to faith in Christ. In Dickens's mind, if his characters imitate Jesus and demonstrate his love, mercy, humility, grace, and compassion—if they demonstrate *Christlikeness*—then sharing a testimony or describing their spiritual journey is superfluous and quite unnecessary. It is "mere profession." Dickens was convinced that Christians were not in need of new ways to claim they were Christians, bigger buildings, more theology or doctrine, or better preaching. What they needed was to be awakened to God's call on their life, to take seriously their responsibilities to imitate Jesus in genuine and concrete ways, and to go about whatever opportunities God had provided for them to serve others. To that end, Dickens wrote to Christians to encourage, exhort, and admonish them toward the imitation of Christ.

It seems clear, then, why Dickens would react almost fiercely against the mere profession of and tradings in Christianity, particularly at the expense of what Jesus called the weightier matters of the law (Matt. 23:23 KJV). Dickens profoundly articulates his disdain for this kind of hypocrisy and ignorance in a scene in *Little Dorrit* in which Arthur Clennam is musing on what course of action he should take in the future especially in regard to a past injustice perpetrated by his family—an injustice which is not yet clearly understood by him at this point in the narrative. Here, Arthur's sense

of duty and honor, of justice and right is set over and against his
mother's "fierce dark teaching":

> He was ready at any moment to lay down all he had, and begin the
> world anew. As the fierce dark teaching of his childhood had never
> sunk into his heart, so that first article in his code of morals was, that
> he must begin, in practical humility, with looking well to his feet on
> Earth, and that he could never mount on wings of words to Heaven.
> Duty on earth, restitution on earth, action on earth; these first, as
> the first steep steps upward. Strait was the gate and narrow was the
> way; far straiter and narrower than the broad high road paved with
> vain professions and vain repetitions, motes from other men's eyes
> and liberal delivery of others to the judgment—all cheap materials
> costing absolutely nothing.[33]

Mrs. Clennam proudly describes her faith as developing from an
upbringing of "wholesome repression, punishment, and fear. The
corruption of our hearts, the evil of our ways, the curse that is upon
us, the terrors that surround us—these were themes of my childhood. They formed my character, and filled me with an abhorrence
of evil-doers."[34] And even though for Arthur there had been provided
"no more real knowledge of the beneficent history of the New Testament, than if he had been bred among idolaters,"[35] fortunately
"the fierce dark teaching of his childhood had never sunk into his
heart."[36] Thus, in Dickens's mind, Arthur is free, and responsible,
to attend to the weightier matters, the concerns of real Christianity,
and he is right to do so.

Obviously, the Christian life, for Dickens, is not simply the mere
profession of faith. Neither is it the contemplative life, whether in
a positive or negative expression; nor is it about speculative theologizing, doctrinal proof-texting, or exclusive creedal claims. Rather,
it is an active life in imitation of Jesus. In a letter to Miss Emmely
Gotschalk (see chapter 2), Dickens attempts to address her deep
concerns over certain theological speculation and spiritual mysteries.
To try to help her, Dickens points her to more significant, practical
matters: "Be earnest—earnest—in life's reality and do not let your
life, which has a purpose in it—every life upon the earth has—fly
by while you are brooding over mysteries. The mystery is not here,
but far beyond the sky. The preparation for it is in doing duty. Our

Saviour did not sit down in this world and muse, but labored and did good."[37]

Dickens made no apologies for such a strong sense of moral responsibility and active faith. Embracing the popular lay Anglicanism of his day, he assumed that there were just a few fundamental doctrines, however vaguely they might be expressed, that genuine Christians readily and agreeably accepted without much of a second thought. Accordingly, for Dickens, doctrine is not of primary concern or determinative of a genuine faith. Neither is the church, with all of its accoutrements and particulars, central to the Christian's duty and responsibility. Instead, the Christian is to be concerned first and foremost with following the teaching and imitating the life of "the Founder of our religion," "our great Master" and the Lord of the church. [38] Like Arthur Clennam, the Christian is to focus on doing justice, loving mercy and walking humbly with God (Micah 6:8), those weightier matters of which our Lord spoke. And Dickens was more than exemplary in practicing what he preached.

Dickens's Own Real Christianity

If Dickens's "good people" are those who are claimed by him as "disciples of the Founder of our religion"; and if they "exhibit . . . some faint reflections of the teachings of our great Master," Dickens himself is no less so.[39] His emphasis on following the teaching and the example of Jesus was no mere rhetorical posturing. He involved himself in whatever seemed to him to be a worthy cause, and he brought whatever resources he could—whether speaking, writing, financial support, or rallying the help of others—to each project with equal amounts of compassion, energy, and commitment. Edgar Johnson has noted of Dickens, "No one more constantly worked for others in the midst of a laborious career."[40] Dickens worked tirelessly on behalf of the poor, the destitute, the disadvantaged, the needy. He wrote as a social journalist to call for and bring about change; he spoke on behalf of a variety of charitable causes; he contributed financially and raised financial support; and he visited the problems personally to see what needed to be done. He planned and organized and rallied help. But Dickens was not simply the fundraiser, the spokesperson, or the organizer for an organization or a person—although he was that at times. Often he was the advocate, the person on the frontline, the one who personally did the hands-on work of whatever cause he found worthy or for whatever person he found in need.

In the hortatory passages of *TLOL*, Dickens urges his children to be constantly alert to the needs of others, particularly those less fortunate than themselves. When Dickens recounts Jesus's gathering his disciples, he emphasizes that Jesus "chose them from among Poor Men, in order that the Poor might know—always after that; in all years to come—that Heaven was made for them as well as for the rich, and that God makes no difference between those who wear good clothes and those who go barefoot and in rags."[41] He encourages his children further in the same passage, "Never forget this, when you are grown up. Never be proud or unkind, my dear, to any poor man, woman, or child. . . . [A]lways try to make them better by kind persuading words; and always try to teach them and relieve them if you can. And when people speak ill of the Poor and Miserable, think how Jesus Christ went among them and taught them, and thought them worthy of his care."[42] Dickens was not merely giving lip-service when he wrote to his children this way. He was not prone to ever doing so. He took seriously his responsibility as a follower of Jesus to act on behalf of the poor and less fortunate—and that he did.

It was not uncommon at all for Dickens to find out or be made aware of a personal need and then immediately devise a way to meet the need. On 1 November 1848, for instance, Dickens wrote to his friend, Angela Burdette-Coutts, for her assistance "in getting a highly esteemed and valued old servant of mine . . . into St George's Hospital."[43] Louis Roche, who had accompanied Dickens to Switzerland in 1846 as his courier, was struck with heart problems and Dickens was not exactly sure how to go about finding a vacancy in a hospital suitable to his illness. So, Dickens contacted Burdette-Coutts, whom he believed had some knowledge and contacts to find admittance somewhere for Roche. "I must accomplish it if it can be done," Dickens wrote. It is worth noting that Dickens heard from Coutts the very next day and Roche was admitted almost immediately.

On another occasion, Dickens learned that Edward Elton, an actor, had drowned in a shipwreck off the coast of Ireland. Elton, whose wife had died three years earlier, had seven children who were now left orphaned. Dickens, acting as the chairperson of a committee to raise funds and enlisting the aid of two others, established and managed the Elton Fund on behalf of the children. According to Michael Slater, the committee raised, "within months," £2300.[44] Dickens's correspondence to Angela Burdett-Coutts over a period of about six months reveals that he followed the fortunes of the orphans, actively involving himself in their welfare. Two years after the Elton Fund was established, Dickens wrote to Coutts of his admiration for and the success of Esther Elton, the oldest of the Elton children. He writes, "Esther Elton . . . in her training at the Normal School has uniformly conducted herself in a manner for which no praise could be too high; and has now the choice of two large schools in the country—to one of which she will go, as Mistress, early in the Spring."[45]

In another instance, Dickens engaged himself with the family of John Overs, who had died and was survived by his widow and their six children. Dickens petitioned the Orphan Working School on behalf of the oldest son, John, and requested of Miss Coutts that she "might have opportunity of presenting one of the girls to some other school or charity."[46] John Overs, who was a cabinetmaker by trade, was also an aspiring amateur author who had sent Dickens some poems while Dickens was still editor of *Bentley's Miscellany* in 1839. Dickens eventually helped Overs get some of his poetry published in *Tait's Magazine*, helped with historical background for some short stories Overs was writing, and acted as a mentor for the novice writer. Dickens was also instrumental in helping Overs to publish his *Evenings of a Working Man*, a collection of verse and prose, for which Dickens had written a preface. When it was learned that Overs had tuberculosis, Dickens enlisted the best physician he could find and was able to help find less strenuous work for him.

Because of his celebrity and his reputation as one ready to help the poor, Dickens was besieged regularly by what he called "begging-letters." With regard to such letters, Slater remarks, "The begging-letter writers he had always with him, of course, and here the remarkable thing is the number of individual cases he actually made time to follow up."[47] The point here is not that Dickens was besieged by such letters; rather, the point is that he would read them and involve himself if he was convinced of a need and if he could be of help. This fact highlights Dickens's seemingly constant readiness to help others, which he saw as a sacred duty. And consistent with his convictions, he made no parade of his involvements either in the helping of individuals or in his support and activity on behalf of more public endeavors. For Dickens, this was no more and no less than the practice of real Christianity.

Dickens and the Ragged School Movement

One such endeavor to which Dickens had become committed was the establishment and development of what were known as Ragged Schools. Ragged Schools began probably around 1800 and initially advertised themselves as free schools that taught adults and children on Sundays and on two week-day evenings.[48] According to Dickens scholar Philip Collins, these schools were "founded locally and independently in London and in some provincial cities by good-hearted citizens, usually humble laymen, to give some religious instruction to the very poorest children."[49] Dickens was an advocate and supporter in the early days of the schools when they were just becoming publicly recognized.

In 1844, Samuel R. Starey is credited with organizing almost twenty independent schools into the Ragged School Union. In 1856, the journalistic arm of the Ragged School Union, *The Ragged School Union Magazine*, succinctly stated the Ragged Schools' purpose: "The great aim of Ragged Schools, we confess and rejoice, is, to impart religious instruction. Other objects they undoubtedly have; but these are all subordinated to the chief end of bringing neglected and ignorant children within reach of the doctrine of Christ. His religion is adapted to every class and every type of fallen humanity."[50] The "other objects" to which this description refers were no small concerns. In addition to religious instructions, students of Ragged Schools were taught to read, write, and do arithmetic and might be trained in tailoring, cobbling, or needlework. Ragged School should not be confused with Sunday schools. Ragged Schools were a comprehensive educational enterprise, but with a biblical foundation.

Apparently acting as an agent of sorts of Angela Burdett-Coutts, Dickens visited one of the Ragged Schools and then wrote to her about the visit. It would be an understatement to say that Dickens was taken aback by what he observed. "I have very seldom seen, in all the strange and dreadful things I have seen in London and else-where," Dickens writes, "anything so shocking as the dire neglect of soul and body exhibited in these children." Dickens was impressed with the teachers at the school—"extremely quiet, honest, good men. You may suppose they are, to be there at all," he remarks. But he was perplexed by the prospects of their task: "To gain their [the students'] attention in any way, is a difficulty quite gigantic. To impress them, even with the idea of a God, when their own condition is so desolate, becomes a monstrous task."[51] Nevertheless, Dickens relates to Miss Coutts that students have knowledge of the Saviour and the day of judgment, which they have evidently learned at the school. One child that he notes in particular—"really a clever child"—told Dickens "that God was no respecter of persons, and that if he prayed . . . 'as if he meant it,' and didn't keep company with bad boys, and didn't swear and didn't drink, he would be as readily forgiven in Heaven, as the Queen would."[52]

If Dickens was visiting the school to provide Miss Coutts with a report as to whether or not to offer support, his conclusions and rec-ommendation are unmistakable: "The moral courage of the teachers is beyond all praise. They are surrounded by every possible adversity, and every disheartening circumstance that can be imagined. Their office is worthy of the apostles. . . . I need not say, I am sure, that I deem it an experiment most worthy of your charitable hand."[53] Obvi-ously, Dickens himself was also persuaded of the value of supporting the school as well as the larger enterprise. He recognized the Schools' shortcomings and their uphill struggle, but he seemed encouraged by the endeavor. He was impressed with what he referred to as the Scotch system of elementary education employed by the schools. But because of the appalling conditions he encountered at the school he visited, he was less than confident that the larger endeavor would meet with much encouragement and support.[54] Perhaps that is why he was ready to be both advocate and supporter. "There is a kind of delicacy," he so astutely observes, "which is not at all shocked by the existence of such things, but is excessively shocked to know them."[55] Still, Dickens's resolve was steady: "Whether this effort will succeed, it is quite impossible to say. But that it is a great one, begin-ning at the right end, among thousands of immortal creatures, who cannot, in their present state, be held accountable for what they do, it is *as* impossible to doubt." As such, Dickens himself was ready to get behind the effort.

Dickens's support was active and involved and he was considered by the Ragged School Union an ally and a friend all his life. His public support of the movement in journalistic efforts was invaluable. As Collins points out, a number of articles on the Ragged Schools appeared in his *Household Words*.[56] Dickens wrote one article himself, "A Sleep to Startle Us" (13 March 1852, and cowrote another, "Boys to Mend" (11 September 1852), with Henry Morley. He was also ready to use any influence he might have—as Charles Dickens—to appeal to the government on behalf of the Ragged Schools. At the request of Starey, Dickens approached the Committee of Council on Education concerning a possible grant, but the government refused to take any action. Undaunted, Dickens pledged to write to Lord John Russell on the matter. It is not known what effect, if any, that correspondence produced.

Collins indicates that Dickens had also written an open letter in the *Daily News*, 4 February 1846, during his brief tenure as editor there, concerning the Ragged Schools, asking readers to observe the schools firsthand and involve themselves in their support. Interestingly, Dickens's endorsement is qualified: "I have no desire to praise the system pursued in the Ragged Schools; which is necessarily very imperfect, if indeed there be one. So far as I have any means of judging of what is taught there, I should individually object to it, as not being sufficiently secular, and as presenting too many religious mysteries and difficulties, to minds not sufficiently prepared for their reception." Nevertheless, he confirms his support for the work: "But I should very imperfectly discharge in myself the duty I wish to urge and impress on others, if I allowed any such doubt of mine to interfere with my appreciation of the efforts of these teachers, or my true wish to promote them by any slight means in my power." It appears, then, that Dickens was behind the Ragged School "experiment." But he obviously had certain reservations about the pedagogy.

For Dickens, the educational process was not made better or more effective or more spiritual by couching it in Christian language and bringing Bible verses to bear on it. According to his letter to Miss Coutts, Dickens clearly agrees with the Ragged schoolmasters that their charges first be taught the difference between right and wrong. But his conviction that the curriculum is not "sufficiently secular" was a conviction that he wished to impress upon her. What Dickens means by this, of course, is that wisdom dictates that in the course of education students be taught to read and write as a first priority. But even more basic—to any attempt at education—was finding some point of contact on which to begin. Dickens wrote of the students to Miss Coutts, "To find anything within them—who know nothing of affection, care, love, or kindness of any sort—to which it is possible to appeal, is, at first, like a search for the philosopher's stone." On this basis and in this context Dickens's words and reasoning concerning the adjustment of particular Christian content—what he refers to as "the viciousness of insisting on creeds and forms"— make sense. Dickens insists that "to talk of catechisms, outward and visible signs, and inward and spiritual graces, to these children is a thing no Bedlamite would do, who saw them."[57] And he continues, "To get them, whose whole lives from the moment of their birth, are one continued punishment, to believe even in the Judgment of the Dead and a future state of punishment for their sins, requires a System in itself."[58]

Dickens was not objecting to Christian teaching in the schools or to the scriptural foundation of the curriculum. Rather, he was calling for a more judicious implementation of those elements for these particular students. It is "of vital importance," Dickens writes to Starey, 24 September 1843, "that no persons, however well intentioned, should perplex the minds of these unfortunate creatures with religious mysteries that young people with the best advantages can but imperfectly understand."[59] It is notable that this quote is part of a request Dickens made to Starey expressly concerning "visitors," or visiting volunteer teachers. Dickens asked that such volunteers be requested to confine their questions and instructions to the broad truths taught in the school by Starey and his full-time teachers.

Certainly, this concern for the teaching of broad Christian truths suited to one's audience was a real one for Dickens, but it was specific and understandable. *TLOL* is his own response to this same concern. What rankled Dickens was the tendency of some to take what he believed were the simple yet profound truths of the Scriptures and transform them into complex and confusing doctrines.

Dickens would rail against such a tendency almost whenever the opportunity presented itself. Obviously, he hoped to make an impact on the Ragged Schools in this regard.

Dickens's willingness to support the Ragged Schools despite reservations about certain aspects of their teaching may not be as remarkable as his accommodating himself to the fact that the Ragged Schools' headquarters was located in Exeter Hall, the bastion of dissenting Evangelicalism. Dickens writes in his article "The Niger Expedition" published in *The Examiner*, 19 August 1848, "It might be laid down as a very good general rule of social and political guidance, that whatever Exeter Hall champions, is the thing by no means to be done."[60] Dickens's tongue was not very far in his cheek when he wrote those words. Specifically, in this particular article, he was addressing the Evangelical preoccupation with overseas missions. He was incensed by what he saw as their unhealthy interest in the heathen of other nations to the neglect of those needy "heathen" in their own country. Dickens could never understand how Evangelicals could ignore the plight of the poor, of children, and of the disadvantaged right in their own backyard. There was too much need, too much to be done, too much to be undone, too much not to be ignored. The Evangelical preoccupation with overseas mission at the expense of the pressing needs "at home" was a theme that Dickens would return to again and again in his fiction. Perhaps his most scathing and yet most powerful passage in this regard is found in *Bleak House*, concerning Jo, the street sweeper, who represents the destitute of London's slums:

> "He [Jo] is not one of Mrs. Pardiggle's Tockahoopo Indians; he is not one of Mrs. Jellyby's lambs, being wholly unconnected to Borrioboola-Gha; he is not softened by distance and unfamiliarity; he is not a genuine foreign-grown savage; he is the ordinary home-made article. Dirty, ugly, disagreeable to all the senses, in body a common creature of the common streets, only in soul a heathen. Homely filth begrimes him, homely parasites devour him, homely sores are in him, homely rags are on him: native ignorance, the growth of English soil and climate, sinks his immortal nature lower than the beasts that perish. Stand forth, Jo, in uncompromising colours! From the sole of thy foot to the crown of thy head, there is nothing interesting about thee."[61]

Likely, Dickens was willing to set aside his suspicion concerning anything coming out of Exeter Hall in the case of the Ragged Schools, for those in the movement were involving themselves in precisely what he believed they should. As such, the Ragged Schools movement exemplified what Dickens believed was one expression of the real Christianity that the church was to exhibit. The Ragged Schools movement went into the worst parts of London to minister to those whom the church, the government, and society were ignoring and neglecting. How could Dickens ignore such a ministry? In fact, he couldn't. And he didn't. Despite his reservations about the Ragged Schools and his distaste for Exeter Hall and its products, Dickens remained a supporter and advocate of the schools for many years.

Dickens and Urania Cottage

It is clear that Dickens and Angela Burdett-Coutts formed an effective partnership in social justice causes and charitable endeavors. Miss Coutts was one of the wealthiest women in Victorian England and was more than generous with her great fortune. Dickens had an incomparable sense of human nature and unfailing compassion for the poor and destitute, whether children or adults. Miss Coutts, often relying on Dickens to investigate and assess various opportunities for charitable assistance, trusted his assessments and was confident in his advice. In the initial stages of their involvement together in the Ragged School movement, Dickens writes to Forster of Miss Coutts (particularly concerning Dickens's own suggestions for initial improvement of the schools): "I have no doubt she will do whatever I ask her in the matter. She is a most excellent creature, I protest to God, and I have most perfect affection and respect for her."[62]

"[Dickens] was not only the creative imagination behind many of Miss Coutt's efforts," Edgar Johnson remarks, "but their directing force and executive arm."[63] In addition to their work on behalf of the Ragged Schools, they worked together on improving living conditions for the poor, either by means of renovating slums or by clearing and redeveloping them. Dickens himself took charge of this latter work even to the extent of developing plans for anything from landscaping to the installation of sanitary facilities and running water. The project in which Dickens seems to have immersed himself the most, however, was what would become known as Urania Cottage, a private "Home for Fallen Women at Shepherd's Bush" where prostitutes were rehabilitated and prepared for emigration.

A woman who became a resident of Urania Cottage did so voluntarily and was given the responsibility for her own reclamation. Dickens writes to Miss Coutts in his initial letter regarding the Urania Cottage project, "A woman or girl coming to the asylum, it is explained to her that she has come there for useful repentance and reform, and because her past way of life has been dreadful in its nature and consequences, and full of affliction, misery, and despair to herself. Never mind society while she is at that pass. Society has used her ill and turned away from her, and she cannot be expected to take much heed of its rights or wrongs."[64] These words certainly speak to the basic approach that was to be taken in the rehabilitation of the women who would enter Urania Cottage; but they also speak rather poignantly to Dickens's understanding of human nature and his belief that the home will benefit society only as it benefits each woman and reforms her understanding first of herself and then of her place in and responsibility to society.

The first reference to "the asylum," as Dickens initially referred to Urania Cottage, is in his correspondence with Miss Coutts on 26 May 1846. The letter is quite long, which seems to indicate that Dickens gave considerable time and thought to the project. Much of Dickens's correspondence to Miss Coutts over the period of a quarter of a century is taken up to one degree or another with the subject of Urania Cottage, and it is clear from that correspondence that Dickens accepted and maintained a key role in the project. He worked out the functional and administrative organization of the home; he shopped for and made arrangements for the purchase of the structure in which it would be housed; he planned and oversaw the remodeling of the house to accommodate the project; he handpicked and recruited much of the staff to present to Coutts for her approval; and he supervised and directed the school for many years.

Almost exactly one year after the date of his first letter to Miss Coutts on the subject, Dickens wrote to her on 23 May 1847, to inform her that he had located a suitable lodging for the project, and it appears that he entered into terms for the lease of the property in June of that same year. On 26 August 1847, Dickens wrote to Coutts,

"I hope we shall be ready, very early in October, to shew you the Institution in perfect order."[65] A letter composed by Dickens on 28 October 1847 indicates that the home did not open until sometime in November of 1847.

It was important to Dickens that the institute be called a "Home," and he tells Miss Coutts so directly in his letter of 28 October. For Dickens, it was necessary that Urania Cottage be an archetypal home. That is, it would be a place of comfort, beauty, warmth, shelter, and safety—but it would also be a place that would need to be made into a home by the women residents themselves. They would learn the necessary skills and do the daily chores that would make the house a home. "In this home," Dickens writes to the residents, "which stands in a pleasant country lane and where each may have her little flower-garden if she pleases, [you] will be treated with the greatest kindness: will lead an active, cheerful, healthy life: will learn many things it is profitable and good to know, and being entirely removed from all who have any knowledge of [your] past career, will begin life afresh and be able to win a good name and character."[66] And, of course, "What they would be taught in the house, would be grounded in religion ['the system of Christianity.'[67]], most unquestionably. It must be the basis of the whole system."[68]

Angela Burdett-Coutts was a devout Christian and was probably an Anglican Evangelical, as is evidenced especially in her generous and varied support of the established church. And while her religious persuasion was not determinative of her charitable commitments, it was important to her, as it was to Dickens, that her projects be distinctly Christian in character. The Urania Cottage project was no exception. Dickens reassured her that the project would be grounded in Christian teaching. "But," he notes in a letter to her, "it is essential in dealing with this class of persons to have a system of training established, which, while it is steady and firm, is cheerful and hopeful."[69] This is likely a measured caution aimed at Miss Coutts to remind her that a strong dose of Mrs. Clennam's distorted Calvinistic religion was not what these women needed. In a later letter, Dickens writes, "I have great faith in the soundness of your opinions in reference to the religious instruction; knowing you to be full of that enlarged consideration in this case, without which nothing hopeful or useful can be done."[70]

As Dickens made preparation for the opening of Urania Cottage and the admission of its first residents, he decorated the living room with two plaques: one with an inscription from a sermon of Jeremy Taylor and one with an inscription from a sermon of Isaac Barrow. Both Taylor and Barrow were seventeenth-century Anglican churchmen whose writings were still popular and familiar in the nineteenth century. Dickens also hung a plaque with an inscription of his own regarding order, punctuality, and good temper and another displaying Jesus's teaching on duty to God and to neighbor. "In each bedroom is another Inscription," Dickens writes to Miss Coutts, "admonishing them against ever lying down to rest, without being affectionate and reconciled among themselves."[71] Dickens wrote a short welcoming note that the supervising matron read individually to each of the new residents as they arrived. He even selected and marked certain prayers in the Book of Common Prayer that the supervising matron could use temporarily. Finally, Dickens wrote an "appeal" that was read to potential residents and given to them in written form. In this "Appeal to Fallen Women," Dickens directly and firmly outlines the privileges of entering Urania Cottage and the great possibilities that are available to the residents should they pursue them. He writes of the life that each of the potential residents is currently living and the new life which could be opened up. He writes of duty, honor, accountability, responsibility, and hard work. And he cautions them, "But you must solemnly remember that if you enter this Home without such constant resolutions, you will occupy, unworthily and uselessly, the place of some other unhappy girl, now wandering and lost; and that her ruin, no less than your own, will be upon your head, before Almighty God, who knows the secrets of our breasts; and Christ, who died upon the Cross to save us."[72]

According to the extant correspondence between them, Dickens and Angela Burdett-Coutts worked together on the Urania Cottage project for at least a decade. The last letter from Dickens to Miss Coutts to make reference to Urania Cottage was written on 20 July 1857, and indicates that Dickens had made arrangements to do some physical renovation there. This reference, like so many others in their correspondence in which Dickens informs Miss Coutts of the goings-on at Shepherd's Bush, can be reasonably read to suggest that Dickens was still as involved as ever in the project and likely remained so for some time.

Some Final Considerations

Dickens's real Christianity was neither a literary device nor a pious facade. He worked tirelessly on behalf of others, according to his Christian convictions concerning the imitation of the teaching and the character of Jesus. It is no small thing that while Dickens was engaged in his various charitable endeavors, he was employed in his vocation as a novelist. In fact, between the years 1843 and 1857, Dickens wrote *Martin Chuzzlewit*, *A Christmas Carol* and four other Christmas books, *Dombey and Son*, *David Copperfield*, *Bleak House*, *Hard Times*, and *Little Dorrit*. He established the *Daily News* and began his weekly journal, *Household Words*. He did all of this while working relentlessly for the Ragged Schools and for Urania Cottage (and other of Miss Coutts's charitable endeavors); providing support and financial assistance to the Elton orphans, the Overs family, and Bertha White;[73] supporting Mrs. Caroline Chisholm's Family Colonization Loan Society;[74] speaking and writing on behalf of the Metropolitan Sanitary Association and sanitary reform; and speaking on behalf of and supporting hospitals, athenaeums, and mechanics institutes.[75] These, of course, are the things we know about. Other involvements of his have certainly gone unrecorded.

The point here is not to suggest that real Christianity was to be demonstrated in busy-ness. Nor is it to suggest that Dickens's example is a model or pattern to be adopted by everyone. Rather, the point is to indicate that Dickens made time to serve others and to give himself freely to the needs of others, even in the midst of a schedule such as his. Dickens's purpose was not simply to stay busy. His purpose was to rise up to the teaching of Jesus and to imitate his example. Clearly Dickens's idea of real Christianity was not mere rhetoric.

Dickens was convinced that such a practice of Christianity was born out of character and heart. It was not mere moral striving that sought to perform good works. In thinking of the life of faith, Dickens began with Jesus—his person, his character, his motivation. That is where the imitation of Jesus was grounded and from where it proceeded. For Dickens, it was really that simple. And to whatever end such an attitude and approach might lead did not much matter. For whatever the end, it would be indubitably "real Christianity."

6

Dickens and the Church

Dickens's relationship with the church is both provocative and instructive. Certainly some would maintain that Dickens had no relationship with the church, other than that of being its enemy. On the surface, that appears to be a fair claim. But things are never as simple with Dickens as they may first appear, especially when it comes to something so charged as Christian thought in the early to mid-Victorian age. Granted, Dickens was often scathing in his criticism of the church and churchmen, but his always sounded like the voice of reform from within the church rather than dissent from without. A positive and affirming approach to concerns and shortcomings is, it seems, today's conventional wisdom, at least in the church. That was not Dickens's approach. He faced what he perceived as shortcomings in the church head-on, challenging the church and calling for careful attention and resolute correctives to lingering problems. Dickens goaded, chastised, lampooned, and chided the church in the hope that it might become a community of true disciples—that is, single-minded followers and imitators of Jesus. This aspect of Dickens's faith is extremely instructive for those who are willing to listen to and interact with him.

Growing up, Dickens, much like other Victorians, did not have a home life that was particularly religious. Dickens's parents were Anglicans, but certainly of the disengaged, popular-lay stripe; that is, they were not overly concerned with regular attendance or any sort of religious observances. His sister Fanny would recollect later in her life, "I was brought up in the Established Church but, I regret to say, without any serious ideas of religion. I attended Divine worship as a duty, not as a high privilege."[1] Because it was convenient, the family attended a Nonconformist Baptist chapel near their home when Dickens was just a youth, an experience he remembered as being less than pleasant. Perhaps his distaste for Evangelicalism of the dissenting sort developed from his earlier experience; or maybe his later opinions colored his recollections. Likely, this aversion to Evangelicalism is a complex combination of any number of social, religious and personal factors. In any event, it is the Evangelical, the Nonconformist, the Dissenter who typically takes it on the chin in Dickens's work.

That he received some sort of religious training, however, is likely. His first real educational experience came in the school of the Oxford-educated Mr. William Giles, whose father was the Reverend William Giles, the minister at the chapel the Dickens family attended. While Dickens had less than fond memories of sitting in chapel under the senior Giles, his schooling under Mr. William Giles appears to have been one of the rare highlights of his early childhood. It is certainly likely, under the circumstances, that there would have been a religious component to his lessons and education. At any rate, it seems clear that whatever experiences may have contributed to his spiritual formation, Dickens developed a conspicuously Christian worldview and passionate vision for the life of faith in his formative years, one that continued to mature as he grew older.

Dickens in the Nineteenth-Century English Religious Landscape

Dickens seems to have been hardly affected at all by what historians typically call the Victorian crisis of faith. In fact, it seems that Dickens's faith remained notably settled and consistent throughout his entire life. In spite of his brief flirtation with Unitarianism in the early 1840s, Dickens remained within the fold of popular lay Anglicanism. Dickens biographer John Forster notes that Dickens did, indeed, "take sittings" in the Little Portland Street Unitarian chapel but "after two or three years" stopped attending. Forster remarks further, "Upon essential points he had never any sympathy so strong as with the leading doctrines of the Church of England; to these, as time went on, he found himself able to accommodate all minor differences."[2] Forster adds that Dickens's "unswerving faith in Christianity itself, apart from sects and schisms . . . had never failed him at any period in his life."[3]

Still, Dickens's faith developed and was established at a time when traditional thought in so many disciplines was being reimagined and redefined in Great Britain. Religious thought was not immune to such trends, of course, and Victorians had many options available to them in terms of religion. The Anglican Church consisted of three parties: High Church, Low Church, and Broad Church. Those of a more conservative and traditional Anglican persuasion would have found a comfortable place in the High Church party. Those Anglicans leaning toward or embracing the Evangelical religion of the heart would have been labeled Low Church. The Broad Church category—not a party at all in the same sense as the High Church and Low Church parties—tended to draw the enlightened academic and those of a similar mind, who demanded broader doctrinal and ecclesial horizons. Outside the establishment were the Evangelicals, Methodists, Baptists, and other Dissenters and Nonconformists. Further outside the fold of mainstream religious thought were the Unitarians.

There were also those who were intent upon recasting Christianity for contemporary life. To them, Christianity as it was understood and practiced in the church had become outdated. That is, it was old and primitive and was becoming obsolete. The solution for this group was to reinterpret Christianity and bring it up-to-date for a new humanity in a new and progressive age. This notion and concern would eventually be taken up and articulated by some Broad Churchman and in *Essays and Reviews*. Still, others insisted that Christianity had become used up. Christianity needed much more than simply reinterpretation and updating: it needed to be dismantled and resurrected in a new secular form preserving its moral core and discarding its supernatural husk. Just such an idea materialized in the 1830s and 1840s in the Religion of Humanity. Driven by August Comte's Positivism and an insipient religious humanism, the Religion of Humanity offered options outside the boundaries of even the broadest Christian thinking.

It is against just such a religious landscape, then, that Dickens's Christian convictions and worldview developed. In the 1840s, when Dickens's Christian thought was becoming solidly established and settled—more mature—the established church was becoming unsettled and struggling for stability. The High Church party was experiencing its own internal upheaval as the Tractarians were challenging a more orthodox Anglicanism with Anglo-Catholicism. Anglican Evangelicals had become complacent in their position and the successes achieved by an earlier generation. They seemed quite satisfied to maintain their current status. Dickens was convinced, and rightfully so, that the two parties, together comprising the church, had become preoccupied with themselves as an institution and spent the better part of their time and energy in squabbles over polity and doctrine. Concurrently, the Broad Church was attempting to take advantage of these unsettled circumstances to establish its voice and make inroads into the mainstream.

The exercise of attempting to situate Dickens within such a diverse religious landscape, one in which the lines of distinction were often blurred, will not render precise results in terms of identifying him with a particular party or even placing him comfortably within the overlaps. In the end, the attempt to pigeonhole Dickens in this manner is not what really matters anyway. Because of what it can reveal along the way about Dickens and his relationship to the church, however, the exercise will prove to be a worthwhile and productive one.

Charles Dickens: The Reluctant Layperson

Dickens's sometimes ferocious criticism of the church naturally raised eyebrows in the nineteenth century just as it does today. In fact, it is often Dickens's scathing criticism by itself that understandably gives many the impression that he wanted no part of the church.

One particularly noteworthy example of Dickens's criticism is his 1843 article in the *Examiner* entitled, "Report of the Commissioners Appointed to Inquire into the Condition of Persons Variously Engaged in the University of Oxford."[4] The University of Oxford, Dickens points out in the article, is an institution "established for the Manufacture of Clergymen." His "report," then, is the result of his "inquiry" into such "manufacture," its "findings" highlighting the "Prevailing Ignorance" at the university. Dickens reports, among other findings: "A vast number of witnesses being interrogated as to what they understood by the words Religion and Salvation, answered Lighted Candles. Some said water; some, bread; others, Little boys; others mixed the water, lighted candles, bread and little boys up together, and called the compound, Faith." His report continues with the observation that, even though one particular schoolboy in Derbyshire was not able to spell "'Church' . . . there was no doubt that the persons employed in the University of Oxford can all spell Church with great readiness, and, indeed, very seldom spell anything else."[5]

Of course, Dickens's criticism was not reserved only for High Church Anglicans. Evangelicals, especially of the dissenting or nonconformist sort, were the most frequent targets of his censure and caricatures. Reverend Chadband in *Bleak House* is the typical Dickensian caricature of the Evangelical preacher—self-important, smug, and quite insensible to any genuine Christian feeling or teaching. After a pretentious reproach by Chadband directed toward Jo, the street sweeper—not, of course, for Jo's benefit, but to impress those who were within earshot—Jo is left thinking of himself as an "unimprovable reprobate" who "won't never know nothink." Afterwards, in a penetrating indictment of Chadband and his distorted version of Christianity, Dickens writes, in a remarkable editorial aside: "It may be, Jo, that there is a history so interesting and affecting even to minds as near the brutes as thine, recording deeds done on this earth for common men, that if the Chadbands, removing their own persons from the light, would but show it thee in simple reverence, would but leave it unimproved, would but regard it as being eloquent enough without their modest aid—it might hold thee awake, and thou might learn from it yet!"[6]

The idea expressed in this observation is one that recurs in Dickens: that of the garrulous preacher who loves to hear himself preach and is always ready to point a condemning finger, but who, in reality, stands in the way of the truth of the New Testament and renders inaudible the words of Jesus. In Dickens's mind, these imposters are far from bringers of good news; nor are they persons who can simply be ignored, for they are pretenders who have a negative impact on those who hear them and are liable to cause much damage and harm. They are the Stigginses, the Clennams, the Pecksniffs, the Jellybys, the Pardiggles. In Dickens's mind, they are dangerous and he takes it upon himself to expose them.

Perhaps one of Dickens's clearest and most direct comments on his perception of and antipathy for Evangelicalism and Dissent occurs in the preface to the 1867 edition of *The Pickwick Papers*. His comments are intended to provide clarity to those who were offended by and critical of his Pickwickian satire on Christian themes. And yet, as is obvious, there is no apology or retraction here. In fact, there is really only a staunch reiteration of those convictions he held at the time he wrote *The Pickwick Papers* in 1836:

> Lest there should be any well-intentioned persons who do not perceive the difference . . . between religion and the cant of religion, piety and the pretence of piety, a humble reverence for the great truths of Scripture and an audacious and offensive obtrusion of its letter and not its spirit in the commonest dissensions and meanest affairs of life, to the extraordinary confusion of ignorant minds, let them understand that it is always the latter, and never the former, which is satirized here. Further, that the latter is here satirized as being, according to all experience, inconsistent with the former, impossible of union with it, and one of the most evil and mischievous falsehoods existent in society—whether it establish its headquarters, for the time being, in Exeter Hall, or Ebenezer Chapel, or both. It may appear unnecessary to offer a word of observation on so plain a head. But it is never out of season to protest against that coarse familiarity with sacred things which is busy on the lip, and idle in the heart; or against the confounding of Christianity with any class of persons who, in the words of Swift, have just enough religion to make them hate, and not enough to make them love, one another.[7]

This is as bold and clear a statement as Dickens makes, apart from his satire, about the reasons for his distaste for Evangelicalism and

Dissent, at least as he perceived them. What may give the statement an even greater significance is that it connects the religious sentiments Dickens held earlier in his life to those he apparently continued to hold in his later life. This preface was written in 1867, three years before his death, when he was fifty-five years old, concerning material in a book, *The Pickwick Papers*, he wrote in 1836 when he was in his early twenties. In other words, Dickens's convictions about such "course familiarity with sacred things" remained essentially unchanged throughout his lifetime.

In light of material of this sort, it is certainly understandable why some see Dickens as a Christian outsider, if not an outright enemy of Christianity. Such a conclusion seems all but confirmed by his correspondence with friends Albany Fonblanque and Cornelius Felton. In an 1843 letter to Fonblanque, Dickens openly discusses his frustration with the High Church party and does not withhold provocative comment: "I find I am getting horribly bitter about Puseyism. Good God to talk in these times of most untimely ignorance among the people, about what Priests shall wear, and whither they shall turn when they say their prayers.—They had best not discuss the latter question too long, or I shrewdly suspect they will turn to the right about: not easily to come back again."[8] As Dickens saw things, the established church had become totally out of touch with its people and oblivious to its mission. The church's preoccupation with its own ecclesial minutiae in the face of what he saw as dire social conditions—conditions the church should be addressing and actively attempting to alleviate—raised Dickens's ire to extreme levels.

Ire raised, Dickens had written similarly to his American friend Felton on 2 March of the same year: "Disgusted with our Established Church, and its Puseyisms, and daily outrages on common sense and humanity, I have carried into effect an old idea of mine, and joined the Unitarians, who would do something for human improvement if they could; and who practice Charity and Toleration."[9] Not only is this another disenchanted criticism of the church, it also includes the clear declaration by Dickens that he had "joined the Unitarians." For so many, this is the clear and final evidence of Dickens's religious persuasion and renders any further discussion of his Christianity moot. Dickens was a Unitarian. He said so.

While such a conclusion, without question, appears reasonable and is understandable, I do not believe it is accurate. I argue in greater detail elsewhere against the notion that Dickens was ever a Unitarian by creed or any serious faith or doctrinal connection,[10] but a few pertinent points should be made here. The fact is, there is no compelling evidence to suggest that Dickens became a Unitarian. And to maintain that his involvement with Unitarianism was more than a "flirtation" (to borrow Noel Peyrouton's description)—little more than a tantrum—is difficult to sustain. Indeed, his attraction to Unitarianism seemed to depend more upon his admiration for the American Unitarian William Ellery Channing, whom he had met on his first visit to America, and his relationship to the Unitarian clergyman, the Reverend Edward Tagart, than upon Unitarianism as a system of theistic belief. Surely, that the Unitarians "practiced Charity and Toleration" held great attraction for him, but just what exactly Dickens meant when he said he had "joined the Unitarians" is never explained or played out in any conspicuous or practical way. In the end, no substantial evidence challenging the veracity and accuracy of Forster's remarks about Dickens and Unitarianism (see above) has been brought forward.

Dickens and the Broad Church[11]

Still, Dickens's relationship to the church was a tenuous one at best, and because his views have been branded as reflecting a broad Christianity, or the broadest Christian thought, Dickens is often identified with a more liberal strain of Christianity. As a result, Dickens is sometimes associated (wrongly, I believe) with Broad Church Anglicanism.

As I have already suggested, the Broad Church party was largely a movement within the academy. By and large, its impact at the popular level in Dickens's day was negligible. The Broad Church movement was advanced by a relatively small group of academics and others of quite diverse backgrounds, interests, and theological persuasions. For instance, Samuel Taylor Coleridge, often considered one of the pioneers of the Broad Church movement, stood alongside of Richard Whately, both as Broad Churchmen. Thomas Arnold, also recognized as one of the fathers of the Broad Church movement, shared a place in the Broad Church with the likes of Benjamin

Jowett and F. D. Maurice. Each of these men was distinct in how he thought about the church, about the Bible, and about doctrine. But they were all considered Broad Churchmen.

In October of 1853, W. J. Conybeare wrote his important and influential article in the *Edinburgh Review* entitled "Church Parties." Conybeare wrote that the Broad Church movement was still not considered a recognized church party: "Those whom we now describe [the Broad Church movement] have so little organization or mutual concert of any kind that they can scarcely be called a party at all."[12] Margaret Crowther, in her *Church Embattled*, refers to the Broad Church not as a party but as "a restless and critical attitude of mind." She maintains that the Broad Church was composed of a group brought together more by their common ability as individuals to incite controversy and opposition than by any shared ideas or vision.[13] The Broad Church, then, offered very little by way of group identity or doctrinal solidarity. Consequently, to situate Dickens—or anyone else, for that matter—in the Broad Church movement, in reality, says very little about him.

Nevertheless, at first glance, situating Dickens within the Broad Church movement seems sound and reasonable. In fact, there are a number of critics and scholars who classify Dickens as a Broad Churchman. But Dickens's affinity with the Broad Church is actually rather superficial. First, and significantly, Dickens was not critically engaged or intellectually invested in the biblical and theological issues that captivated the Broad Churchmen.[14] He certainly seems to have understood many of the issues, but where such concerns did not touch the practical course of Christian living or did not come to bear directly upon the life of faith, he had little use for them and was convinced that they were of little or no import to the Christian or to the church.

Second, while Dickens appears to have been sympathetic to some of the fundamental ideas of Broad Churchmen, his interests and his leanings were actually quite different. Like most Broad Churchmen, Dickens was certainly in favor of the church easing doctrinal restrictions and qualifications for clergy, for instance, but he showed no real interest in or even knowledge of the broader notions of "comprehension," a major tenet of the Broad Church movement.[15] Again, Dickens's clear preference for the New Testament over the Old Testament appears to be a point of contact with the Broad Church movement, but in the end, his concern was not a historical-critical one as with Broad Churchmen; rather, it was more a pastoral-functional one. That is, Dickens seems to have been unconcerned with the historical, textual, or compositional components of the Old Testament. His concern almost always seems to be with the "injudicious use" of the Old Testament in Christian teaching and moral instruction.

Finally, Dickens, like Broad Churchmen, was a progressive thinker in some respects. Yet, when it concerned the Bible and things biblical, Dickens was prone to see things through traditional lenses and then accommodate more progressive ideas to a more traditional view. This is, in fact, just how Dickens came to terms with the impact of the new science on a biblical cosmogony (see chapter 3). And his composition of *TLOL* as a harmony of the Gospels speaks loudly of his view of the Gospels as reliable historical documents, a rather traditional view that many Broad Churchmen would be unwilling to accept.

The more his religious views and practices are scrutinized, then, the more Dickens begins to resemble the typical Anglican that Francis Knight has described (see chapter 1). The Christian themes that occupied Dickens's thinking and the religious ideas about which he seems to have held the most definite opinions—the ideas and themes he developed most elaborately in his work—reflect those core beliefs that Knight describes. Even his more progressive, allegedly inconsistent, and sometimes seemingly improvised views would not have been unusual for a mid-nineteenth-century Anglican layperson. So, while it is a common inclination for some to situate Dickens in Broad Church Anglicanism or to insist that Dickens eventually gave up on the establishment and became a Unitarian, it seems more likely that "upon essential points he had never any sympathy so strong as with the leading doctrines of the Church of England; to these, as time went on, he found himself able to accommodate all minor differences," as Forster notes, and so, was able to find a tolerable place within the boundaries of a popular lay Anglicanism.[16]

Dickens and Religion

It is from the perspective of this simple, popular lay-Anglican faith that Dickens approached and criticized the church. But Dickens did not criticize the church simply because it was church; in fact, Dickens criticized the church because it was *not* the church—not it, at least, as he understood "church" in light of its New Testament description. Without question, Dickens did stand aloof from the church, but as far as we know, he never advocated disestablishment, nor was he ready to abandon the church altogether.

Dickens wanted the church to be what it was intended to be. And it was certainly not in his mind simply the bastion of dogma, an outlet for the distribution of the sacraments, or a dispensary where one might receive a dose of religion. Instead, the church was to be a community of committed disciples of Jesus, and thus an agency of social change and cultural transformation. For Dickens, the institutional rigmarole was superfluous and deadening. All that really mattered was that the church take seriously its call by God and the claim of Jesus upon it.

George Orwell's following observation about Dickens, then, makes sense: "He was essentially a Bible-Christian, as he took care to make plain when writing his will. In any case, he cannot properly be described as a religious man. He 'believed,' undoubtedly, but religion in the devotional sense does not seem to have entered much into his thoughts."[17] Orwell was right. Dickens was not a religious man and likely would have cringed at the designation being applied to him. Indeed, Dickens seems to have been deliberate in avoiding anything that could smack of cant or conspicuous religiosity. Religion suggested false piety and paraded spirituality. Those whom Dickens criticized were "religious." Unquestionably, the description was not one to which Dickens would have aspired or laid claim.

For Dickens, his "real Christianity" was not religion (or religious). It was, in fact, the opposite of religion. Dickens's real Christianity, as we have seen, was a faith lived out in service to others, and if the church was to be anything, it was to be the guardian and facilitator of that simple fact. As far as Dickens could see, the church was not actively and conspicuously engaged in such an endeavor. In fact, pursuing such a course was not even on the church's agenda. Dickens, therefore, employed all the tools and talents at his disposal to get the church's attention, hopeful that it might awaken and right itself. But he also hoped, through his satire, parody, and caricature, to awaken the Christian conscience, so that even if the institution failed to rise to the occasion, individual Christians might succeed in its place. And, of course, as was demonstrated in the previous chapter, Dickens was more than ready to lead the way. Forster touches on this, to some degree, in his comments on Dickens's purpose in his second Christmas Book, *The Chimes* (1844): "He was to try to convert Society, as he had converted Scrooge, by showing that its happiness rested on the same foundations as those of the individual, which are mercy and charity not less than justice. . . . In varying forms this ambition was in all his life."[18]

By 1864 Dickens was still anxious for the church and its lack of any sign of "real Christianity" within it, and he complained of its lack of fortitude and resolve to be what God intended it to be. He laments to Cerjat (25 October) of the "indecent squabbles" and infighting in the church and that Jesus himself is being more or less ignored. Moreover, he muses, "How our sublime and so-different Christian religion is to be administered in the future I cannot pretend to say, but that the Church's hand is at its own throat I am fully convinced." Finally, in an almost prophetic declaration, he closes his comments on the church to Cerjat: "The Church that is to have its part in the coming time must be a more Christian one, with less arbitrary pretensions and a stronger hold upon the mantle of our Saviour, as He walked and talked upon this earth."[19] In a very real sense, this, at once, sums up Dickens's concerns for the church and provides his basic principle for the realization of its calling.

Dickens Speaks to the Church

It seems to me that Dickens has quite a bit to say to the church today, for many of his fundamental concerns provide healthy reminders to us of what the church should look like and what it must be. As in each of the previous sections in which we have considered what Dickens might have to say to Christians today, I'm not sure he tells us anything new. Nonetheless, his powers of observation and his knack of turning a phrase deliver his reminders in a fresh and engaging manner. And because Dickens was a Christian and because what he wrote was rooted deeply in an uncompromising Christian worldview and in his passionate convictions, we would be wise to read Dickens alert to what he might teach us about the church. While there are quite a few things we could observe here, I would like to suggest five reminders from Dickens to the church.

Keep a Critical Eye on Yourself and Your Teaching

First, and perhaps most obvious, is his reminder to us, the church, to keep a critical eye on ourselves. That means being ready to call ourselves, as the church, on our complacency, our self-preoccupation, our tendency toward maintaining the status quo, and whatever other maladies might beset us. It means being ready to challenge ourselves as the church when we fail to live up to our sacred calling. And while this is certainly necessary on the global level, it is absolutely imperative that it happens on the local level and on a regular basis. The apostle Paul told Timothy, "Pay close attention to yourself and your teaching" (1 Tim. 4:16), which J. B. Phillips translates: "Keep a critical eye both upon your own life and on the teaching you give." Paul was speaking to Timothy as an individual, certainly, but he was speaking to him also as a pastor. Surely, by extension, the fundamental principle applies to the church as well.

It matters, then, that the church is constantly and consistently being assessed both by those who form it and by those who lead it. This is not a call for criticism that is reckless or divisive. But it is a call for a bold approach that seeks the good of the church. Some, of course, would say that Dickens's criticism of the church *was* reckless and divisive; that it was criticism for the sake of criticism. In fact, Dickens's criticism of the church grew out of his passionate convictions concerning the role of the church in the England in which he lived, and those convictions were born of his reflection on the life and teaching of Jesus.

Dickens's praise for the Unitarians as those who "would do something for human improvement if they could; and who practice Charity and Toleration" revealed, at least in part, his understanding of what the role of the church is to be in the world. The church must be a body of Christ followers who are ready to serve others and be the love of Christ in the places where God situates them. Dickens is not trying to argue here that social action makes one a Christian or that social action is the only thing the church is to be about. Rather, he is arguing that those who are Christians will involve themselves in social action. His criticism, then, is directed toward the church's failure to be and do according to its calling.

There are some who would say that the church should not be criticized. They are not averse to what they term as constructive suggestion; but criticism, they claim, is destructive and unhelpful. They are the ones who might support the idea of a suggestion box being placed in the foyer. Dickens, of course, would want a criticism box at every exit from the sanctuary. Suggestions are fine, but suggestions are usually the proposal of an idea or simply an idea itself. Criticism gets directly at the problem and identifies it in order to realize an informed solution. Sometimes a criticism is nothing more than a complaint or grumbling, and complaints are certainly unhelpful, if not destructive. The church doesn't need complaints or complainers (grumblers), but it needs more than suggestions. It often needs criticism.

A consideration of Jesus's criticisms of the religious establishment is enormously instructive in this regard. Jesus certainly never hesitated to level criticism at the religious leaders of his day or the religious establishment. Our failure to learn some important lessons from these challenges by Jesus stems from the fact that we fail to recognize that the Pharisees were the conservative Evangelicals of their day. They are us. Even more importantly, when we seek to arrive at some understanding of Jesus's criticism of them, we will miss the important lessons if we believe that every criticism of Jesus against the Pharisees was a severe rebuke toward a group of impostors and deceivers. Without question, Jesus used strong words in many of his confrontations with the religious leaders. Think of the woes pronounced on the Pharisees in Matthew 22. But it is hard to imagine that our Lord did not criticize so that the minds of the religious leaders might be changed, that there would be repentance, and that they might get it right.

When Jesus called the Pharisees and religious leaders hypocrites, he was calling them play-actors. That is, he was maintaining that they were just going through the motions in their religion. So often, we take that as an epithet and as strong words of reprimand to those who were trying to deliberately deceive others. That the religious leaders were on the whole deceivers and impostors seems unlikely. Considering what we know about the Pharisees in the time of Jesus and their relationship to the people of the land, it seems more likely that they were not aware that they were play-actors, just going through the motions. They believed that they, in fact, had it right. If we allow this perspective to inform our understanding, it begins to look as though Jesus was trying to help them see that they were just going through the motions; that they had gotten it all very wrong and very mixed up, and that he was hopeful they might be brought back and righted.

The point here is twofold. First, Jesus never hesitated to be critical. Sometimes Jesus's criticisms were deservedly scathing; other times they were necessarily careful. But they were more often corrective than not. And that is the second point: criticism does not need to be seen or understood as destructive or unhealthy. Dickens's criticism of the church seemed negative; it is difficult for criticism not to be negative to some degree. But it tended to be spot on. Dickens was never trying to be destructive with his criticism. Indeed, he was attempting to rouse the church to its senses so that it might be what God intended it to be. In the end, Dickens's criticism would prove positive and constructive. And where the church ignored it, it did so to its own hurt.

Focus

A second reminder that Dickens provides for the church emerges directly from his criticism of it. That is, Dickens reminds us to keep the peripherals on the periphery and keep the focus on what the church is to be about. This involves, first, establishing and maintaining a sharp focus on who and what the church is to be and then, second, having a firm grasp on the mission and role of the church in the community in which God has placed it. Again, this is to be a central concern of the church on the global level, but it must be of necessity a priority especially on the local level as well.

If the church is going to establish a clear focus, of first importance is the recognition that it is the body of Christ of which he is the head. And while Dickens likely would not have couched it in these particular terms, he firmly grasped that Jesus must be at the center of this enterprise called the church—or it is not the church—and that all ministries, programs, and workings of the church are vitally connected to Jesus. This reality provides the definitive and fundamental focus of the church. That is, this is where everything that the church is and does begins and ends. Jesus is at the center and must remain there always. He is the Head of the church, he is Exemplar for the church, he is Creator and Sustainer in the church, he is Lord, he is Saviour; the church's identity is derived from Christ, as is the meaning and substance of its ministry. Most everything else about the church can and will change. But the centrality of Jesus can never change without distorting and rendering powerless the entire organism.

It becomes imperative, then, that the church remains alert to this centrality of Jesus. This is especially important to the local church. Pushing Jesus to the periphery can happen rather easily in the concern to meet needs with various ministries and the pressure to create attractive and meaningful programs. It is unlikely that it ever happens intentionally—but it can happen if we lose focus. How does it happen that a program emphasizing Bible study or discipleship pushes Jesus to the periphery? Are not these programs Christ-centered and Christ-oriented? Or how does it happen that a ministry that serves the social needs of the community pushes Jesus to the periphery? Aren't such programs developed to provide opportunity to imitate Jesus and to serve others in Jesus's name? Of course they are. But such very excellent and necessary programs and ministries as these can become simply programs and ministries, inadvertently losing connection with the Head and pushing Jesus from the center.

A program that emphasizes Bible study can easily become a largely intellectual pursuit or an exercise in bibliolatry and, then, just as easily, an end in itself. No longer is it a means by which we encounter the living Christ and build a substantial relationship with him. When this happens, Jesus has already been moved to the periphery. Unless we deliberately and intentionally maintain the centrality of Jesus in such programs, such subtle drift can easily occur. A social outreach program can easily become a self-congratulatory effort in good works and a scoring of points with God if it is not an expression of the love and service of Christ. And, again, becoming an end in itself rather than the conduit of Jesus's love and compassion, it has pushed Jesus to the periphery already. Such missteps as these rarely, if ever, happen intentionally, but without deliberately recognizing the centrality of Jesus as Head of the church, his body, they happen more than we might like to admit. The church, leadership and laity, share the responsibility here and must be deliberately vigilant in this concern. The health of any church depends on this single-minded recognition.

From this focus on the centrality of Jesus and the determination to keep peripheral things on the periphery, a second necessity that will help us keep a clear focus follows: it is essential that the local church know what it is to be about in the community in which God has placed it. This isn't simply about being a church in the community. It is about how, precisely, our church will be the church in the community in which God has placed and called us. An instructive parallel is provided by considering the events that gave rise to "the law of the situation." In 1904 Mary Parker Follet, the first management consultant in America, coined this phrase, which was identified in the answer to the question, "What business are we *really* in?" Follett was consulting with a window blind manufacturer and helped the leadership of the company understand that they were not simply in the window blind business but that they were really in the lighting control business.[20] That simple question and its answer had a dramatic impact on the future of that company and its survival. And every church and its leadership must continually pose just such a question to clarify what it is to be about and keep the peripherals on the periphery.

Operating according to just such a principle can help pastors avoid the myth that there is a single model upon which all churches can be built. There is not. The local church—any local church—must consider its location, its community, its time, and its people and develop and continually adapt its ministry accordingly. While it may not sit well with our twenty-first century corporate mind-set, the example we see in the early church was not a particularly proactive one. In fact, the church seems to have been rather reactive. That is, the church and its people reacted to the needs of the community in its time and place. Just so, the local church can benefit from such an example today as it identifies needs, meets needs, and adapts its service to meet the changing needs of the community.

For instance, the ministry of a church in, say, a semi-rural setting in South Bend, Indiana is not going to provide a functional model for a church on the northeast side of Akron, Ohio—except by some odd coincidence. Because these communities are unique, each church will have to learn for itself what it is to be about in its respective community. Once the church has learned to be and do what God has called it to, it then can go about being and doing that. Everything—from worship to programming, from philosophy of ministry to management of facilities, from organizational structure to missional strategy—is to be determined by the clearly defined notion of what God has called the church to be and do in its community, in its time, and with its people.

Again, it is quite unlikely that Dickens would have couched his ideas in any of the language or concepts that I have articulated here. Nevertheless, his concern for being the church as God intended it to be, maintaining a sharp and clear focus, and keeping the peripherals on the periphery is an important reminder for the church today.

Minister to the Other

Dickens's criticism of the church often spoke to the fact that it was an institution that had become preoccupied with itself. Not only had it apparently abandoned its calling to an outward focus of serving others but it also had lost touch with its people. A portion of his article in the *Examiner*, "Report of the Commissioners Appointed to Inquire into the Condition of Persons Variously Engaged in the University of Oxford" (cited above) was given to this subject. And Dickens's letter to Fonblanque (cited above) hints in the same direction: "Good God to talk in these times of most untimely ignorance among the people, about what Priests shall wear, and whither they shall turn when they say their prayers."

A third reminder that Dickens provides, then, concerns being alert to the malady of the ingrown church. Many churches today, both large and small, find that much of their energy, human resources, and facilities are being utilized just to make church happen. Once more, this is seldom done by strategy or by plan. It just happens. And before anyone is even aware of it, the church has become ingrown—that is, all of its resources are being used up just to perpetuate itself. Years ago, I heard Dr. Anthony Campolo relate the story of an oil refinery that was being touted as the example of cutting-edge technology, engineering, and aesthetics. It was a facility that was years ahead of its time and would be the standard for evaluating such facilities for years to come. When the refinery was up and running, the first group to tour it was awestruck. It was more magnificent than the hype that had surrounded it. Toward the end of the tour, one of the guests, anticipating more wonder, asked if the group would be touring the shipping department. The tour guide, who happened to be the plant manager, composed and confident, responded without missing a beat: "There is no shipping department. Everything that we produce here goes back into the facility to keep it running."

As is regularly the case with Campolo's illustrations, this one is brilliant, and it captures the idea of the ingrown church perfectly. The church does not exist simply to keep itself running. Its energies, its efforts, and its resources are to be spent on ministering to others and to the Other. Without a doubt, the church must be conscientious in keeping itself and its people spiritually fit; but that is never to be an end in itself. The worship, the teaching, the discipleship, the spiritual disciplines, the pursuit of holiness—all of these things are necessary and important, but only to the end that they make the church effective as salt and light. The German theologians of an earlier generation used to emphasize the fact that Jesus didn't say *become* the salt of the earth and the light of the world; he said we *are* the salt of the earth and the light of the world. So *be* that.

That means going outside the church and being what we are outside the church. However one might see the church and perceive its functions, its focus in all of its ministry is to be outward. Even the equipping of the saints ultimately has an outward focus. And as pastors, teachers, and leaders, we have a responsibility to free those whom God has placed under our pastoral care from an unhealthy dependence on the church. That is, we enable and empower them to be salt and light in their worlds; we equip them to stand in God's grace in their homes, schools, and places of work; we bolster them to move out to serve in the mundane events and situations of their lives; and then we entrust them to the Spirit of God to be and do all of that.

It doesn't take a futurist to know that the church that will lead the way in the coming days will be the church that understands that its energy and efforts must be spent outside the walls of the church. For this is nothing new; it has always been the case. Dickens understood this and he provides us some excellent reminders in his work that the church must embrace an uncompromising outward focus while guarding itself carefully against becoming ingrown.

Playing Church or Being the Church?

A fourth reminder that Dickens offers concerns an idea that he introduced in his 1867 preface to *The Pickwick Papers* (see above). In speaking of "the difference . . . between religion and the cant of religion, piety and the pretence of piety," Dickens clarified earlier allusions to "obtrusive professions of and tradings in religion" and "mere professions of religion" in letters to Davies (1856) and Macrae (1861), respectively. In each case, Dickens was distinguishing between genuine devotion in an authentic expression of Christianity and the superficial religiosity of pseudo-spirituality. In other words, Dickens reminds us that there is an important difference between religiosity and the life of faith; between playing church and being the church.

If we take our cue from these quotes from Dickens, we will begin to get an idea of what I will refer to as religion or religiosity—what Dickens was describing with his phrases "the cant of religion," "mere professions of religion," and "tradings in religion." As I pointed out above, religion suggests false piety and paraded spirituality. It is characterized by words without supporting actions and behaviors; it smacks more of showmanship than of humble selflessness; it deceives its subjects by convincing them to think more highly of themselves than they should; it focuses on the letter of the law rather than its spirit but quite often aspires to neither. In a word, religion is pretense. Religion is deadly and deadening. And Dickens reminds us to be alert to the danger of religion and religiosity in order that we are being the church—not just playing church.

Religion prefers to emphasize and embrace the externals. It relishes the ritual and the observance without concern for the substance of those things. It takes great care with the facade of Christianity and little notice of the essential core. Dickens saw this clearly and precisely, and he writes about it in his "Report of the Commissioners Appointed to Inquire into the Condition of Persons Variously Engaged in the University of Oxford" when he suggests that High

Churchmen are being trained to define salvation and religion in terms of bread, water, lighted candles, or altar boys, and end up defining faith by mixing all four. Dickens's "Report" also finds that those persons variously engaged at Oxford invest singular importance in the color of the clerical gown, the posture assumed in prayer, and the direction the priest should face in prayer.

Dickens's point, of course, is that the externals take on such a significant and central role in religion and religiosity that, in the end, they alone become the substance and the meaning of religion. In this way, then, religion produces churchianity—the mere playing of church rather than being the church. And so Dickens refers to "mere professions" because that is all churchianity is; or he speaks of "tradings in religion" because churchianity uses the facade of Christianity to whatever expedient serves its end at the moment. In either case, churchianity is, at once, a misconstruction and a deception of what the church should be and what real Christianity looks like.

Those who practice churchianity today, once more, often practice it inadvertently. They do so primarily because they are unaware of the meaning of genuine Christianity and the life of faith. Or they choose to busy themselves with the work, programs, and function of the church, leaving little time or emotional energy for nurturing an intimate relationship with Jesus. Either way, a relationship with the church substitutes for an experiential relationship with Christ. Unfortunately, in our rush to compete with activities of the world and other churches, to establish programs to reach the desires of our congregants, and to be relevant, we in church leadership often provide enough distractions to keep our people comfortably engaged in churchianity without ever having to consider its substance or value—or its difference from genuine Christianity.

Dickens recognized "playing church" as the misconstruction and the deception that it is and put the full force of his voice and his pen behind warning people of its dangers. We would be wise to hear Dickens on this and to heed the reminders he provides.

And Now a Word to the Preacher

The fifth reminder that Dickens provides comes by way of advice to pastors, teachers, and leaders in the church. As we have seen, when it came to the Scriptures, Dickens rooted his understanding of Christianity and the life of faith firmly in the New Testament. And within the New Testament, he emphasized the Gospels, although he would not have advocated dispensing with the rest of the New Testament by any means. We've also established that at the core of Dickens's "real Christianity" was the life and teaching of Jesus. It's no surprise, then, that he refers to the story of Jesus as it comes to us in the Gospels as "a most affecting history," and, "a blessed history." For Dickens, this story constituted the core and the essence of the message of the preacher. As a result, Dickens's advice to pastors, teachers, and leaders is to get out of the way and simply tell that story.

Earlier in this chapter, I introduced the Reverend Chadband, Dickens's caricature of the nonconformist or Evangelical lay preacher. And you will recall Dickens's editorial rebuke of Chadband for having dressed down Jo in the particular way that he did. It is in that rebuke that Dickens speaks to pastors, teachers, and leaders about "a history so interesting and affecting" that even—and especially—those with minds "as near the brutes" as Jo's might be moved by it and learn from it. And Dickens emphasizes what becomes his advice: tell that blessed history—the story of Jesus—without embellishment and stay out of the way.

Dickens's advice here is given, of course, in the immediate context of the narrative of *Bleak House*, but he offers the same advice more directly and more completely in an essay from *The Uncommercial Traveller* that he entitled "Two Views of a Cheap Theatre."[21] The basic framework of the essay consists of Dickens's visits to the Britannia Theatre in London on two consecutive January evenings. On Saturday evening Dickens attended a pantomime and a play there; on Sunday evening he attended a church service. One thing Dickens attempts in the essay is to contrast the audiences and their responses on the consecutive evenings. But it is clear, too, that Dickens is more interested in commenting on the church service and the audience in attendance. (The Saturday night entertainment and audience is meant to act, it would seem, as a control group of sorts.) Among Dickens's observations about the church service, the most interesting ones are those about the preacher and his preaching. In these Dickens offers his advice to preachers and to his readers—even today—who will hear him.

This essay is certainly intended as Dickens's advice to the church, and while he begins with some mild criticism leveled at the church service as a whole and at the oratorical skill of the presiding minister, he is surprisingly positive in his description and assessment of the service and his experience. Before he offers his advice in earnest, he begins with a simple yet profound observation that at once previews his basic theme: "'A very difficult thing,' I thought, when the discourse began, 'to speak appropriately to so large an audience, and to speak with tact. Without it, better not to speak at all. Infinitely better, to read the New Testament well, and to let *that* speak. In this congregation there is indubitably one pulse; but I doubt if any power short of genius can touch it as one, and make it answer as one.'"[22] The audience for the service is estimated by Dickens to be around four thousand and in this context he must have been thinking seriously about the dynamic of preaching and communicating to such a large and apparently diverse group. By observing that it would be difficult "to speak with tact," Dickens certainly means that it would be difficult to make use of language with the skill, discretion, and good judgment necessary for effective communication to such a group. His solution: simply read the New Testament aloud to the audience. While this may seem naïve and simplistic, it speaks to Dickens's view of the power of the story of Christ and of the ability of the New Testament to speak for itself.

Dickens is not especially impressed with the minister's skill as a public speaker or with the minister's "understanding of the general mind and character of his audience."[23] Nevertheless, Dickens praises "the large Christianity of [the minister's] general tone" and appreciates the emphasis throughout the sermon on "Our Saviour" and that the message about Christ from the Gospels was quite sufficient. Most importantly, of these general elements of the sermon, Dickens observed, "And it was a most significant and encouraging circumstance that whenever he struck that chord, or whenever he described anything which Christ himself had done, the array of faces before him was very much more earnest, and very much more expressive of emotion, than at any other time."[24] It would seem that at this point in the essay Dickens had expanded his advice to the preacher from simply reading from the New Testament to now include more focused attention on Christ. That is, whatever might turn people's attention to Jesus, whether in the Gospels or elsewhere in the New Testament, would be a good and profitable thing.

Finally, Dickens makes one last set of observations, which must take "precedence of all others": "In the New Testament there is the most beautiful and affecting history conceivable by man, and there are the terse models for all prayer and for all preaching. As to the models, imitate them, Sunday preachers—else why are they there, consider? As to the history, tell it. . . . You will never preach so well, you will never move them so profoundly, you will never send them away with half so much to think of."[25] While it is imperative that we take Dickens's words literally, it would be anachronistic to suggest that we apply them literally. Nevertheless, there is good advice here in his emphasis on the biblical models and patterns, on the centrality of Jesus, and on the sufficiency of the Scriptures.

During the course of his essay, Dickens mentions a couple of the minister's illustrations and indicates that they seemed to lack any real connection to reality or to the audience to whom the sermon was addressed. So, Dickens asks, "Which is of better interest: Christ's choice of the twelve poor men to help in those merciful wonders among the poor and rejected," or an illustration employed by the preacher? And why force this particular illustration "when you have the widow's son to tell me about, the ruler's daughter, the other figure at the door when the brother of the two sisters was dead, and one of the two ran to the mourner, crying, 'The Master is come and calleth for thee'" (John 11:28 KJV)?[26] With this in mind, Dickens concludes, "Let the preacher who will thoroughly forget himself and remember no individuality but one, and no eloquence but one, stand up before four thousand men and women at the Britannia theatre any Sunday night, recounting that narrative to them as fellow creatures and, he shall see a sight!"[27] Notably, Dickens's focus is, once again, upon Jesus and the Scriptures as the source and content for the preacher's message.

When read conscientiously and alertly, almost all of Dickens's criticisms and comments upon the church and upon Christians can be taken as advice. "Two Views of a Cheap Theatre," though, is the one piece in which Dickens gave advice directly and deliberately. As pastors and teachers, we might be tempted in our weaker and lesser moments to respond, "Who asked you?" After all, Dickens was a layperson. What would a layperson know about preaching and pastoring? That is a question we would be wise to think about very carefully before dismissing it. I suspect our congregants could teach us quite a bit about both. Certainly Dickens has much to teach us in this short essay. In the passages considered, there are, among others, four reminders.

First, and remarkably, Dickens speaks to the idea of communication and rhetoric, specifically the communication of ideas to a group of people. Preaching and teaching for Dickens was not simply about dispensing information, nor was it about articulate and eloquent expression. Rather, he saw preaching as just one more way of communicating ideas to others: in this case, Truth. The one who will seek to do so must always be alert to language, how it works, and how it communicates. Dickens, of course, understood this as well as anyone, but it is extremely interesting—and telling—that he observed this in the church service from the beginning.

Second, and no surprise, Dickens reminds us of the centrality of Jesus and the Scriptures in the preaching and teaching enterprises. He recommends that the entire endeavor begin and end with Jesus and the New Testament. Moreover, the best illustrations, Dickens maintains, are those taken directly from the Scriptures.

Third, and in spite of himself, Dickens recognizes the dynamic of the Holy Spirit in the act and ministry of preaching and teaching. I say "in spite of himself" because Dickens never mentions the Holy Spirit here or elsewhere in his writing—except perhaps in veiled allusions—and it is unlikely, although not impossible, that when he hints at the dynamic involved in the process of addressing an audience in a sermon or lesson, he is thinking of the Holy Spirit. Nevertheless, he certainly recognized that what happens in the sermon and in teaching, particularly in terms of communication from speaker to hearer, is something more than mere public speaking.

Finally, permeating all that Dickens observed and thought about is the idea captured in his brilliant phrase from the 1867 preface to *The Pickwick Papers*: "the coarse familiarity with sacred things."[28] In the act of preaching and teaching, there must be a certain propriety, a certain respect, a certain care taken with the handling and communication of the content. For Dickens, the preacher or the teacher is never engaged in a mundane or common act. There is sacred purpose and effect here, and anyone engaging in the role of preacher or teacher must be aware of that and respond accordingly. It is no small thing to declare God's Word to an audience of people in an attempt to turn their attention to who Jesus is and what difference Jesus makes. Those who engage in preaching and teaching are held to a stricter accountability and so should approach their task, both in preparation and delivery, with a clear sense of that enormous responsibility. Dickens understands this and so he provides a reminder—along with some good advice—for our benefit.

Sometimes it seems that Dickens thought more carefully, more passionately, and more astutely about the church and the life of faith than many churchmen. And while he could seem unrelenting in his criticism of the church, he clearly offered it some timely advice. From where I stand, that advice resonates in ways that sting, that rouse, that rebuke, that motivate, that unsettle, that encourage. And it finds a way to remind us of what God wants the church to be in our time. This is our time, and we have been afforded some extraordinary opportunities to lead the church into the future. Perhaps Dickens's voice will play some small part in moving the church in the right direction. Or, perhaps not. But, as he wrote to his friend Cerjat (see above), one thing is certain: "The Church that is to have its part in the coming time must be a more Christian one, with less arbitrary pretensions and a stronger hold upon the mantle of our Saviour, as He walked and talked upon this earth."[29]

7

Reading (and Hearing) Dickens

No one can turn a phrase so cleverly and with such meaning, nor present a description with such precision and imagination as Dickens. Hear him in the final sentence of *Little Dorrit*, as Amy and Arthur leave St. George's Church: "They went quietly down into the roaring streets, inseparable and blessed; and as they passed along in sunshine and shade, the noisy and the eager, and the arrogant and the forward and the vain, fretted and chafed, and made their usual uproar."[1] Or again, in the final two sentences of *Oliver Twist*: "But, if the spirits of the Dead ever come back to earth, to visit spots hallowed by the love—the love beyond the grave—of those whom they knew in life, I believe that the shade of Agnes sometimes hovers round that solemn nook. I believe it none the less because that nook is in a Church, and she was weak and erring."[2]

Of course, there are any number of concise, seemingly almost incidental, observations that Dickens has phrased that are just as clever and full of meaning as longer passages and that stand by themselves as enduring and classic. Certainly "Bah! Humbug!" is so common as to have become clichéd. Likewise, his "It was the best of times, it was the worst of times," which opens *A Tale of Two Cities*. And his closing of that same novel is perhaps one of the best known conclusions in literature—apart from his own "God bless Us, Every One!" which closes *A Christmas Carol*—"It is a far, far better thing that I do, than I have ever done; it is a far, far better rest that I go to than I have ever known." To these can be added the less familiar but equally memorable remarks; for instance, Dickens wrote to his youngest son, Edward, upon Edward's departure for Australia in 1868: "But this life is half made up of partings, and these pains must be borne."[3] And from Nicholas Nickleby: "The power to serve is as seldom joined with the will, as the will is with the power, *I* think."[4]

Perhaps it is Dickens's pithy descriptive characterizations, however, that function most effectively to endear him to readers. In his *Martin Chuzzlewit*, for instance, Dickens describes Colonel Diver as "a man who was oppressed to inconvenience by a sense of his own greatness."[5] Similarly, from *Our Mutual Friend*: "Mr. Podsnap was well to do, and stood very high in Mr. Podsnap's opinion." Indeed, Mr. Podsnap "never could make out why everybody was not quite satisfied, and he felt conscious that he set a brilliant social example in being particularly well satisfied with most things, and, above all other things, with himself."[6] And in *The Mystery of Edwin Drood*, Dickens adroitly presents Mr. Grewgious, who "had a scanty flat crop of hair, in color and consistency like some very mangy yellow fur tippet; it was so unlike hair, that it must have been a wig, but for the stupendous improbability of anybody's voluntarily sporting such a head."[7]

You may or may not forgive me for the shameless indulgence in some of Dickens's classic expression, but the simple point here is that Dickens's adeptness with words and language are an invitation to read him. His novels are far from ordinary and much of that has to do with his mastery of written expression and his use of language. Of course, there is much more to entice us to read Dickens, and I hope that the themes introduced in this book may serve as some enticement. Indeed, one of my hopes in writing this book has been that it will inspire some readers to pick up Dickens for the first time and draw others back to Dickens to read him with a fresh vision and a new orientation. And as Dickens reminds us of some very important ideas about the life of faith in fresh and urgent ways, perhaps we might learn from him, broadening our categories of thinking about Christianity and the Christian life positively and meaningfully.

Beginning with Dickens

For some, reading Dickens can seem intimidating to a degree, even cumbersome perhaps. But reading Dickens should be enticing and enjoyable. Some basic suggestions might help to ease readers into Dickens. For those intimidated by the length of Dickens's novels—most are right around eight hundred to nine hundred pages—there are some shorter works to enjoy. *A Christmas Carol* is an excellent (re)introduction to Dickens. It is certainly one of his best stories[8] and one of his outstanding pieces of writing. When reading *A Christmas Carol*, be sure to give careful attention to the all-important conversation early in the story between Scrooge and Marley's ghost. The meaning of Scrooge's reclamation, not to mention the entire story, turns on that portion of the book. But *A Christmas Carol* is only one of Dickens's five Christmas Books. *The Haunted Man* (1848), his last Christmas Book, while perhaps not as well crafted as *A Christmas Carol*, is nevertheless a delightful work with as strong, if not stronger, a spiritual message as *A Christmas Carol*. Pay close attention to what Dickens does with hurt, memory, and forgiveness in *The Haunted Man*.

Of course, short is not always better when it comes to Dickens, but he did write several comparatively shorter novels that have become both favorites and classics. *A Tale of Two Cities* (1859), *Great Expectations* (1860–1861), and *Hard Times* (1854) are Dickens's shortest novels (if we count the Christmas Books as novellas), each one less than five hundred pages in length. And it is sometimes forgotten that *Oliver Twist* (1837–1839) is also a comparatively short novel, less than five hundred pages as well. *A Tale of Two Cities* is noteworthy for its theme of resurrection based on what is surely one of Dickens's favorite New Testament passages, John 11 in which Lazarus is raised from the dead. Watch for the transformation—and what I would argue is the radical conversion—of Sydney Carton grounded firmly in Jesus' proclamation, "I am the resurrection, and the life."

In *Great Expectations*, pay close attention to Joe Gargery. He is one of Dickens's "good people." And look for the themes of both offering and seeking forgiveness. *Oliver Twist* is one of Dickens's earliest novels, yet many of the themes that he will develop with more complexity in his later writing, especially Christian themes, are introduced here. In *Oliver Twist*, you see glimpses of Dickens's concept of God, gain insight into Dickens's uncanny ability to read and understand the human condition, and get a sense of what Angus Wilson, A. E. Dyson, and Humphry House speak of concerning Dickens's understanding of the evil in our world.

While these shorter works can certainly furnish an adequate introduction to Dickens and his work, if we desire to appreciate all that Dickens has to offer, I think a persuasive argument can be made for starting with his best work over what may be perceived as his more manageable work. In his, *Leslie Stephen: The Godless Victorian*, Noel Annan observes rather astutely, "We are accustomed to summing people up when their career is over because we imagine that only then can we form a judgment on a man's contribution to his times; but we will get a truer picture if we see people at the height of their powers when their achievements, or indeed, their failures are still before them."[9] While Annan's book is about Leslie Stephen, this general observation could certainly apply to Dickens. And if Annan's observation is accurate, we might get a true picture of Dickens from his work beginning in the early 1840s through the 1850s. For Dickens, this was, indeed, a period of imaginative power and creativity like the one to which Annan refers.

In 1843, Dickens wrote to Forster, "I feel my power now more than I ever did."[10] And in his biography of Dickens, Edgar Johnson says of Dickens's claim, "It was no idle boast. . . . His imaginative energy had never been more electric."[11] Dickens's words to Forster would certainly have referred to his writing and imaginative power in *Martin Chuzzlewit* (1843–1844) and *A Christmas Carol* (1843). In fact, when Dickens wrote of feeling his power as never before, he was speaking specifically of *Martin Chuzzlewit*. But this period of heightened power could also include *Dombey and Son* (1846–1848), *The Chimes* (Dickens's second Christmas Book [1844]), and even *David Copperfield* (1849–1850), *Bleak House* (1852–1853), and *Little Dorrit* (1855–1857).

Given this, the best introduction to Dickens, after *A Christmas Carol*, will probably not be one of his shorter pieces. Of course, embarking on the task of selecting the Dickens novel that best introduces him is usually not very different from naming one's favorite Dickens novel. Let me try to do so, nonetheless, since sometimes having some suggestions to consider is better than floundering with no direction at all. I am convinced that *Bleak House* and *Little Dorrit* are the novels that best represent the full scope of both Dickens's consummate skill and urgent message.

Bleak House is at once a love story, a social commentary, and a detective novel. And *Bleak House* is uncompromising in its Christian worldview. In it, Dickens deals directly, and in penetrating ways, with such Christian themes as the church, the Providence of God, and "real Christianity," as well as love, forgiveness, and generosity. We have already considered Esther's portrayal in *Bleak House* as a true disciple of Jesus. But watch for the love and the generosity of spirit of John Jarndyce. He, too, is one of Dickens's "good people." Even the minor characters—Charley, Allan Woodcourt, and George Rouncewell—are noble characters of honor and integrity and exhibit "some faint reflections of the teachings of our great Master." Dickens's caricatures—the Reverend Chadband, Mrs. Pardiggle and Mrs. Jellyby—as we have seen, serve not only to illustrate important Christian themes but also to provide comic relief. Don't sell them short; they might teach us a great deal.

In terms of his Christian thought and message, *Little Dorrit* may be Dickens's most important novel. Dennis Walder has written, "There is no more profound or original expression of the religious aspect of Dickens's imagination than *Little Dorrit*."[12] And Michael Slater suggests that the dynamic which drives Little Dorrit is "the earnest love, self-sacrifice and active New Testament goodness of a gentle young woman pitted against the 'prison' world of fraud, confusion, corrosive pretence, sycophancy, Old Testament vengefulness and criminal irresponsibility, as well as sheer, diabolic evil represented by her polar opposite in the novel, the 'gentlemanly' villain Rigaud/Blandois."[13]

Reading *Little Dorrit* is especially rewarding if you attend closely to the characterizations of both Amy Dorrit and Mrs. Clennam. Everything Dickens says about them is significant. Give attention especially to how their lives confront one another and how they develop individually. Watch how Amy serves and at what cost. Watch, too, as Arthur Clennam struggles with life, his past, and how he will do the right thing generally and in the specific situations in which he finds himself. Most of all, listen carefully for the Christian voice of Dickens. It is heard on every page of the novel.

A Few Things to Remember When Reading Dickens

Once you have decided what to read by Dickens, you may want a plan for working your way through his work. One way of reading Dickens is to read him according to the number. That means reading Dickens much the way a nineteenth-century reader would have read him, at least logistically speaking. Most of Dickens's novels were first published serially, or in installments, before they were published as bound books. These installments were referred to as numbers and were composed of a few chapters, usually three or four. These numbers were published sometimes as stand-alones or in magazines or publications that ran either monthly or weekly. Many Dickens enthusiasts enjoy reading Dickens along these lines. For instance, *Bleak House* originally appeared in monthly numbers that ran for nineteen months,[14] from March 1852 to September 1853. The point here, of course, is not taking nineteen months to read *Bleak House*, but reading it in smaller pieces, making it more manageable, and getting a sense of the dramatic structure of Dickens's work. Oxford University Press, the publisher of The Oxford World's Classics editions of Dickens's novels indicates the number divisions of the original publication in the table of contents.

Of course, there is no single "right" way to read Dickens. The important matter is that you read. In this regard, I am reminded of an observation Kevin Vanhoozer makes while discussing, of all things, hermeneutics, particularly the question of authority in the humanities. While challenging a basic postmodern deconstructionist argument, he asks rhetorically, "Why watch Shakespeare rather than TV sitcoms, or read Milton rather than Marvel comics? Why poetry rather than pornography? Why, indeed? Does it not have something to do with our ideas about the culture that we believe will best cultivate those 'humane' and 'humanitarian' virtues we most cherish?"[15] He certainly could have added, "Why read Dickens rather than DC comics?" But his point is well-taken nevertheless. We read Dickens because it is a good thing to do, because it cultivates in us ideas about honor, about propriety, about integrity, about love, about forgiveness, about things that matter and make a difference, even if our culture screams back at us, "They do not!" Finding a way to read Dickens is a good thing.

The Protests

But some will protest: "Dickens wasn't an artist. He got paid by the word and compromised his art to write long books to make money." Or: "Dickens wasn't a Christian. He simply gave a superstitious and sentimental reading audience what they wanted: a dose of religion and overdrawn, mawkish scenes of domestic and societal life." I may not have phrased them in the manner or as precisely as some might wish, but such protestations have been raised academically, critically, and popularly about Dickens and his work time and again. And I believe they should be addressed, if only briefly.

Perhaps Dickens did get paid by the word (although, I'm not so sure expressing it in such a way communicates accurately the contractual arrangements) and perhaps not. But it is certain that Dickens wrote to make a living. Writing was his job. So, he did write books to make money and, in fact, we know that *A Christmas Carol*, for instance, was conceived and written from a concern for income. Does that nullify the value of *A Christmas Carol*? Or might his concern for income render any of Dickens's work suspect? Everything we know about Dickens suggests at least two things about his attitude toward money: (1) his first concern was not the accumulation of wealth and (2) he was rather generous with the money that he earned. In the larger context, claims that Dickens wrote simply to make money carry very little weight. To say that Dickens wrote to earn money is little different from saying one goes to work each day to earn money. As to Dickens's art, it stands on its own.

To this is connected indirectly a second protest or complaint about Dickens's writing. Some still insist that the religious or Christian elements in Dickens's work were nothing more than concessions to a reading public that required a gesture toward God and religion here and there and that Dickens was savvy enough to know how to work his audience in just this way. This seems unlikely and implausible. Considering what we have seen in this book, either those who accuse Dickens of simply appeasing his audience with a dose of religion are wrong or Dickens was one of the greatest pretenders and deceivers history has known. Not only do we read in Dickens consistent and pervasive themes of Christianity and the life of faith but also we see that Dickens's work as a whole is undergirded by a conspicuous and solid Christian worldview. Add to this the personal declarations of his letters, and the argument that Dickens's religion is superficial and hollow is hard to sustain.

Another vein of this same protest maintains that some of Dickens's characters are overidealized and that some of his scenes, especially his death scenes, often drift into sentimentalism. If, in fact, some of Dickens's characters seem overidealized, they are intentionally so. That is, Dickens intended to show the ideal, the example, the committed follower of Jesus. Such characters are not mistakenly or overzealously blown out of proportion. Rather, they are measured and deliberate creations intended to portray true Christian disciples. Joseph Gold brilliantly answers those who criticize Dickens on this: "These characters are the artists of being human; they create whole worlds. It is our inadequacy, not their unreality, that makes us shy of their love and compassion."[16] That is, it is our failure to see these characters correctly, not a flaw in Dickens's skill of characterization.

The same might be said about the claims of sentimentalism in Dickens: these, too, indicate our failure as readers. George Santayana writes: "I must confess, though the fault is mine and not his, that sometimes his absoluteness is too much for me. When I come to the death of little Nell, or to What the Waves were always Saying, . . . I skip. I can't take my liquor neat in such draughts, and my inner man says to Dickens, Please don't. But then I am a coward in so many ways! There are so many things in this world that I skip, as I skip the undiluted Dickens!"[17] What we consider sentimentalism today was apparently the way life was in Dickens's day. Nell's death is not sentimentalized. It is, in fact, a proper Victorian death and burial for a character so loved by Dickens's readers that he was practically required to write her death as he did. Neither is Paul Dombey's death sentimentalized.[18] It is life in reality—full and human. To reduce it to an alleged sentimentality is to eviscerate the reality and cheat ourselves. Like Gold, Santayana insists that we must read and understand Dickens on his terms not ours. If not, we are more likely to distort and dilute him than to hear him clearly and read him in all his fullness. Our world is not Dickens's world, and if we insist on forcing him into our limited and limiting vision, we might as well leave him alone.

The last protest that we should address is that the crumbling of Dickens's marriage during the 1850s and final separation from

Catherine in 1858 reveals that his Christianity was not genuine. While Dickens was never divorced, he and Catherine never reconciled. Much has been written about this period in Dickens's life and much has been made of Dickens's relationship with the actress Ellen Ternen. Many take for granted that an alleged affair between Dickens and Ternen was the cause of Dickens's failed marriage and his separation from Catherine. The latest chapter in the speculation is that Ternen gave birth to a child fathered by Dickens.

While I am not anxious to defend Dickens here, I believe it is important to be fair and to admit, as does Michael Slater, there is really very little in all of this that we know for certain. Much of what is claimed as fact is instead speculation and sometimes borders on sensationalism. Significantly, I think, we have definite clues that Dickens's marriage was troubled several years before he met Ellen Ternen, and it is unlikely that she was the cause of this trouble. *David Copperfield*, which Dickens wrote in 1849–1850 and is typically understood as semiautobiographical, contains David's very pertinent and very wise reflections on his marriage to Dora and on marriage in general. But one such reflection that echoes throughout the latter portion of the novel after David and Dora are married is perhaps the most telling: "There can be no disparity in marriage like unsuitability of mind and purpose."[19] In another place, David reflects on his marriage, "Thus it was that I took upon myself the toils and cares of our life, and had no partner in them."[20] Reflections such as these are conspicuous enough, but they also find expression in Dickens's life. Dickens writes to Angela Burdett-Coutts on 9 May 1858, "I believe my marriage has been for years and years as miserable a one as ever was made. I believe that no two people were ever created, with such an impossibility of interest, sympathy, confidence, sentiment, tender union of any kind between them, as there is between my wife and me."[21] While none of this is meant to excuse Dickens from culpability, I believe it can provide some necessary perspective for a very undisciplined area of Dickens studies.

Some would insist that Dickens's failed marriage does in fact pass judgment on his work. Others, in light of his failed marriage, would even go so far as to disqualify his Christian voice. That certainly doesn't seem to be a wise or even fair course of reasoning. If what Dickens says has any ring of truth to it, if it contains wisdom that is genuine, if it can speak to our hearts in profound and transformative ways, what he says does so not because truth, genuine wisdom, and transformation come from Dickens but because these things belong to God. Even human failure is unable to disqualify that.

A Final Word

As I write these words, my desk is cluttered and piled with Dickens books. Two that I see are about Dickens; the other dozen are his work. And there are at least another dozen or so sitting on my shelves. Collectively, they are the voice of Dickens. Sometimes that voice shouts out. Other times it nudges and cajoles. Most of the time, however, it seems that it reasons and persuades, challenges and commands thought, and hopes to make me a little better for having listened to it.

In this book, we have been listening for Dickens's Christian voice. It is my hope that it has been heard and, having been heard, might somehow make a difference. As I have emphasized repeatedly through this volume, Dickens was neither theologian, Bible scholar, nor churchman. But as he speaks to the human condition with his extraordinary strength of observation and through the lens of his uncompromising Christian worldview, he invites us—almost requires us—to listen. Indeed, it is sometimes difficult to ignore that voice. Not because it is brash and demanding; more so because it is engaging and rings true.

And while Dickens's Christian voice provides us so much to consider, perhaps it reaches its finest moment—if not its most penetrating one—in the kind urgings of Amy Dorrit:

> Be guided, only by the healer of the sick, the raiser of the dead, the friend of all who were afflicted and forlorn, the patient Master who shed tears of compassion for our infirmities. We cannot but be right if we put all the rest away, and do everything in remembrance of Him. There is no vengeance and no infliction of suffering in His life, I am sure. There can be no confusion in following Him, and seeking for no other footsteps, I am certain![22]

Notes

Introduction

1. Dickens writes in his will (12 May 1869), "I rest my claims to the remembrance of my country upon my published works, and to the remembrance of my friends upon their experience of me in addition thereto." See John Forester, *The Life of Charles Dickens* (London: J. M. Dent & Sons, 1927), 2:422.

2. Two more biographies rate at least an honorable mention. Peter Ackroyd's *Dickens* (London: Guild, 1990) is enormous—just shy of 1200 pages—but extremely readable and engaging. Also, Fred Kaplan's *Dickens: A Biography* (Baltimore: Johns Hopkins University Press, 1998) is noteworthy.

3. Joseph Gold, *Charles Dickens: Radical Moralist* (Minneapolis: University of Minnesota Press, 1972), 10.

4. Charles Dickens, *The Life of Our Lord* (New York: Simon and Schuster, 1999), 122.

5. George Orwell, "Charles Dickens," *Critical Essays* (London: Secker and Warburg, 1960), 52.

Chapter 1 Charles Dickens: That Great Christian Writer

1. G. K. Chesterton, *Chesterton on Dickens* (San Francisco: Ignatius Press, 1989), 409.

2. For the most recent scholarly treatments of Dickens's religious thought and orientation, see Dennis Walder's seminal *Dickens and Religion* (London: George Allen & Unwin, 1981; London: Routledge, 2007); Andrew Sanders, *Charles Dickens: Resurrectionist* (London: Macmillan 1982); Janet Larson, *Dickens and the Broken Scriptures* (Athens: University of Georgia Press, 1985); Carolyn W. de la L. Oulton, *Literature and Religion in Mid-Victorian England: From Dickens to Eliot* (Hampshire: Palgrave Macmillan, 2003); Gary Colledge, *Dickens, Christianity and "The Life of Our Lord": Humble Veneration, Profound Conviction* (London: Continuum, 2009).

3. C. T. Watts, ed., *The English Novel: Questions in Literature* (London: Sussex Books, 1976), 55.

4. Humphry House, *The Dickens World* (London: Oxford University Press, 1941), 131. See House's entire discussion, 106–32. Although it does not carry the same weight it did in the mid- to late twentieth century, it is still recognized as one of the most important discussions of Dickens and religion.

5. Sir Arthur Quiller-Couch, *Charles Dickens and Other Victorians* (London: Cambridge University Press, 1927), 65.

6. Philip Collins, *Dickens and Education* (London: Macmillian, 1964), 59.

7. Robert Newsom, *Charles Dickens Revisited* (New York: Twayne, 2000), 70–71.

8. David Macrae, *Amongst the Darkies and Other Papers* (Glasgow: John S. Marr & Sons, 1880), 127.

9. Ibid.

10. Andrew Sanders, *Charles Dickens: Resurrectionist* (London: Macmillan, 1982), 118.

11. Dickens uses this phrase in an oft-quoted letter to Rev. R. H. Davies penned on Christmas Eve 1856: "I discountenance all obtrusive professions of and tradings in religion, as one of the main causes why real Christianity has been retarded in this world." John Forster, *The Life of Charles Dickens* (London: J. M. Dent & Sons, 1927), 2:380.

12. I will say more about this essay, "Two Views of a Cheap Theater," in chapter 6.

13. See Charles Dickens, *Little Dorrit*, The Oxford Illustrated Dickens (Oxford: Oxford University Press, 1989), 28–30.

14. Charles Dickens, *Little Dorrit*, The Oxford Illustrated Dickens (Oxford: Oxford University Press, 1989), 29.

15. Charles Dickens, *The Letters of Charles Dickens*, ed. Madeline House, Graham Storey, Kathleen Tillotson, Pilgrim Edition (Oxford: Clarendon House, 1965–2004), 1:541.

16. Dickens, *LD*, 29-30.

17. Forster, *The Life of Charles Dickens*, 2:379.

18. It is unlikely that Dickens would have embraced a view of vicarious atonement as it was articulated in the distorted form of Calvinism that he has in mind here. See chapter 4 for a fuller discussion of Dickens's understanding of atonement.

19. Charles Dickens, *David Copperfield*, The Oxford Illustrated Dickens (Oxford: Oxford University Press, 1989), 834.

20. Charles Dickens, *Barnaby Rudge*, The Oxford Illustrated Dickens (Oxford: Oxford University Press, 1989), 188–89.

21. This idea of the imitation of Jesus will be a central concern of both chapter 2 and chapter 4 and will be developed there more substantially.

22. Charles Dickens, *Bleak House*, The Oxford Illustrated Dickens (Oxford: Oxford University Press, 1989), 18, 25, 495.

23. Charles Dickens, *The Life of Our Lord* (New York: Simon & Schuster, 1999), 29.

24. Charles Dickens, *The Pickwick Papers*, Oxford World's Classics (Oxford: Oxford University Press, 1999), xii–xiii. This comes from the 1867 edition preface of *The Pickwick Papers*.

25. Dickens, *BH*, 107.

26. Ibid., 104.

27. Ibid.

28. Ibid., 108

29. Ibid., 109.

30. Ibid., 37.

31. Ibid., 36.

32. Ibid., 42.

33. Ibid., vii.

34. Ibid., 361.

35. Ibid.

36. Macrae, *Amongst the Darkies*, 127.

37. In the chapters that lie ahead, I will maintain that, despite the various religious options available to him in the mid-nineteenth century, and despite what has been written about him on this subject, Dickens was a typical Anglican layperson of the popular sort.

38. For Knight's complete discussion see Frances Knight, *The Nineteenth-Century Church and English Society* (Cambridge: Cambridge University Press, 1995), 21–48.

39. Watts, *The English Novel*, 55.

40. I qualify this with "rarely" and "substantial" to suggest to the reader that while a handful of scholars and critics have indeed discussed Dickens's religion, there has been no real attempt to assimilate their important contributions to the larger discussion of Dickens's work and thought.

41. Note in this regard, Dennis Walder's comment, "In my view it is in *Little Dorrit* that Dickens makes his most serious attempt to find a religious 'answer' to life's painful mysteries" (Walder, *Dickens and Religion*, xiii), as well as Michael Slater's observation, "He [Dickens] had evidently begun to register what was to be the essential dynamic of the story, the earnest love, self-sacrifice and active New Testament goodness of a gentle young woman pitted against the 'prison' world of fraud, confusion, corrosive pretence, sycophancy, Old Testament vengefulness and criminal irresponsibility, as well as sheer, diabolic evil represented by her polar opposite in the novel, the 'gentlemanly' villain Rigaud/Blandois." Michael Slater, *Charles Dickens*, (New Haven: Yale University Press, 2009), 392.

42. Peter Ackroyd, *Dickens* (London: Guild, 1990), 694.

43. G. D. Carrow, "An Informal Call on Charles Dickens by a Philadelphia Clergyman," *The Dickensian* 63 (May 1967): 112–19.

44. Natalie McKnight, "Dickens's Philosophy of Fathering," *Dickens Quarterly* 18 (September 2001), 134.

45. Forster, *The Life of Charles Dickens*, 2:82.

46. Ibid.

47. Slater, *Charles Dickens*, 212.

48. Dickens, Charles Jr., "Glimpses of Charles Dickens," *North American Review* 160 (1895): 525–37, 677–83. Cited in *Dickens: Interviews and Recollections*, ed. Philip Collins (London: Macmillan, 1981), 1:133.

49. Dickens, *Letters*, Pilgrim, 3:482. The "paper" to which Dickens refers here is an article Jerrold had written for a monthly magazine, the *Illuminated Magazine*. The magazine carried articles which regularly commented on social and (apparently) political issues. See note in *Letters*, 3:482.

50. Dickens, *TLOL*, 17.

51. Georgina, Dickens's sister-in-law, once approached Dickens to see if he might consider publishing it. He thought it over for about two weeks and finally decided that, not only would he not publish it, but that it should never be published during his lifetime or the lifetimes of his children.

52. I argue in *Dickens, Christianity and "The Life Of Our Lord": Humble Veneration, Profound Conviction* (London: Continuum, 2009) that *The Life of Our Lord* (*TLOL*) was written over an extended period of time, perhaps three years or more, and that it was completed in the late 1840s. If, for instance, *TLOL* was completed in 1849 (which is likely), Dickens would have had eight children by then, all twelve years of age or under, and five of them between the ages of two and ten. Nine years later, in 1858, Dickens would still have had three children under the age of twelve. This data suggests two things: first, it is quite likely that Dickens wrote *TLOL* with a target age range rather than a particular target age; and second, Dickens would have had a relatively large audience for his "performances" of *TLOL* for a considerable number of years, perhaps as many as twelve.

53. Macrae, *Amongst the Darkies*, 128.

54. Dickens, *Letters*, Pilgrim, 12:202.

55. Forster, *The Life of Charles Dickens*, 2:422.

56. For Dickens, *TLOL* was at once a "little New Testament" and a life of Jesus.

Dickens referred to *TLOL* as a little New Testament in, for instance, a letter to Forster, (Forster 1:395), a letter to Macrae (Macrae 128), and a letter to his son, Edward (Forster 2:379). In a letter to J. M. Makeham (Forster 2:381), Dickens refers to *TLOL* as a "history" of "the life and lessons of our Saviour." He made frequent reference to the New Testament (usually referring specifically to the Gospels) as a "history" (and thus as a life of Jesus). For instance, see *Dombey and Son* (826), *DC* (766), and *LD* (30).

57. Søren Kierkegaard, *Attack Upon Christendom*, trans. Walter Lowrie (Princeton: Princeton University Press, 1972), 30.

58. I do not mean to suggest here that Dickens had read Kierkegaard or that he even knew of him, although they were contemporaries. I only mean to point out that Kierkegaard's thought, at least in this instance, would have resonated with Dickens.

59. George Orwell, "Charles Dickens," in *Critical Essays* (London: Secker and Warburg, 1960), 56.

60. Charles Dickens, *Dombey and Son*, The Oxford Illustrated Dickens (Oxford: Oxford University Press, 1989), 826–27.

61. Charles Dickens, The *Uncommercial Traveller* and *Reprinted Pieces*, The Oxford Illustrated Dickens (Oxford: Oxford University Press, 1989), 38.

62. The letter to Edward is found in Dickens, *Letters*, Pilgrim, 12:188; the letter to Henry in Dickens, *Letters*, Pilgrim, 12:202.

63. Forster, *The Life of Charles Dickens*, 2:422.

64. Ibid., 2:380.

65. Ibid., 2:381.

66. Dickens, *Uncommercial Traveller* and *Reprinted Pieces*, 209.

Chapter 2 Charles Dickens's Jesus

1. Charles Dickens, *The Letters of Charles Dickens*, ed. Madeline House, Graham Storey, Kathleen Tillotson, Pilgrim Edition (Oxford: Clarendon House, 1965–2004), 5:45.

2. Dickens, *Letters*, Pilgrim, 12:202.

3. Charles Dickens, *The Uncommercial Traveller* and *Reprinted Pieces*, The Oxford Illustrated Dickens (Oxford: Oxford University Press, 1989), 37.

4. Dickens, *Letters*, Pilgrim, 12:188.

5. Ibid., 12:202.

6. Charles Dickens, *Little Dorrit,* The Oxford Illustrated Dickens (Oxford: Oxford University Press, 1989), 792.

7. Philip Collins, *Dickens and Education* (London: Macmillian, 1964), 54.

8. The original handwritten manuscript is currently kept in the United States at the Free Library of Philadelphia. For an excellent and thorough discussion of the history of the manuscript, see Robert Hanna's unpublished dissertation, *"The Life of Our Lord* as a Primer for Christian Education" (PhD diss., University of North Carolina at Greensboro, 1995).

9. Dickens had allowed a handwritten copy of his manuscript to be made for the children of his friend Mark Lemon. Winnifred Matz (see "My Copy of 'The Children's New Testament,'" *The Dickensian* 30, no. 230, [Spring,1934]: 89) also refers to her father making a copy early in the twentieth century from the Lemon copy.

10. *TLOL* was published in serial form in the United States in almost two hundred different newspapers, and in Great Britain the Associated Newspapers published it in their *Daily Mail.*

11. Hermann Reimarus's fragments "Concerning the Story of the Resurrection" and "The Goal of Jesus and His Disciples" (published posthumously, 1774–78), along with Friedrich Schleiermacher's lectures on the life of Jesus (beginning in 1819), provided the impetus for modern historical-critical lives of Jesus. But it was due to the momentum created by David Freidrich Strauss's *Das Leben Jesu, kritisch bearbeitet* (1834) and George Eliot's 1846 English translation of it (*The Life of Jesus Critically Examined*) that modern critical lives of Jesus began to be accepted and began to appear regularly in Great Britain after 1860.

Great Britain had been rocked by the publication of *Essays and Reviews* in 1860, and so 1860 became a watershed. *Essays and Reviews,* written by six Anglican churchmen and an Anglican layman, radically changed the method and study of the Scriptures in Great Britain almost overnight. See more on *Essays and Reviews* on pages 84-86.

12. Harmonies were actually early efforts to try to come to terms with the historical Jesus. The significance here is that the harmony was composed according to the presupposition that the canonical Gospels (1) were in basic agreement and (2) were reliable historical documents providing a true portrait of Jesus.

13. A life of Jesus combines historiography, biographical interest, commentary, and argument to reconstruct the life of Jesus and find therein the historical Jesus. A life, at least in the nineteenth century, would read more like a commentary on the Gospels than like a Gospel itself. Lives asked historical questions and proposed answers. Lives are composed upon the presupposition that a more historical approach will provide a more accurate understanding of Jesus's life.

14. For a thorough discussion of *TLOL* as a serious expression of Dickens's Christian thought, see Gary Colledge, *Dickens, Christianity and "The Life of Our Lord": Humble Veneration, Profound Conviction* (London: Continuum, 2009).

15. Dickens's letter to Forster of 28 June 1846 is often understood to indicate that Dickens wrote *TLOL* in a very short time, perhaps in a couple sittings, and finished it on that Sunday morning (see *Letters,* Pilgrim, 4:573 and accompanying n. 2). Gladys Storey notes, however, "In November, 1846 he took his wife and family, Georgina Hogarth, and servants to Paris. They lived in a furnished house, 48 Rue de Courcelles, Faourbourg St. Honoré. Here he wrote part of the little history of the New Testament for his children." Gladys Storey, *Dickens and Daughter* (London: Frederick Muller, 1939), 78. It is unclear why the editors of the Pilgrim *Letters,* while recognizing Storey's comments, maintain that the letter of 28 June 1846 "suggests that he [Dickens] completed it [*TLOL*] in June."

16. Juvenile harmonies were often called and even titled lives of Jesus. See my unpublished dissertation, "Revisiting the Sublime History: Dickens, Christianity and *The Life of Our Lord*" (PhD diss., University of St. Andrews, 2007), for a thorough analysis of *TLOL* as a harmony and a comparison of *TLOL* with other juvenile harmonies.

17. In the 1840s, Dickens was drawn to Unitarianism and went so far as to write to his friend Cornelius Felton that he had "joined the Unitarians" (see *Letters,* Pilgrim, 3:455–56). If, in fact, Dickens actually embraced Unitarian doctrine, the use of the titles Saviour and Son of God would take

on quite a different meaning than they have in the trinitarian orthodoxy of nineteenth-century Anglicanism. Elsewhere I thoroughly discuss Dickens's foray into Unitarianism and his alleged Unitarian sympathies. See Colledge, *Dickens*, 84–135. Suffice it to say here that there are no compelling reasons to suspect that Dickens ever strayed from his assent to a popular lay Anglicanism into committed Unitarianism. Consequently, the discussion in this chapter of the ascriptions "Our Saviour" and "Son of God" will consider them exclusively from the more orthodox perspective and will exclude material on Dickens and Unitarianism.

18. Charles Dickens, *The Life of Our Lord* (New York: Simon & Schuster, 1999), 38.

19. Dickens, *TLOL*, 27, 121.

20. Ibid., 85.

21. Ibid., 109.

22. Urania Cottage, or Urania House, was a project in which Dickens participated with the wealthy heiress Angela Burdett-Coutts. A private "Home for Fallen Women at Shepherd's Bush," Urania Cottage was a home for the rehabilitation of prostitutes, readying them for emigration normally to Australia. See more on Urania Cottage in chapter 5.

23. Charles Dickens, *Letters from Charles Dickens to Angela Burdett-Coutts, 1841–1865*, ed. Edgar Johnson (London: Jonathan Cape, 1953), 100.

24. Charles Dickens, *Hard Times*, The Oxford Illustrated Dickens (Oxford: Oxford University Press, 1989), 274.

25. Dickens, *HT*, 274.

26. Again, Dickens's alleged Unitarian sympathies come into play in this discussion. As with the title "Our Saviour," Unitarians would have felt comfortable with strictly qualified use of the title "Son of God." My discussion here is based on the more thorough and comprehensive argument in my *Dickens, Christianity and "The Life of Our Lord": Humble Veneration, Profound Conviction* (London: Continuum, 2009), and will concentrate on Dickens's Anglican understanding of Jesus as Son of God.

27. For the orthodox Anglican, Jesus's deity and messianic office were integrally linked, such that it was understood that Jesus did not become the Son by virtue of

an appointment as Messiah; rather, because Jesus was the eternal son of God, he was designated Messiah.

28. Dickens, *TLOL*, 28, 59.

29. Ibid., 110.

30. Ibid., 54–55.

31. That the inclusion of an episode is significant, however, does not necessarily mean that its inclusion is determinative of a particular idea, concept, or doctrine. Correspondingly, the absence of an episode in *TLOL* may be significant but not necessarily determinative of a particular idea, concept, or doctrine.

32. Dickens, *TLOL*, 38.

33. Ibid., 49–50.

34. Ibid., 110. Dickens renders his account in part, "The guards, terrified at these sights, said to each other, 'Surely this was the Son of God!'" Likely, Dickens is following Matthew's narrative, which includes a collective declaration of Jesus as Son of God by the centurion "and they that were watching with him".

35. Ibid., 115.

36. Charles Dickens, *David Copperfield*, The Oxford Illustrated Dickens (Oxford: Oxford University Press, 1989), 685.

37. Dickens, *LD*, 775.

38. Ibid., 702.

39. Charles Dickens, *A Tale of Two Cities*, The Oxford Illustrated Dickens (Oxford: Oxford University Press, 1989), 200.

40. David Macrae, *Amongst the Darkies and Other Papers* (Glasgow: John S. Marr & Sons, 1880), 128.

41. Charles Dickens, *Miscellaneous Papers* (New York: Chapman & Hall, 1908), 40.

42. Depending on the precise dating of *TLOL*, it is almost a certainty that the writing of *Dombey and Son* and *TLOL* overlapped.

43. Charles Dickens, *Dombey and Son*, The Oxford Illustrated Dickens (Oxford: Oxford University Press, 1989), 226.

44. Dickens, *Letters*, Pilgrim, 6:25–26.

45. Dickens, *TLOL*, 122.

46. Ibid., 49.

47. Ibid., 64.

48. Ibid., 88.

49. Ibid., 52.

50. Ibid., 38.

51. Ibid., 51–52.

52. Ibid., 36–37.

53. For further examples of Jesus's compassion in *TLOL*, see Dickens's exhortation to his children (33–34); the account of the healing of the leper (35–36); the account of the sinful woman at the home of Simon the Pharisee (49–51); and the account of the raising of Lazarus (83–85).

54. Dickens, *TLOL*, 28–29.

55. Ibid., 29.

56. Ibid., 69.

57. Dickens's original manuscript of *TLOL* is kept at the Free Library of Philadelphia. William Lang, Head of the Rare Books Department there and Joel Sartorius provided their assistance as well as an office space in which I was able to study the manuscript. Donald Root, also of the Free Library of Philadelphia acted as liaison in procuring my micrcofilm copy of the manuscript.

58. Dickens, *TLOL*, 17.

59. Ibid., 61.

60. Ibid., 50.

61. Ibid., 50–51.

62. John Forster, *The Life of Charles Dickens* (London: J. M. Dent & Sons, 1927), 2:381.

63. The parables in *TLOL* include: the parable of the unmerciful servant (61–62), the parable of the workers in the vineyard (62–63), the parable of the good Samaritan (69–71), a parable on humility (71), the parable of the feast of the poor (71–72), the parable of the prodigal son (73–76), the parable of the rich man and Lazarus (76–77) and the parable of the publican and the Pharisee (77–78).

64. Other teaching in *TLOL* includes: a brief mention of the Sermon on the Mount (35), Simon and the two debtors (50), the narrative of the woman taken in adultery (65–66), the Greatest Commandment (69–70), the widow's contribution (79–80), the footwashing (88), the Last Supper (93–94), Jesus's being ill-used at the crucifixion by the soldiers (103), Jesus and the two disciples on the road to Emmaus (116), and post-resurrection, pre-ascension teaching in the epilogue (118).

65. Dickens, *TLOL*, 76.

66. Ibid., 63.

67. Ibid., 71.

68. Ibid., 78.

69. Ibid., 33.

70. Ibid., 79–80.

71. Ibid., 76.

72. See Gerald F. Hawthorne, *Philippians*, in The Word Biblical Commentary, vol. 43 (Waco: Word Books, 1983), 75–96.

73. Standiford's 2008 offering, *The Man Who Invented Christmas*, was titled after Rogers's 1988 article of the same name in London's *Sunday Telegraph*.

74. Charles Dickens, *Christmas Books*, The Oxford Illustrated Dickens (Oxford: Oxford University Press, 1991), 19.

75. Dickens, *CB*, 20.

Chapter 3 Charles Dickens: Theologian?

1. Charles Dickens, *The Letters of Charles Dickens,* ed. Madeline House, Graham Storey, Kathleen Tillotson, Pilgrim Edition (Oxford: Clarendon House, 1965–2004), 10:253.

2. Edward Parsons, *The Providence of God Illustrated* (London: Hamilton, Adams; Leeds: J. Y. Knight, 1836), 1.

3. Charles Dickens, *Bleak House*, The Oxford Illustrated Dickens (Oxford: Oxford University Press, 1989), 180.

4. Anonymous, "On God's Providence," Burn's Series of Narratives and Tracts, 1841.

5. Charles Dickens, *David Copperfield*, The Oxford Illustrated Dickens (Oxford: Oxford University Press, 1989), 161. See also John Forster, *The Life of Dickens* (London: J. M. Dent & Sons, 1927), 1:25, where Dickens writes these exact words to his eventual biographer as he recollects some of his own past in Warrens Blacking.

6. Dickens, *DC*, 213.

7. Charles Dickens, *Oliver Twist*, The Oxford Illustrated Dickens (Oxford: Oxford University Press, 1989), 242.

8. Dickens, *BH*, 509.

9. K. J. Fielding, *The Speeches of Charles Dickens* (Oxford: Oxford University Press, 1960), 49.

10. Charles Dickens, *American Notes* and *Pictures from Italy*, The Oxford Illustrated Dickens (Oxford: Oxford University Press, 1989), 200–201.

11. Charles Dickens, *Christmas Books*, The Oxford Illustrated Dickens (Oxford: Oxford University Press, 1989), 154.

12. Charles Dickens, *A Child's History of England* and *Master Humphrey's Clock*, The Oxford Illustrated Dickens (Oxford: Oxford University Press, 1989), 224.

13. Charles Dickens, *Barnaby Rudge*, The Oxford Illustrated Dickens (Oxford: Oxford University Press, 1989), 188.

14. Walter Houghton, *The Victorian Frame of Mind, 1830–1870* (New Haven: Yale University Press, 1957), 66.

15. T. W. Heyck, "From Men of Letters to Intellectuals: The Transformation of Intellectual Life in Nineteenth-Century England," *Journal of British Studies* 20 (Fall 1980), 158–83.

16. The *Bridgewater Treatises* are a collection of volumes commissioned by the Royal Society at the bequest of Francis Henry Egerton, the eighth Earl of Bridgewater, and overseen by Davies Gilbert, as works that were expressly intended to demonstrate "the Power, Wisdom, and Goodness of God, as Manifested in the Creation" (Thomas Chalmers, *On the Power Wisdom and Goodness of God as Manifested in the Adaptation of the External Nature to the Moral and Intellectual Constitution of Man*, vol. 1 [London: William Pickering, 1839], 9). These treatises are serious scientific works of natural theology by respected authors of the day including Thomas Chalmers, William Whewell, and William Buckland. A *Ninth Bridgewater Treatise* was written by Charles Babbage. This was not, however, an authorized volume of the original *Treatises*, but was Babbage's own undertaking intended by him to correct some of what he perceived as deficiencies in the originals. Notably, Dickens cited Babbage's *Treatise* in a speech to the Birmingham and Midland Institute in September of 1869.

17. Dickens, *Letters*, Pilgrim, 10:253.

18. This is just a short list of the deaths that Dickens would confront in his life. The list includes many other family and friends.

19. Magarete Holubetz, "Death-bed Scenes in Victorian Fiction," *English Studies: A Journal of the English Language and Literature* 67 (February 1986): 14.

20. For a much more elaborate treatment of the social conventions surrounding death in the Victorian period, see Philippe Ariès, Margarete Holubetz, and Pat Jalland in the bibliography. For a thorough treatment of Nell's death, see Gary Colledge, *Dickens, Christianity and "The Life of Our Lord": Humble Veneration, Profound Conviction* (London: Continuum, 2009).

21. Dickens, *Letters*, Pilgrim, 1:268.

22. Ibid., 1:259–68.

23. Pat Jalland, *Death in the Victorian Family* (Oxford: Oxford University Press, 1996), 123.

24. James Hervey, *Meditations and Contemplations* (London: W. Suttaby, 1808), 10.

25. Dickens, *Letters*, Pilgrim, 6:356.

26. Ibid., 6:355.

27. Ibid., 6:357.

28. Ibid., 1:259, n. 1.

29. Michael Wheeler, *Heaven, Hell and the Victorians* (Cambridge: Cambridge University Press, 1994), 121.

30. Ibid.

31. Francis Knight, *The Nineteenth-Century Church and English Society* (Cambridge: University Press, 1995), 57.

32. Ibid., 51.

33. Wheeler, *Heaven, Hell and the Victorians*, 120–21.

34. Charles Dickens, *The Old Curiosity Shop*, The Oxford Illustrated Dickens (Oxford: Oxford University Press, 1989), 281–82.

35. Charles Dickens, *The Life Of Our Lord* (New York: Simon & Schuster, 1999), 17.

36. Dickens, *Letters*, Pilgrim, 5:297.

37. Dickens, *BH*, 871.

38. Dickens, *Letters*, Pilgrim, 1:632.

39. Charles Dickens, *Miscellaneous Papers* (New York: Chapman & Hall, 1908), 35.

40. Charles Dickens, *Great Expectations*, The Oxford Illustrated Dickens (Oxford: Oxford University Press, 1991), 434.

41. Dickens, *DC*, 686.

42. Dickens, *Letters*, Pilgrim, 1:568.

43. Dickens, *BR*, 496.

44. Ibid., 420.

45. Charles Dickens, *A Tale of Two Cities*, The Oxford Illustrated Dickens (Oxford: Oxford University Press, 1989), 314.

46. Ibid., 315.

47. Dickens, *BR*, 474.

48. Dennis Walder, *Dickens and Religion* (London: Routledge, 2007), 63.

49. Dickens, *OT*, 408.

50. Ibid., 368.

51. Walder, *Dickens and Religion*, 63.

52. C. T. Watts, ed., *The English Novel: Questions in Literature* (London: Sussex Books, 1976), 56.

53. Humphry House, *The Dickens World* (London: Oxford University Press, 1941), 112.

54. *Charles Dickens: A December Vision, and Other Thoughtful Writings*, ed. Neil Philip and Victor Neuburg (New York: Continuum Publishing Company, 1987), 21.

55. Dickens, *Letters*, Pilgrim, 2:257.

56. Charles Dickens, *Oliver Twist*, Penguin Classics (London: Penguin Books), 456. From the preface to the 1841 edition of *Oliver Twist*.

57. Ibid., 460.

58. Ibid., 356.

59. Ibid., 134.

60. Ibid., 456.

61. Dickens, *BR*, 129.

62. Ibid.

63. Dickens, *TLOL* 44–45.

64. The boy is described as a lunatic (Matt. 17:15[KJV]), or an epileptic, in the story, and some nineteenth-century commentators appeal to Matthew 4:24 to point out the biblical distinction between madness/epilepsy and demon possession. "And his fame went throughout all Syria; and they brought unto him all sick people that were taken with divers diseases and torments, and those which were possessed with devils, and those who were lunatic, and those that had the palsy; and he healed them" (Matt. 4:24 KJV). The "lunatic" and the "possessed" are distinguished here. In this way, then, some commentators argue that demon possession was just a primitive understanding of madness/epilepsy or some other infirmity.

65. Hermann Olshausen, *Commentary on the Gospels: Adapted Expressly for Preachers and Students*, vol. 1, trans. H. B. Creak (Edinburgh: T&T Clark, 1847), 274.

66. Thomas Arnold, *Christian Life: Sermons Preached Mostly in the Village Church of Laleham, 1820–1828*, rev. ed., ed. Mrs. W. E. Forster, vol. 1, *Sermons* (London: Longmans, Green and Co. 1878), 150–51.

67. Perhaps Adam Clarke made the most perceptive and clever comments regarding this larger discussion: "Certain doctors in both sciences, divinity and physic, gravely tell us, that these demoniacs were only common madmen, and that the disease was supposed, by the superstitious Jews, to be occasioned by demons. But with due deference to great characters, may not a plain man be permitted to ask by what figure of speech can it be said that "two diseases *besought,—went out—filled a herd of swine—rushed down*
a precipice, &c." Adam Clarke, *The Gospels Harmonized: With Notes, Explanatory, Experimental and Practical. . .* , ed. Samuel Dunn (London: Thomas Tegg & Son, 1836), M3–4.

68. Frederick Buechner, *Listening to Your Life* (San Francisco: HarperSanFrancisco, 1992), 295.

69. Henry Thiessen, *Lectures in Systematic Theology* (Grand Rapids: Eerdmans, 1989), 5.

70. Forster, *The Life of Charles Dickens*, 2:422.

71. Dickens, *Letters*, Pilgrim, 12:188.

Chapter 4 Charles Dickens: Resurrectionist

The title for this chapter is borrowed from the brilliant book of Professor Andrew Sanders entitled *Charles Dickens: Resurrectionist* (1982). For all intents and purposes, a resurrectionist is a body-snatcher. Professor Sanders explains in his introduction that upon one particular occasion, Dickens was asked to leave his name—which was to be delivered to Vincent Dowling—with the proprietors of a restaurant. Dickens mischievously left a makeshift calling card that read: Charles Dickens, Resurrectionist, In search of a subject. Professor Sanders, then, playfully chose this title for his book dealing with the extent to which Dickens drew on his faith in his treatment of death and resurrection in his work.

1. Charles Dickens, *The Letters of Charles Dickens*, ed. Madeline House, Graham Storey, Kathleen Tillotson, Pilgrim Edition (Oxford: Clarendon House, 1965–2004), 3:485.

2. Dickens's use of the term "snuffling" here is slightly derogatory and is an obvious signal that he is writing to a Dissenting or Nonconformist Evangelical—or at least Dickson gave the impression of being one and Dickens is addressing him as such.

3. Angela Burdett-Coutts, a close family friend, was an Evangelical. As far as we know, Dickens had the highest respect for Coutts and collaborated with her often on a number of philanthropic endeavors. Coutts regularly sought out Dickens's opinions and advice on projects before she committed any of her considerable financial support. It seems that

Dickens had a grave distaste for the cant and the spectacle with which nineteenth-century dissenting Evangelicals were associated. It is likely that Dickens parodies and caricatures are directed more toward these Dissenters than to Anglican Evangelicals.

4. Pusey was a High Churchman and a key figure in the Oxford Movement.

5. Edward Bouverie Pusey, *Parochial Sermons*, vol. 3, rev. ed. (London: Rivingtons, 1873), 20.

6. Humphry House, *All In Due Time: The Collected Essays and Broadcast Talks of Humphry House* (London: Rupert Hart-Davis, 1955), 183–84.

7. Ibid., 189.

8. Charles Dickens, *Mr. and Mrs. Charles Dickens: His Letters to Her*, ed. Walter Dexter (London: Constable and Co., 1935), 266–68.

9. This prayer takes on a special poignancy when we realize that Dickens composed it for and included it in the letter he wrote to Catherine to inform her of the death of their infant daughter, Dora. Being in poor health herself, Mrs. Dickens was away at the time "to try the air and the water in Malvern."

10. Charles Dickens, *Dombey and Son*, The Oxford Illustrated Dickens (Oxford: Oxford University Press, 1989), 826–27.

11. Charles Dickens, *David Copperfield*, The Oxford Illustrated Dickens (Oxford: Oxford University Press, 1989), 679–87.

12. Charles Dickens, *Barnaby Rudge*, The Oxford Illustrated Dickens (Oxford: Oxford University Press, 1989), 128–31, 564–65.

13. Charles Dickens, *The Life Of Our Lord* (Simon & Schuster, 1999), 63.

14. Dickens, *TLOL*, 76.

15. Dickens, *DC*, 725.

16. Dickens includes this story in *TLOL* and renders it conspicuously as a story of forgiveness rather than as a story of Jesus's resourcefulness in avoiding entrapment over an issue involving the passing of magisterial judgment. The episode functions in *TLOL* as the climactic story of a series of teachings and parables on forgiveness that takes up the major portion of chapter six.

17. Dickens, *TLOL*, 122.

18. Certainly the issue of the extent of the atonement was also a fundamental question in the nineteenth century, but Dickens did not seem very much bothered by that.

19. W. J. Conybeare, "Church Parties," *Edinburgh Review* (October 1853), 142.

20. Lant Carpenter, the eminent nineteenth-century Unitarian, writes, "The power or disposition of God to pardon sinners on repentance, was not affected by the Death of Christ; nor is the exercise of his Pardoning Mercy, except as far as sinners are brought by means of that event, into a state in which God can, consistently with his Holiness and his Justice grant them his mercy and his grace." Lant Carpenter, *Lectures on the Scripture Doctrine of Atonement* (London: J. Green, 1843), xii. Harriet Martineau further clarifies the Unitarian position: "We . . . reject the notion that any part of the punishment of sin can be escaped through the sacrifices, or mediation, or intercession of any being whomsoever." Harriet Martineau, *The Essential Faith of the Universal Church; Deduced from the Sacred Records* (London: Unitarian Association, 1831), 36.

21. See Thomas Erskine, *The Unconditional Freeness of the Gospel: In Three Essays*, 2nd ed. (Edinburgh: Waugh & Innes, 1828); *The Brazen Serpent; or, Life Coming Through Death* (Edinburgh: Waugh & Innes, 1831). For Campbell, see John McLeod Campbell, *The Nature of the Atonement* (Edinburgh: Handsel Press, n.d.; repr., Grand Rapids: Eerdmans, 1996). The full text of all three books can be read online for free at www.archive.org, although the Eerdmans/Handsel print copy of Campbell's *The Nature of Atonement* includes a most valuable introduction by James B. Torrance.

22. The subtlety that distinguishes Erskine's view and what he emphasizes is his use of "belief" in a common and familiar sense, not a theological one. And what he labored to teach was that repentance and faith are not conditions for forgiveness. Rather, the sort of belief or faith that Erskine had in mind was that which affirmed, "Through Christ's work on the Cross, God forgave my sin. I have been pardoned and I embrace that pardon." That is, for Erskine, repentance and faith are simply affirmations of the pardon that God has already bestowed.

23. Charles Dickens, *The Uncommercial Traveller* and *Reprinted Pieces*, The Oxford Illustrated Dickens (Oxford: Oxford University Press, 1989), 36.

24. Charles Dickens, *Bleak House*, The Oxford Illustrated Dickens (Oxford: Oxford University Press, 1989), 270.

25. Charles Dickens, *Little Dorrit*, The Oxford Illustrated Dickens (Oxford: Oxford University Press, 1989), 774.

26. Dickens, *LD*, 29.

27. Dickens, *Letters*, Pilgrim, 1:586.

28. Dickens, *LD*, 127.

29. Ibid.

30. See Philip Collins, *Dickens and Crime* (London: Macmillan, 1962), 5–93, esp. 82–93.

31. Ibid., 82.

32. Ibid., 89.

33. Dickens, *BR*, 355.

34. Charles Dickens, *The Old Curiosity Shop*, The Oxford Illustrated Dickens (Oxford: Oxford University Press, 1989), 241.

35. Dickens clearly allowed this designation. He just felt it should not be the necessary point of emphasis. In "Two Views of a Cheap Theatre" he notes that to be called "fellow-creatures" surely includes "the other designation (fellow-sinners) and some touching meanings over and above." See Charles Dickens, *The Uncommercial Traveller* and *Reprinted Pieces*, The Oxford Illustrated Dickens (Oxford: Oxford University Press, 1989), 36.

36. Charles Dickens, *Oliver Twist*, Penguin Classics (London: Penguin Books, 2003), 460.

37. Charles Dickens, *Oliver Twist*, The Oxford Illustrated Dickens (Oxford: Oxford University Press, 1989), xvii.

38. Charles Dickens, *"Gone Astray" and Other Papers from Household Words*, ed. Michael Slater (London: J. M. Dent, 1998), 397.

39. For Dickens, the pattern penitent is the prisoner who makes false or hypocritical claims of conversion for manipulative ends.

40. Charles Dickens, *Christmas Books*, The Oxford Illustrated Dickens (Oxford: Oxford University Press, 1997), 396.

41. Charles Dickens, *Selected Journalism, 1850–1870*, ed. David Pascoe (London: Penguin Books, 1997), 10.

42. Richard Chenevix Trench, *Notes on the Miracles of Our Lord*, 2nd ed. (London: John W. Parker, 1847), 400.

43. Hermann Olshausen, *Biblical Commentary on the Gospels and On the Acts of the Apostles*, vol. 4, trans. John Gill and William Lindsay (Edinburgh: T&T Clark, 1850), 10.

44. Charles Dickens, *A Tale of Two Cities*, The Oxford Illustrated Dickens (Oxford: Oxford University Press, 1997), 299.

45. Dickens, *TTC*, 356.

46. Dickens, *D & S*, 867–68.

47. Dickens, *OT*, 305.

48. *Charles Dickens: A December Vision, and Other Thoughtful Writings*, ed. Neil Philip and Victor Neuburg (New York: Continuum Publishing Company, 1987), 77–78.

49. Ibid., 78.

50. Dickens, *OT*, 415.

51. The Foundling Hospital was, in the time *Little Dorrit* is set, a home for fatherless children. Dickens was a patron of the hospital and had rented a pew in the chapel of the hospital until he moved his family to Devonshire Terrace (1840).

52. Dickens, *LD*, 18.

53. Dickens, *D & S*, 48.

54. Ibid., 666.

55. Ibid., 681.

56. Ibid., 605.

57. This is the contrast employed by James Torrance in his introduction to John MacLeod Campbell, *The Nature of Atonement* (Edinburgh: Hansel Press, 1996), 1–17.

58. K. J. Fielding, *The Speeches of Charles Dickens* (Oxford: Oxford University Press, 1960), 404.

59. Dickens, *TLOL*, 20.

60. Dickens, *CB*, 137.

61. Ibid., 378–79.

62. Dickens, *BH*, 877.

Chapter 5 Real Christianity

1. The child's hymn is written by Harriet Parr (Holme Lee) as part of her story, "Poor Dick's Story," in *The Wreck of the Golden Mary*. *The Wreck of the Golden Mary* is the Christmas story in the extra Christmas number of *Household Words* in 1856. The hymn is noteworthy:

> Hear my prayer, O! Heavenly Father,
> Ere I lay me down to sleep;
> Bid the Angels, pure and holy,
> Round my bed their vigil keep.
>
> My sins are heavy, but Thy mercy
> Far outweighs them every one;
> Down before Thy Cross I cast them,
> Trusting in Thy help alone.

Keep me through this night of peril
Underneath its boundless shade;
Take me to Thy rest, I pray Thee,
When my pilgrimage is made.

None shall measure out Thy patience
By the span of human thought;
None shall bound the tender mercies
Which Thy Holy Son has bought.

Pardon all my past transgressions,
Give me strength for days to come;
Guide and guard me with Thy blessing
Till Thy Angels bid me home.

Christmas stories such as *The Wreck of the Golden Mary* were typically collaborations between Dickens and his literary friends and acquaintances, with Dickens providing the basic framework and writing the linking and bridging sections. This hymn is a part of one of those linking or bridging sections, and this is perhaps why Dickens writes to Davies that Dickens himself was the author. Moreover, as Dickens brings this story to close, he himself adds:

"After awhile Dick drew his coat up over his head and lay down to sleep. 'Well, poor Dick!' thought I, 'it is surely a blessed thing for you that—
None shall measure out God's patience,
By the span of human thought;
None shall bound the tender mercies
Which His Holy Son has bought.'"

Two observations are pertinent here: (1) While Parr is typically credited with the authorship of the hymn, it would have to receive Dickens's approval to remain part of the story. Dickens was notorious for keeping a tight reign on anything that was printed in his journals and was never hesitant to edit, cut, or adapt material from his contributors. (2) It is telling that Dickens chose to end the story by reprising a stanza of the hymn as the final word. That would be Dickens's decision, not Parr's. See *Charles Dickens's Uncollected Writings from Household Words, 1850–1859*, ed. Harry Stone, vol. 2 (Bloomington: Indiana University Press, 1968), 564–69, for a full discussion.

2. John Forster, *The Life of Charles Dickens*, (London: J. M. Dent & Sons 1927), 2:380.

3. David Macrae, *Amongst the Darkies and Other Papers* (Glasgow: John S. Marr & Sons, 1880), 127.

4. Ibid.

5. Ibid.

6. Forster, *The Life of Charles Dickens*, 2:380.

7. Charles Dickens, *The Life Of Our Lord* (New York: Simon & Schuster, 1999), 122.

8. Forster, *The Life of Charles Dickens*, 2:381.

9. Sir Henry Fielding Dickens, *The Recollections of Sir Henry Dickens, K. C.* (London: William Heinemann, 1934), 41.

10. I am not maintaining here that Dickens was familiar with the idea of righteousness or faithfulness in the Hebrew Scriptures. I am only suggesting that the sense in which Dickens used the word "faithful" seems to reflect the Hebrew idea.

11. Charles Dickens, *Mr. and Mrs. Charles Dickens: His Letters to Her*, ed. Walter Dexter (London: Constable and Co., 1935), 266–67.

12. Dickens, *TLOL*, 50–51.

13. Ibid., 62.

14. This story is of one of Dickens's many Christmas stories and comes from the extra Christmas number (or edition) of *Household Words*, 1854.

15. Charles Dickens, *Great Expectations*, The Oxford Illustrated Dickens (Oxford: Oxford University Press, 1991), 455.

16. Ibid., 439.

17. Charles Dickens, *Dombey and Son*, The Oxford Illustrated Dickens (Oxford: Oxford University Press, 1989), 680.

18. Charles Dickens, *Little Dorrit*, The Oxford Illustrated Dickens (Oxford: Oxford University Press, 1989), 47.

19. Ibid., 789.

20. Charles Dickens, *Bleak House*, The Oxford Illustrated Dickens (Oxford: Oxford University Press, 1989), 18.

21. Dickens, *TLOL*, 29.

22. Dickens, *D & S*, 323.

23. Ibid., 198.

24. Ibid., 471–79, 822–27.

25. Dickens, *TLOL*, 17.

26. Dickens, *LD*, 71.

27. Ibid., 72.

28. Charles Dickens, *The Old Curiosity Shop*, The Oxford Illustrated Dickens (Oxford: Oxford University Press, 1989), 344.

29. Macrae, *Amongst the Darkies*, 127.

30. Dickens has often been criticized for his overidealized characters. It seems, however, that Dickens deliberately and

intentionally overidealized his heroes and heroines in order to demonstrate what genuine Christianity should look like.

31. Charles Dickens, *Christmas Books*, The Oxford Illustrated Dickens (Oxford: Oxford University Press, 1997), 20.

32. Ibid.

33. Dickens, *LD*, 319.

34. Ibid., 739

35. Ibid., 42.

36. Ibid.

37. Charles Dickens, *The Letters of Charles Dickens*, ed. Madeline House, Graham Storey, Kathleen Tillotson. Pilgrim Edition. 12 vols. (Oxford: Clarendon House, 1965-2004), 6:25-26.

38. Macrae, *Against the Darkies*, 127.

39. Ibid.

40. Charles Dickens, *Letters from Charles Dickens to Angela Burdett-Coutts, 1841–1865*, ed. Edgar Johnson (London: Jonathan Cape, 1953), 10.

41. Dickens, *TLOL*, 33.

42. Ibid.

43. Dickens, *Letters from Charles Dickens to Angela Burdett-Coutts*, 131.

44. Michael Slater, *Charles Dickens* (New Haven: Yale University Press, 2009), 217–18. While it is notoriously difficult even to suggest what that £2300 might look like today, it certainly is fair to say that this was a large sum of money in the nineteenth century and could have sustained Elton's large family comfortably for a few years.

45. Dickens, *Letters from Charles Dickens to Angela Burdett-Coutts*, 70.

46. Ibid., 61–62.

47. Slater, *Charles Dickens*, 341.

48. Philip Collins, "Dickens and the Ragged Schools," *The Dickensian* 55.2, no. 328 (Spring 1959): 95.

49. Ibid., 95.

50. *The Ragged School Union Magazine* 8, no. 85, (January 1856), 232.

51. Dickens, *Letters from Charles Dickens to Angela Burdett-Coutts*, 51.

52. Ibid., 52.

53. Ibid., 53–54.

54. This had less to do with the schools and more to do with external circumstances beyond the control of the schools. Since the schools were privately funded by the charitable contributions of individuals alone, funds were limited. The government would not provide any substantial grants since the schools were broadly religious and not specifically Anglican.

55. Dickens, *Letters from Charles Dickens to Angela Burdett-Coutts*, 54.

56. Dickens was the editor of *Household Words* and had great control over what was published in its pages. If something was published in *Household Words*, chances are it met Dickens's approval and he supported it.

57. Dickens, *Letters from Charles Dickens to Angela Burdett-Coutts*, 51.

58. Ibid.

59. Dickens, *Letters*, Pilgrim, 1:541.

60. Collins, "Dickens and the Ragged Schools," 97.

61. Dickens, *BH*, 640–41.

62. Forster, *The Life of Charles Dickens*, 282.

63. Dickens, *Letters from Charles Dickens to Angela Burdett-Coutts*, 18.

64. Ibid., 78–79.

65. Ibid., 95.

66. Ibid., 99

67. Ibid., 108.

68. Ibid., 80.

69. Ibid., 80.

70. Ibid., 101.

71. Ibid., 106.

72. Ibid., 100.

73. Bertha White was a woman who had been engaged for fourteen years and whose fiancé was taken ill and died suddenly just before the wedding. Miss White, who entered the room of her fiancé just moments before he expired, flung herself out of a fourth floor window but miraculously survived the fall. Her father was paralyzed, in debt, and without means. Dickens enlisted the support of Miss Coutts and others to help the family.

74. The Family Colonization Loan Society was an organization that aided those poor people who wished to emigrate to Australia. Dickens wrote a number of articles in *Household Words* on emigration, including an article that outlined the operation of The Family Colonization Loan Society in particular and praised Mrs. Chisholm for her work.

75. Athenaeums and mechanics institutes were institutions founded to provide both educational and recreational opportunities for the working class. The athenaeum tended to be more academic while the mechanics institute was more practical and trade

oriented. Dickens typically recognized the opportunities afforded in both as having a spiritual component as well. In a speech at the Manchester Athenaeum on 5 October 1843, Dickens said: "I think it is grand to know, that, while her factories re-echo with the clanking of stupendous engines, and the whirl and rattle of machinery, the immortal mechanism of God's own hand, the mind, is not forgotten in the din and uproar, but is lodged and tended in a palace of its own." He would add toward the end of his speech, "The benefits he acquires in such a place are not of a selfish kind, but extend themselves to his home, . . . nor can it ever fail to lead to larger sympathies with man, and to a higher veneration for the great Creator of all the wonders of this universe." K. J. Fielding, *The Speeches of Charles Dickens* (Oxford: Oxford University Press, 1960), 49.

Chapter 6 Dickens and the Church

1. Peter Ackroyd, *Dickens* (London: Guild, 1990), 44.

2. John Forster, *The Life of Charles Dickens* (London: J. M. Dent & Sons, 1927), 1:282–83.

3. Ibid., 1:283.

4. Dickens's title suggests the nature of his parody. Numerous official government papers and reports were published in the nineteenth century that were Parliamentary "Report[s] of the Commissioners Appointed to Inquire into the Condition of [fill in the blank]." A few examples will give a better feel for Dickens's parody: "Report of the Commissioners Appointed to Inquire into the Sanitary State of the Army in India" (1863); "Report Of The Commissioners Appointed to Inquire into the Condition and Treatment of the Prisoners Confined in Birmingham Borough Prison, and the Conduct, Management, and Discipline of the Said Prison, Together with Minutes of Evidence." (1854); "Report of the Central Board of His Majesty's Commissioners Appointed to Collect Information in the Manufacturing Districts, as to the Employment of Children in Factories and as to the Propriety and Means of Curtailing the Hours of Their Labour with Minutes of Evidence and Reports by the District Commissioners" (1853).

5. Charles Dickens, *"The Amusements of the People" and Other Papers: Reports, Essays and Reviews, 1834–51*, ed. Michael Slater (London: J. M. Dent, 1996), 62.

6. Charles Dickens, *Bleak House*, The Oxford Illustrated Dickens (Oxford: Oxford University Press, 1989), 361.

7. Charles Dickens, *The Pickwick Papers*, Oxford World's Classics (Oxford: Oxford University Press, 1999), 724–25.

8. Charles Dickens, *The Letters of Charles Dickens*, ed. Madeline House, Graham Storey, Kathleen Tillotson, Pilgrim Edition (Oxford: Clarendon House, 1965–2004), 3:462–63.

9. Ibid., 3:455–56.

10. See Gary Colledge, *Dickens, Christianity and "The Life of Our Lord": Humble Veneration, Profound Conviction* (London: Continuum, 2009), 84–88.

11. For a fuller discussion of Dickens and the Broad Church movement, see Gary Colledge, *Dickens, Christianity and "The Life of Our Lord."*

12. W. J. Conybeare, *Essays, Ecclesiastical and Social Printed with Additions from the Edinburgh Review* (London: Longman, Brown, Green, & Longmans, 1855), 147.

13. M. A. Crowther, *Church Embattled: Religious Controversy in Mid-Victorian England* (Devon: David & Charles, 1970), 29–30.

14. The topics and subtopics of the essays in *Essays and Reviews* can be seen as exemplary of some of the concerns of the Broad Churchmen. These would include, for instance, the primacy of the historical-critical method in biblical studies; the meaning of the inspiration of Scripture; the bearing of the new sciences, especially geology, on Mosaic cosmology; the spiritual elements in the Scriptures over and against the scientific and historical elements; and the dawning of a new epoch of knowledge, learning, and education in the history of the world taking place in the nineteenth century. Dickens indicates in a letter to de Cerjat that he had read *Essays and Reviews*, and he demonstrates in that same letter that he understands the essential points of Jowett and some others. But we have no evidence at all that Dickens was ever inclined to engage these issues with any serious attention. Perhaps this is an argument from silence, but an argument from silence can be cogent if the silence is conspicuous.

15. Broad Churchmen employed this term, "comprehension," to describe twin ideas. On the one hand, comprehension referred to the loosening of doctrinal requirements especially to allow for a greater inclusiveness among clergy. The Church of England was losing many clergy because of its insistence that all clergy strictly adhere doctrinally to the Thirty-Nine Articles. Broad Churchmen campaigned aggressively for a relaxing of such requirements so that the Church would not lose some of its brightest and best clerical thinkers. On the other hand, and perhaps more importantly, comprehension referred to the idea of relaxing doctrinal and ecclesial limitations that resulted in the narrow sectarianism both within and outside of the Church. That is, the Church of England needed to take the lead in initiating reforms that would bring in and accommodate Dissenters and Nonconformists of any and all sorts, thereby creating a comprehensive and unified Church. It should be remembered that those in the Broad Church movement were still Churchmen—that is, they were Anglicans. As such, most were still committed to the Church of England and to its survival and longevity. And most were convinced that the survival and longevity of the Church depended on certain necessary reforms. One such reform was comprehension.

16. Forster, *The Life of Charles Dickens*, 1:282–83.

17. George Orwell, "Charles Dickens," in *Critical Essays* (London: Secker and Warburg, 1960), 57.

18. Forster, *The Life of Charles Dickens*, 1:335–36.

19. Dickens, *Letters*, Pilgrim, 10:444.

20. John Naisbitt, *Megatrends: Ten New Directions Transforming Our Lives* (New York: Warner Books, 1982), 58–59, 85–86.

21. "Two Views of A Cheap Theatre" originally appears in Dickens's weekly journal *All the Year Round*, 25 February 1860. Later Dickens's pieces from *All the Year Round* would be compiled in his volume *The Uncommercial Traveller*.

22. Charles Dickens, *The Uncommercial Traveller* and *Reprinted Pieces*, The Oxford Illustrated Dickens (Oxford: Oxford University Press, 1989), 35.

23. Dickens, *The Uncommercial Traveller*, 35.

24. Ibid., 37.

25. Ibid., 38–39.

26. Ibid., 39. The three particular Gospel episodes that Dickens employs here are the three instances in the Gospels in which Jesus raises the dead to life. These were favorites of Dickens. They recur conspicuously throughout his writing and all three are included in *TLOL*.

27. Ibid.

28. Charles Dickens, *The Pickwick Papers*, The Oxford Illustrated Dickens (Oxford: Oxford University Press, 1989), xiii.

29. Dickens, *Letters*, Pilgrim, 10:444.

Chapter 7 Reading (and Hearing) Dickens

1. Charles Dickens, *Little Dorrit*, The Oxford Illustrated Dickens (Oxford: Oxford University Press, 1989), 826.

2. Charles Dickens, *Oliver Twist*, The Oxford Illustrated Dickens (Oxford: Oxford University Press, 1989), 415.

3. John Forster, *The Life of Charles Dickens* (London: J. M. Dent & Sons, 1927), 2:379.

4. Charles Dickens, *Nicholas Nickelby*, The Oxford Illustrated Dickens (Oxford: Oxford University Press, 1989), 248.

5. Charles Dickens, *Martin Chuzzlewit*, The Oxford Illustrated Dickens (Oxford: Oxford University Press, 1989), 260-261.

6. Charles Dickens, *Our Mutual Friend*, The Oxford Illustrated Dickens (Oxford: Oxford University Press, 1989), 128.

7. Charles Dickens, *The Mystery of Edwin Drood*, The Oxford Illustrated Dickens (Oxford: Oxford University Press, 1989), 84.

8. *A Christmas Carol* is one of five Christmas books written by Dickens from 1843–1848. And while it is certainly a story, it should not be confused for one of his Christmas stories. Dickens wrote a number of Christmas stories, usually co-written with other authors, which appeared in the holiday issues of his periodicals *Household Words* and *All the Year Round* from 1850–1867.

9. Noel Annan, *Leslie Stephen: The Godless Victorian* (Chicago: University of Chicago Press, 1984), 1.

10. Forster, *The Life of Charles Dickens*, 1:289.

11. Edgar Johnson, *Charles Dickens: His Tragedy and Triumph* (London: Victor Gollanz, 1953) 1:469.

12. Dennis Walder, *Dickens and Religion* (London: Routledge, 2007), 195.

13. Michael Slater, *Charles Dickens* (New Haven: Yale University Press, 2009), 392.

14. There were twenty numbers to *Bleak House*. The September 1853 number was a double number.

15. Kevin Vanhoozer, *Is There Meaning in This Text? The Bible, the Reader, and the Morality of Literary Knowledge* (Grand Rapids: Zondervan, 1998), 22.

16. Joseph Gold, *Charles Dickens: Radical Moralist* (Minneapolis: University of Minnesota Press, 1972), 9.

17. George Santayana, "Dickens," in *The Dickens Critics*, ed. George H. Ford and Lauriat Lane Jr. (Ithaca, NY: Cornell University Press, 1961), 145, cited in Joseph Gold, *Charles Dickens: Radical Moralist* (Minneapolis: University of Minnesota Press, 1972), 9.

18. Paul's death is narrated in chapter 14, "What the Waves were always Saying," of *Dombey and Son*.

19. Dickens, *DC*, 660.

20. Ibid., 646.

21. Charles Dickens, *Letters from Charles Dickens to Angela Burdett-Coutts, 1841–1865*, ed. Edgar Johnson (London: Jonathan Cape, 1953), 354.

22. Dickens, *LD*, 792.

Selected Bibliography

Ackroyd, Peter. *Dickens*. London: Guild Publishing, 1990.

Annan, Noel. *Leslie Stephen: The Godless Victorian*. Chicago: University of Chicago Press, 1984.

Arnold, Thomas. *Principles of Church Reform*. London: SPCK, 1962.

———. *Sermons Chiefly on the Interpretation of Scripture*. London: B. Fellowes, 1845.

———. *Sermons*. Vol. 1 of *Christian Life. Sermons Preached Mostly in the Village Church of Laleham, 1820–1828*. Revised edition. Edited by Mrs. W. E. Forster. London: Longmans, Green, 1878.

Belsham, Thomas. *The Present State of the Religious Parties in England.* . . . London: R. Hunter, 1818.

Bickersteth, Edward. *A Harmony of the Four Gospels.* . . . London: R. B. Seeley and W. Burnside, 1832.

Branks, William. *Heaven Our Home: We Have No Saviour But Jesus, No Home But Heaven*. Edinburgh: William P. Nimmo, 1863.

Buechner, Frederick. *Listening to Your Life*. San Francisco: HarperSanFrancisco, 1992.

Campbell, John McLeod. *The Nature of the Atonement*. Edinburgh: Handsel Press. Reprint of the first edition, with an introduction by James B. Torrance. Grand Rapids: Eerdmans, 1996.

Carpenter, Lant. *Lecuters on the Scripture Doctrine of Atonement, or of Reconciliation through Our Lord and Saviour Jesus Christ*. London: J. Green, 1843.

Carrow, G. D. "An Informal Call on Charles Dickens." *Dickensian* 63 (1967): 112–19.

Chadwick, Owen, ed. *The Mind of The Oxford Movement*. Stanford, CA: Stanford University Press, 1967.

———. *The Secularization of the European Mind in the 19th Century*. Cambridge: Cambridge University Press, 1975.

———. *The Victorian Church, Part I*. London: Oxford University Press, 1966.

Chalmers, Thomas. *On the Power, Wisdom, and Goodness of God as Manifested in the Adaptation of External Nature to the Moral and Intellectual Constitution of Man*. London: William Pickering, 1833.

———. *The Evidence and Authority of Christian Revelation*. Edinburgh: William Blackburn; Oliphant, Waugh, and Innes, 1814.

Chesterton, G. K. *Charles Dickens*. 20th ed. London: Methuen, 1943.

———. *Chesterton on Dickens*. San Francisco: Ignatius Press, 1989.

Clarke, Adam. *Christian Theology*. Edited by Samuel Dunn. 2nd ed. London: Thomas Tegg & Son, 1835.

———. *The Gospels Harmonized: With Notes, Explanatory, Experimental, and*

Practical. . . . Edited by Samuel Dunn. London: Thomas Tegg & Son, 1836.

Cockshut, A. O. J. *Anglican Attitudes: A Study of Victorian Religious Controversies.* London: Collins, 1959.

———, ed. *Religious Controversies of the Nineteenth Century.* London: Methuen, 1966.

Colledge, Gary. *Dickens, Christianity and "The Life of Our Lord": Humble Veneration, Profound Conviction.* London: Continuum, 2009.

———. *"The Life of Our Lord* Revisited." *Dickens Studies Annual: Essays on Victorian Fiction.* Vol. 36. Edited by Stanley Freidman, Edward Guiliano, Anne Humpherys, and Michael Timko. New York: AMS Press, 2005.

Collins, Philip. *Dickens and Crime.* London: Macmillan, 1962.

———. *Dickens and Education.* London: Macmillian, 1964.

———. "Dickens and the Ragged Schools." *Dickensian* 55 (1959): 94–109.

———, ed. *Dickens: Interviews and Recollections.* 2 vols. London: Macmillan, 1981.

Connell, J .M. "The Religion of Charles Dickens." *Hibbert Journal* 36 (1938): 225–34.

Conybeare, W .J. *Essays, Ecclesiastical and Social Printed with Additions from the Edinburgh Review.* London: Longman, Brown, Green, & Longmans, 1855.

Cross, Anthony J. "Charles Dickens, Edward Tagart and Unitarianism." *Faith and Freedom: A Journal of Progressive Religion* 42 (Summer 1989), 59–66.

Crowther, M. A. *Church Embattled: Religious Controversy in Mid-Victorian England.* Devon: David & Charles, 1970.

Davis, Earle. *The Flint and the Flame: The Artistry of Charles Dickens.* Columbia: University of Missouri Press, 1963.

Dexter, Walter. *The Love Romance of Charles Dickens: Told in His Letters to Maria Beadnell (Mrs. Winter).* London: Argonaut Press, 1936.

Dickens, Charles. *American Notes* and *Pictures from Italy.* The Oxford Illustrated Dickens. Oxford: Oxford University Press, 1989.

———. *Barnaby Rudge.* The Oxford Illustrated Dickens. Oxford: Oxford University Press, 1989.

———. *Bleak House.* The Oxford Illustrated Dickens. Oxford: Oxford University Press, 1989.

Charles Dickens: A December Vision, and Other Thoughtful Writings. Edited by Neil Philip and Victor Neuburg. New York: Continuum Publishing Company, 1987.

———. *Christmas Books.* The Oxford Illustrated Dickens. Oxford: Oxford University Press, 1997.

———. *David Copperfield.* The Oxford Illustrated Dickens. Oxford: Oxford University Press, 1989.

———. *Dombey and Son.* The Oxford Illustrated Dickens. Oxford: Oxford University Press, 1989.

———. *"Gone Astray" and Other Papers from Household Words.* Edited by Michael Slater. London: J. M. Dent, 1998.

———. *Great Expectations.* The Oxford Illustrated Dickens. Oxford: Oxford University Press, 1991.

———. *Hard Times.* The Oxford Illustrated Dickens. Oxford: Oxford University Press, 1991.

———. *Letters from Charles Dickens to Angela Burdett-Coutts, 1841–1865.* Edited by Edgar Johnson. London: Jonathan Cape, 1953.

———. *The Letters of Charles Dickens.* Edited by Madeline House, Graham Storey, Kathleen Tillotson. Pilgrim Edition. 12 vols. Oxford: Clarendon House, 1965–2004.

———. *The Life of Our Lord.* Edited by Neil Philip. Morristown, NJ: Silver Burdett Press, 1987.

———. *The Life of Our Lord: Written for His Children During the Years 1846 to 1849.* New York: Simon & Schuster, 1999.

———. *Little Dorrit.* The Oxford Illustrated Dickens. Oxford: Oxford University Press, 1989.

————. *Martin Chuzzlewit*. The Oxford Illustrated Dickens. Oxford: Oxford University Press, 1989.

————. *Master Humphrey's Clock* and *A Child's History of England*. The Oxford Illustrated Dickens. Oxford: Oxford University Press, 1989.

————. *Miscellaneous Papers*. New York: Chapman & Hall, 1908.

————. *Mr. and Mrs. Charles Dickens: His Letters to Her*. Edited by Walter Dexter. London: Constable, 1935.

————. *The Mystery of Edwin Drood*. The Oxford Illustrated Dickens. Oxford: Oxford University Press, 1989.

————. *Nicholas Nickleby*. The Oxford Illustrated Dickens. Oxford: Oxford University Press, 1989.

————. *The Old Curiosity Shop*. The Oxford Illustrated Dickens. Oxford: Oxford University Press, 1989.

————. *Oliver Twist*. The Oxford Illustrated Dickens. Oxford: Oxford University Press, 1989.

————. *Oliver Twist*. Penguin Classics edition. London: Penguin, 2003.

————. *Our Mutual Friend*. The Oxford Illustrated Dickens. Oxford: Oxford University Press, 1989.

————. *The Pickwick Papers*. The Oxford Illustrated Dickens. Oxford: Oxford University Press, 1989.

————. *The Pickwick Papers*. Oxford World's Classics edition. Oxford: Oxford University Press, 1999.

————. *Selected Journalism, 1850–1870*. Edited by David Pascoe. London: Penguin Books, 1997.

————. *A Tale of Two Cities*. The Oxford Illustrated Dickens. Oxford: Oxford University Press, 1989.

Dickens, Henry. *The Recollections of Sir Henry Dickens, K.C.* London: William Heinemann, 1934.

————. *Memories of My Father*. London: Victor Gollancz, 1928.

Dickens, Mamie. *Charles Dickens: By His Eldest Daughter*. London: Cassell, 1911.

Ellis, Ieuan. *Seven against Christ: Study of "Essays and Reviews."* Leiden: E. J. Brill, 1980.

Erskine, Thomas. *The Brazen Serpent; or, Life Coming Through Death*. Edinburgh: Waugh & Innes, 1831.

————. *The Unconditional Freeness of the Gospel: In Three Essays*. 2nd ed. Edinburgh: Waugh & Innes, 1828.

Essays and Reviews. London: John W. Parker & Son, 1860.

Fielding, K. J. *Charles Dickens: A Critical Introduction*. 2nd. ed. London: Longmans, Green, 1965.

————. *The Speeches of Charles Dickens*. Oxford: Oxford University Press, 1960.

Forster, John. *The Life of Charles Dickens*. 2 vols. London: J. M. Dent & Sons, 1927.

Frazee, John P. "Dickens and Unitarianism." *Dickens Studies Annual: Essays on Victorian Fiction*. Vol. 18. Edited by Michael Timko, Fred Kaplan, and Edward Guiliano. New York: AMS Press, 1989.

Fyfe, Aileen. "The Reception of William Paley's *Natural Theology* in the University of Cambridge." *British Journal for the History of Science* 30 (1997): 321–35.

Fyfe, Aileen and John van Wyhe. "Victorian Science and Religion." *The Victorian Web*. Edited by George P. Landow. Last modified 11 June 2002. www.victorianweb.org/science/science&religion.html.

Gold, Joseph. *Charles Dickens: Radical Moralist*. Minneapolis: University of Minnesota Press, 1972.

Griffiths, Michael. *The Example of Jesus*. Downers Grove, IL: InterVarsity, 1985.

Hanna, Robert. "Charles Dickens' *The Life of Our Lord* as a Primer for Christian Education." PhD diss. University of North Carolina at Greensboro, 1995.

————, ed. *The Dickens Christian Reader*. New York: AMS Press, 2000.

————. "*The Life of Our Lord*: New Notes of Explication." *Dickensian* 95 (1999): 197–205.

Hardy, Barbara. *The Moral Art of Dickens*. London: Athlone Press, 1970.

Hawthorne, Gerald. *Philippians*. Vol. 43 of The Word Biblical Commentary. Waco: Word Books, 1983.

Hemstadter, Richard J., and Bernard Lightman, eds. *Victorian Faith in Crisis: Essays on Continuity and Change in*

Nineteenth-Century Religious Belief. London: Macmillan Academic and Professional, 1990.

Hemstadter, Richard J., and Paul T. Phillips, eds. *Religion in Victorian Society: A Sourcebook of Documents.* Lanham, MD: University Press of America, 1985.

Hervey, James. *Meditations and Contemplations.* London: W. Suttaby, 1808.

Heyck, T. W. "From Men of Letters to Intellectuals: The Transformation of Intellectual Life in Nineteenth-Century England." *Journal of British Studies* 20 (Fall 1980), 158–83.

Hilton, Boyd. *The Age of Atonement: The Influence of Evangelicalism on Social and Economic Thought, 1795–1865.* Oxford: Clarendon, 1988.

Hinton, John Howard. *Theology: An Attempt towards a Consistent View of the Whole Counsel of God.* London: Wightman and Cramp, 1827.

Holubetz, Margaret. "Death-bed Scenes in Victorian Fiction." *English Studies: A Journal of English Language and Literature* 67 (February 1986): 14–34.

Houghton, Walter. *The Victorian Frame of Mind, 1830 to 1870.* New Haven, CT: Yale University Press, 1957.

House, Humphry. *All In Due Time: The Collected Essays and Broadcast Talks of Humphry House.* London: Rupert Hart-Davis, 1955.

———. *The Dickens World.* London: Oxford University Press, 1941.

Hughes, James L. *Dickens as an Educator.* London and New York: D. Appleton, 1900.

Hylson-Smith, Kenneth. *Evangelicals in the Church of England, 1734–1984.* Edinburgh: T&T Clark, 1988.

Inglis, K. S. *Churches and the Working Class in Victorian England.* London: Routledge and Kegan Paul, 1963.

Jalland, Pat. *Death in the Victorian Family.* Oxford: Oxford University Press, 1996.

Jay, Elisabeth, ed. *The Evangelical and Oxford Movements.* Cambridge: Cambridge University Press, 1983.

———. *The Religion of the Heart: Anglican Evangelicalism and the Nineteenth-Century Novel.* Oxford: Clarendon Press, 1979.

Johnson, Edgar. *Charles Dickens: His Tragedy and Triumph.* 2 vols. London: Victor Gollanz, 1953.

Jowett, Benjamin. *The Epistles of St. Paul to the Thessalonians, Galatians, Romans: With Critical Notes and Dissertations.* 2 vols. London: John Murray, 1855.

Kaplan, Fred. *Dickens: A Biography.* New York: William Morrow, 1988.

Kent, William Richard Gladstone. *Dickens and Religion.* London: Watts, 1930.

Kierkegaard, Søren. *Attack Upon Christendom.* Translated by Walter Lowrie. Princeton: Princeton University Press, 1972.

Knight, Francis. *The Nineteenth-Century Church and English Society.* Cambridge: University Press, 1995.

Knoepflmacher, U. C. *Religious Humanism and the Victorian Novel.* Princeton: Princeton University Press, 1965.

Lai, Shu-Fang. "Fact or Fancy: What Can We Learn about Dickens from His Periodicals *Household Words* and *All the Year Round?" Victorian Periodicals Review* 34 (2001): 41–53.

Larson, Janet L. *Dickens and the Broken Scripture.* Athens: University of Georgia Press, 1985.

Macrae, David. *Amongst the Darkies and Other Papers.* Glasgow: John S. Marr & Sons, 1880.

Manning, John. *Dickens on Education.* Toronto: University of Toronto Press, 1959.

Martineau, Harriet. *The Essential Faith of the Universal Church; Deduced from the Sacred Records.* London: Unitarian Association, 1831.

McKnight, Natalie. "Dickens's Philosophy of Fathering." *Dickens Quarterly* 18 (September, 2001): 129–38.

Miller, Hugh. *The Testimony of the Rocks; or, Geology In its Bearings on the Two Theologies, Natural and Revealed.* Edinburgh: Thomas Constable, 1857.

Moore, James P., ed. *Sources.* Vol. 3 of *Religion in Victorian Britain.* Manchester: Manchester University Press, 1988.

Muston, C. R. *Recognition in the World to Come; or, Christian Friendship on Earth Perpetuated in Heaven.* London: Holdsworth and Ball, 1830.

Newsom, Robert. *Charles Dickens Revisited.* New York: Twayne Publishers, 2000.

Nockles, Peter Benedict. *The Oxford Movement in Context: Anglican High Churchmanship, 1760–1857.* Cambridge: Cambridge University Press, 1994.

Olshausen, Hermann. *Biblical Commentary on the Gospels, Adapted Especially for Preachers and Students.* Translated by Thomas Brown. Vol. 2. Edinburgh: T&T Clark, 1848.

———. *Biblical Commentary on the Gospels, Adapted Especially for Preachers and Students.* Translated by Thomas Brown and John Gill. Vol. 3. Edinburgh: T&T Clark, 1849.

———. *Commentary on the Gospels, Adapted Expressly for Preachers and Students.* Translated by H. B. Creak. Vol. 1. Edinburgh: T&T Clark, 1847.

———. *Biblical Commentary on the Gospels and On the Acts of the Apostles.* Trans. John Gill and William Lindsay. Vol. 4. Edinburgh: T&T Clark, 1850.

"On God's Providence" Anonymous pamphlet from Burn's Series of Narratives and Tracts, 1841.

Orwell, George. *Critical Essays.* London: Secker and Warburg, 1960.

Oulton, Carolyn W. de la L. *Literature and Religion in Mid-Victorian England: From Dickens to Eliot.* Hampshire, UK: Palgrave Macmillan, 2003.

Parson, Edward. *The Providence of God Illustrated.* London: Hamilton, Adams; Leeds: J. Y. Knight, 1836.

Parsons, Gerald, ed. *Controversies.* Vol. 2 of *Religion in Victorian Britain.* Manchester: Manchester University Press, 1988.

Paz, D. G., ed. *Nineteenth-Century English Religious Traditions: Retrospect and Prospect.* Contributions to the Study of Religion 44. Westport, CT: Greenwood, 1995.

Peyrouton, N. C. "The Life of Our Lord: Some Notes of Explication." *Dickensian* 59 (1963): 102–12.

Pfleiderer, Otto. *The Development of Theology in Germany Since Kant and Its Progress in Great Britain Since 1825.* London: George Allen & Unwin, 1923.

Pope, Norris. *Dickens and Charity.* New York: Columbia University Press, 1978.

Pusey, E. B. *Nine Sermons, Preached before the University of Oxford, and Printed Chiefly between A.D. 1843–1855.* London: J. and F. H. Rivington, 1865.

———. *Parochial Sermons.* Vol. 3. rev ed. London: Rivingtons, 1873.

Qualls, Barry. *The Secular Pilgrims of Victorian Fiction: The Novel as Book of Life.* Cambridge: Cambridge University Press, 1982.

Quiller-Couch, Sir Arthur. *Charles Dickens and Other Victorians.* London: Cambridge University Press, 1927.

Reardon, Bernard M. G. *Religious Thought in the Victorian Age.* London: Longman Group, 1980.

Rowell, Geoffrey. *Hell and the Victorians: A Study of the Nineteenth-Century Theological Controversies Concerning Eternal Punishment and the Future Life.* Oxford: Clarendon, 1974.

Sanders, Andrew. *Charles Dickens.* Oxford: Oxford University Press, 2003.

———. *Charles Dickens: Resurrectionist.* London: Macmillan, 1982.

———. *Dickens and the Spirit of the Age.* Oxford: Clarendon, 1999.

———. *The Victorian Historical Novel, 1840–1880.* New York: St. Martins Press, 1979.

Sanders, Charles R. *Coleridge and the Broad Church Movement.* Durham, NC: Duke University Press, 1942.

Schlicke, Paul, ed. *Oxford Reader's Companion to Dickens.* Oxford: Oxford University Press, 1999. Oxford Reader's is correct. GC.

Shatto, Susan. "A Complete Course, According to Question and Answer." *Dickensian* 70 (1974): 113–20.

Slater, Michael. *Charles Dickens.* New Haven, CT: Yale University Press, 2009.

Sroka, Kenneth. "A Tale of Two Gospels: Dickens and John." *Dickens Studies Annual: Essays on Victorian Fiction.* Vol.

27. Edited by Stanley Friedman, Edward Guiliano, and Michael Timko. New York: AMS Press, 1998.

Standiford, Les. *The Man Who Invented Christmas: How Charles Dickens's "A Christmas Carol" Rescued His Career and Revived Our Holiday Spirits.* New York: Crown Publishers, 2008.

Stanley, Arthur Penrhyn. *The Life and Correspondence of Thomas Arnold, D.D.* 12th ed. 2 vols. London: John Murray, 1881.

Stonehouse, J. H. *Reprints of the Catalogues of the Libraries of Charles Dickens and W. M. Thackeray etc.* London: Piccadilly Fountain, 1935.

Storey, Gladys. *Dickens and Daughter.* London: Frederick Muller, 1939.

Symondson, Anthony, ed. *The Victorian Crisis of Faith.* London: SPCK, 1970.

Tagart, Edward. *The Claims of Unitarian Christianity to the Respectful Consideration of the Reflecting Public. . . .* London: R. Hunter & M. Eaton, 1832.

Taylor, Jeremy. *Holy Dying.* Edited by P. G. Stanwood. Oxford: Clarendon Press, 1989.

Thiessen, Henry. *Lectures in Systematic Theology.* Grand Rapids: Eerdmans, 1989.

Timko, Michael, Fred Kaplan, and Edward Guiliano, eds. *Dickens Studies Annual: Essays on Victorian Fiction.* Vol. 12. New York: AMS Press, Inc., 1983.

Turner, Frank. *John Henry Newman: The Challenge to Evangelical Religion.* New Haven, CT: Yale University Press, 2002.

Vanhoozer, Kevin. *Is There a Meaning in This Text? The Bible, The Reader, and the Morality of Literary Knowledge.* Grand Rapids: Zondervan, 1998.

Vogel, Jane. *Allegory in Dickens.* Tuscaloosa: University of Alabama Press, 1977.

Walder, Dennis. *Dickens and Religion.* London: George Allen & Unwin, 1981.

Ward, David A. "Distorted Religion: Dickens, Dissent and Bleak House." *Dickens Studies Annual: Essays in Victorian Fiction.* Vol. 29. Edited by Stanley Friedman, Edward Guiliano, and Michael Timko. New York: AMS Press, 2000.

Watts, C. T., ed. *The English Novel: Questions in Literature.* London: Sussex Books, 1976.

Welsh, Alexander. *The City of Dickens.* Oxford: Clarendon Press, 1971.

Whately, Richard. *A View of Scripture Revelations Concerning a Future State.* London: B. Fellowes, 1829.

Wheeler, Michael. *Heaven, Hell, and the Victorians.* Cambridge: Cambridge University Press, 1994.

Wigmore-Beddoes, Dennis G. *Yesterday's Radicals: A Study of the Affinity between Unitarianism and Broad Church Anglicanism in the Nineteenth Century.* James Clarke, 1971.

Willey, Basil. *Nineteenth Century Studies: Coleridge to Matthew Arnold.* London: Chatto & Windus, 1949.

Wolff, Robert Lee. *Gains and Losses: Novels of Faith and Doubt in Victorian England.* New York: Garland, 1977.

Wright, Richard. *An Essay on the Divinity of Our Lord Jesus Christ, as Distinguished from His Deity.* Liverpool: F. B. Wright, 1814.

Wright, T. R. *The Religion of Humanity: The Impact of Comtean Positivism on Victorian Britain.* Cambridge: University of Cambridge Press, 1986.

Yates, James. *The Scriptural Meaning of the Title "Saviour" as Applied to Our Lord: A Sermon Preached at Glasgow, July 28, 1822 at the Annual Meeting of the Scottish Unitarian Association.* London: David Eaton, 1823.

Author Index

Subject Index